D0299979

UNITY AND VARIETY

Honeychurch, Devon
A rustic mid-Devon interior: nave and chancel only, benches and box pews, and a 17th-century pulpit.

UNITY AND VARIETY

A History of the Church
in Devon and Cornwall

Edited by
NICHOLAS ORME

Exeter Studies in History No. 29
University of Exeter Press

First published in 1991 by
University of Exeter Press
Reed Hall
Streatham Drive
Exeter EX4 4QR
UK

Produced in conjunction with the
Centre for South-Western Historical Studies,
University of Exeter

Typeset by Kestrel Data, Exeter
Printed in the UK by Short Run Press Ltd, Exeter

British Library Cataloguing in Publication Data
Unity and variety: a history of the church in Devon and Cornwall.
   1. Devon (England). Cornwall (England). Christianity,
   history
   I. Orme, Nicholas   II. Series
   274.23

ISBN 0-85989-355-3

Contents

Illustrations and Text Figures

Plates

Text Figures

Acknowledgements

The editor and publishers gratefully acknowledge permission to reproduce illustrations kindly given by the Royal Commission on Historical Monuments (England) (nos 1, 3-5, 7, 9, 11, 13, 17-18, 21, 23, 26 and 33); the Rt. Revd. the Lord Bishop of Exeter (nos 12, 14, 27-28 and 32); Canon J. A. Thurmer (no 22); Diocesan House, Kenwyn, Truro (no 24); Canon H. Miles Brown (no 25); the Revd. L. M. Malsom (no 29); Buckfast Abbey (no 30); and Mr C. Bryan (no 31). Text Figure 3 is based, also with kind permission, on B. Lynette Olson and O. J. Padel, 'A Tenth-Century List of Cornish Parochial Saints', *Cambridge Medieval Celtic Studies*, 12 (1986), pp 33-71.

Contributors

Dr J. Barry is Lecturer in History at the University of Exeter.

Dr B. I. Coleman is Senior Lecturer in History and Deputy Vice-Chancellor at the University of Exeter.

Professor C. J. Holdsworth is Professor of Medieval History at the University of Exeter.

Professor N. I. Orme is Professor of History at the University of Exeter.

The Revd Dr J. A. Thurmer is Canon Emeritus of Exeter Cathedral.

Dr M. Winter is Director of the Centre for Rural Studies at the Royal Agricultural College, Cirencester.

Foreword

The story of Christianity in Cornwall and Devon is an absorbing one, stretching back over 1,500 years. It tells of people, their achievements and conflicts, worship and fellowship, art and architecture, education and charity—things worth studying in their own right by those who are interested in the past. But Church history is equally valuable for what it teaches us about the present. It shows how the modern Christian Churches and denominations have evolved, and why each has its own distinctive features. It widens our horizons, by revealing the enormous variety of Christian responses to different challenges and situations. And it helps us to understand and respect the traditions of other Christians, reminding us of shared beliefs and practices, and ancestors who once belonged to a single Church. We hope therefore that those who read this book will find it a stimulating aid to study, both of the past and the present, and that the knowledge we gain from history may bring us nearer to Christian unity in the future.

Michael Ball, Bishop of Truro.
Christopher Budd, Roman Catholic Bishop of Plymouth.
Amos S. Cresswell, Chairman, Plymouth and Exeter District,
    The Methodist Church.
R. Gwynne Edwards, General Superintendent, South Western Area,
    The Baptist Union of Great Britain.
Ian Haile, Chairman, Cornwall District, The Methodist Church.
Michael F. Hubbard, Moderator, South Western Province,
    The United Reformed Church.
Hewlett Thompson, Bishop of Exeter.

Introduction

This is the third attempt to write a history of the Church in Devon and Cornwall. The pioneer in the field was H.E. Reynolds, vicar choral and librarian of Exeter Cathedral, whose *Short History of the Ancient Diocese of Exeter* (1050–1894) was published locally in 1895 after it had been offered to and rejected by the S.P.C.K. Sadly, the reader cannot but agree with the Society. Reynolds's work (despite revision) is a haphazard mass of personal reflections and transcripts of records (chiefly from the cathedral, not the diocesan, archives), without framework, argument or cohesion. At more than 450 pages it is not even short. You can browse through its pages for bits of stray information (and you have to browse, because there is no index), but nobody strange to the subject would be able to learn Church history from the book. Even the author omitted it from his entry in *Crockford's Clerical Dictionary*.

The next to tackle the project was R.J.E. Boggis with his *History of the Diocese of Exeter* in 1922. This is a much more significant work. Boggis was a first-class theology graduate, capable parish priest, inspector of schools and author of several books. His autobiography, *I Remember*, is still worth reading, and his diocesan history is clear, informative and well-organised. True, the early chapters are out of date, because they precede the fundamental work of G.H. Doble and Charles Henderson, and Boggis was dependent on the romantic speculations of the then authority, Sabine Baring-Gould. But the rest of the book is careful and still useful, especially as a constitutional history of the Church. Boggis was strong on kings, parliaments, bishops, archdeacons and religious houses—reflecting the emphasis of English historians in his day. His work is complemented, not superseded, by our own volume.

In the years since Boggis wrote, a valuable contribution has been made to the study of Cornish Church history by Canon H. Miles Brown whose books *The Church in Cornwall* and *A Century for Cornwall* (a history of the modern diocese of Truro) appeared in 1964 and 1976 respectively. No large-scale work, however, has been done on the whole region or on Devon, and there are good reasons for attempting the task again in the 1990s. First of all, Boggis's history stops in 1900, so that there is virtually another century to be covered—one which both continues and departs from the Victorian age before it. Secondly, the study of history has changed and developed since the 1920s. We can now correct and amplify much that was previously known, and the horizons of historians and their readers are different. People have become more interested in the history of society as a whole, not just of its leaders, and the role of the ordinary clergy and laity in Church history is more highly valued, reflecting the greater role they play in the Church today. A modern Church historian must therefore deal not simply with political and constitutional matters but with social history as well. Finally, we are more ecumenical. Reynolds and Boggis confined themselves to the Church of England, but modern readers have wider allegiances. The Church of our book is 'the whole congregation of Christian people', including the Catholic Church since the Reformation and the Free Churches. It has not been easy to do justice to every denomination and to combine their histories into one coherent story, but we have at least begun to extend the account beyond the Church of England.

A book of this kind may be expected to have readers from inside and outside the region. For those in Cornwall and Devon we have set out to describe the main religious institutions and developments in the two counties, and to show how they fit into the history of the Church in England as a whole. For readers from outside, we have tried to show how national movements like the missionary saints, monasticism, the Reformation, Protestant dissent and Victorian reform operated within the South West in particular. The 'South West', for the purpose of our book, is defined as Devon and Cornwall. We have also aimed to give the book a distinctive general theme, by tracing an issue which has affected the Church throughout history. This issue gives the book its title, *Unity and Variety*. Religion has always had a unifying tendency. It brings together people to worship and to live as a community; it tends to impose uniformity of belief and practice through creeds, set liturgies and moral codes. But equally, religion leads to variety. It may allow its followers to choose between a range of devotions and activities, and (sadly) it may also give rise to disagreements and quarrels. In the past, unity and variety have sometimes coexisted peacefully, notably before the Reformation and in the twentieth century. At other times, especially between the Reformation and the late Victorian period, they have conflicted, leading to schisms, persecutions and violence. Our chapters on the Church in the South West are intended to throw light on this topic: one which can be related to Church history in other regions and countries, and which is central to understanding the Churches of today.

It is difficult nowadays for a single historian to keep in touch with all the manifold current research on a period of history which covers fifteen hundred years. Our book is therefore the work of a team, whose members' interests and insights differ somewhat from one chapter to another, but collectively help to widen the book's horizons. The first four chapters run chronologically, but the nineteenth century, with its larger historical sources, is divided into two chapters on the Church of England and nonconformity, and the twentieth century contains separate sections on Cornwall and Devon. It should be pointed out that these last two sections are not mutually exclusive. The Cornish one includes some valuable comparative statistics about Devon, while the Devon section sketches some of the general religious developments of the twentieth century, which apply to Cornwall as well. It is suggested, therefore, that these two sections should be read and used together.

We are indebted to a number of people and institutions who have enabled this book to appear. It grew out of papers originally presented at the annual symposium of the Centre for South-Western Historical Studies at the University of Exeter in November 1989, and gratitude is due to the Centre for organising this event. The paper on the twentieth century was given by the bishop of Crediton, the Rt. Revd. P.E. Coleman, who kindly allowed it to be used as the basis for Chapter 7, Part 2, of the present book. Without his knowledge and insights, that chapter could not have been written, and we are greatly indebted to him for his help. Valuable advice and information on the Churches of twentieth-century Devon have also been given by Mr P. Greener, the Ven. R.G. Herniman, Mr I. Marlowe, Mr R.S.F. Thorne and Miss P. Williams, as well as by Dr Caroline Brett, Dr R.A. Higham and Professor Charles Thomas on the Anglo-Saxon period. None of them, however, bears responsibility for any remaining errors. The cover and several of the illustrations are the work of Mr S. Goddard and the maps have been drawn by Mr M. Rouillard, both members of the University's Department of History and Archaeology. The Department, the University, St Luke's Foundation Trust, The Iverdean Trust and The Devonshire Association have all made generous grants towards the cost of researching and publishing the illustrations. Finally, the publication has been ably expedited by Dr J. Barry, the series editor, and Ms Elizabeth Saxby of the University of Exeter Press.

Nicholas Orme,
University of Exeter,
March 1991

Plate 1 St Endellion church, Cornwall
Typically Cornish in standing alone, away from any village, but unique in being staffed by four prebendaries, who even survived the Reformation.

CHAPTER ONE

From the Beginnings to 1050

Nicholas Orme

What faith was his, that dim, that Cornish saint,
Small rushlight of a long-forgotten church,
Who lived with God on this unfriendly shore . . .
(Betjeman, *St Enodoc*)

Beginnings

To reach the beginnings of Christianity in Britain, we have to think ourselves back past all the well-known landmarks of Church history. Past the Oxford Movement and the Free Churches, past the Reformation and the medieval abbeys, past even the romantic Celtic saints, to a time of which there are few visible remains or even mental images of the faith: the Roman period. The earliest evidence for Christianity in the South West of England is a fragment of coarse black pottery, probably fourth-century, with the sign ρ pecked on the outside: a form of the well-known 'chi-rho' symbol containing the first two letters of the Greek word for Christ. It was found during excavations in Exeter in 1945–6, in what had been an area of housing near the present-day South Street, and probably belonged to lowly people.[1] 'Great oaks from little acorns grow.' This humble piece of pot marks the emergence of a faith which has filled the region with churches, parishes and clergy, and has shaped the lives of its people for 1600 years.

Christianity had entered Britain earlier than this. By about the year AD200 Origen and Tertullian, Christian writers in the Mediterranean world, believed that their religion had spread all over the Roman Empire including Britain, one of its remotest provinces. During the hundred years after which they wrote, the Roman persecution of Christians reached Britain too, and produced the first British martyrs of whom St Alban is the most famous. Then, in 313, the Emperor Constantine gave Christianity toleration, and in the fourth century there was a development of public Christian worship, with churches and shrines

I

staffed by bishops and clergy. Three British bishops, of Lincoln, London and York, went to the Council of Arles as early as 314. It is possible that similar developments took place at Exeter, the chief Roman centre in the South West, and that the town acquired a congregation, a church and even a bishop, but we do not know, and the existence of churches elsewhere—in the wide rural spaces of the region—is still a mystery.[2]

Roman political authority disappeared from Britain during the early fifth century. The British people of the South West, the Dumnonii, who had long existed as a distinct nation, regained their independence under a series of kings who probably held a loose political control over the modern counties of Cornwall and Devon and possibly other lands further eastwards. Christianity survived in this Dumnonian kingdom, and the evidence for it becomes stronger after AD400. At Exeter, excavations have revealed a cemetery south-west of the cathedral with graves dating from the fifth to the seventh centuries, in part of what had been the basilica (or civic building) of the Roman town. The graves appear to be those of Christians, and their presence at the centre of the town (as opposed to the earlier Roman practice of burying people outside it) suggests the existence of a church nearby, perhaps in part of the basilica.[3] In the countryside, a number of standing stones with Latin inscriptions begin to survive in the fifth century and go on being found until the seventh: memorials to people who had died.[4] Some 40 or so examples can be certainly identified, 11 between the Exe and the Tamar in what is now Devon, and 31 west of the Tamar in present-day Cornwall. Each stone records a person's name in Latin, and three in Cornwall also use variations of the phrase *hic iacit* ('here lies'), which is found on Christian gravestones in Europe. The people commemorated were mainly men, the size and rarity of their memorials suggesting noble men; the name of one, Rialobranus (on the 'Men Scryfys' in Madron parish), can probably be translated, 'kingly raven'. One or two were erected for women, including Cunaide at Hayle who died aged 33 and Nonnita at Tregony. The stones imply that the local aristocracy had become Christians, and this is confirmed by the earliest literature about the South West. The scholar Gildas, writing in about the mid-sixth century, depicts the contemporary king of Dumnonia, Constantine, as a wicked man but as a Christian rather than a pagan.[5] A hundred years later, the so-called first Life of St Samson mentions a chieftain *(comes)* called Guedianus from north-east Cornwall who lived at about the same time as Constantine. Guedianus and the people he ruled appear to have been baptised, but were still observing certain heathen practices.[6] Altogether, it looks as though the Dumnonii were Christian by about 550, at least in a nominal sense.

The Christianity of the region may have survived in part from Roman times, but it was powerfully reinforced by the arrival of hermit and missionary saints

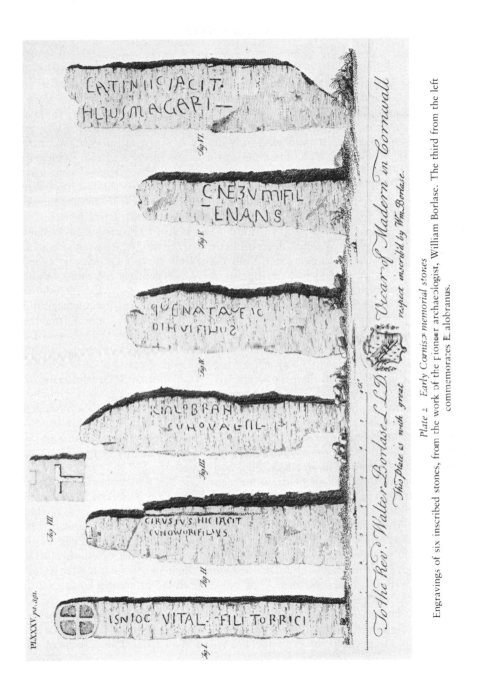

Plate 2 *Early Cornish memorial stones*

Engravings of six inscribed stones, from the work of the pioneer archaeologist, William Borlase. The third from the left commemorates E. alobranus.

from other parts of the Celtic world during the sixth century. This was the 'age of the Celtic saints': of Nectan, Paul Aurelian, Petroc, Piran, Samson, and numerous others. Yet though they have left so many traces of themselves in place-names and church dedications, remarkably little is known about them. The first Life of St Samson is the only early written source; it claims to have been set down in about 620 by an author in Brittany who used an earlier written account, and features a saint who was active in Cornwall about a century previously. According to the Life, Samson was the son of a Welsh nobleman of Dyfed (south-west Wales) and his wife who came from Gwent (the south-east). He was handed over as a child to be taught by St Illtyd (probably at the monastery of Llantwit Fawr in Glamorgan), and grew up to be a monk. He became abbot of a monastery on Caldey Island, and then a bishop. He later travelled to Cornwall and Brittany. On his visit to Cornwall he crossed the 'Severn Sea' from Wales with a number of friends and relations, and landed somewhere on the north-east coast. They made their way to a monastery called Docco, which we can identify as Lanow near St Kew, but the monks there would not receive them, ostensibly on the grounds that Samson's high standards would not accord with their lower ones. Samson continued his journey, and while still in the district of Trigg in north-east Cornwall, came across the chieftain Guedianus and his people who were holding games (including horse racing) in honour of a local idol. The saint remonstrated with them, but his words had no effect until a boy fell off a horse and apparently died. Samson restored him to life, and the people repented. They destroyed the idol, Samson confirmed their baptisms, and the boy promised to become a cleric. Further on in his Cornish travels, Samson destroyed a serpent in a cave and commanded his men to build a new monastery at a place which is not named. He left his father Amon in charge of it and ordained his cousin Henoc as deacon. Finally, he went over the Channel to Brittany where he had a further career, founding the monastery at Dol in which he died and was buried.[7]

Unfortunately, the lives of the other saints are very much later than this.[8] The next with relevant information, the Life of St Paul Aurelian, comes from the late ninth century, 400 years after its hero's lifetime, and the rest are further still from the saints they describe. Such works do not portray the saints as they were, but as people visualised them later on, engaging in all kinds of miraculous and tragic episodes. Still, the names of the saints, the places where they were honoured and the traditions associated with them enable us to infer a few general features of their history. They are represented as coming to the South West, chiefly from South Wales. Most were Welsh, but some like Breage, Erc, Germoe, Ia and Rumon were credited with Irish origins. This is possible, because the descendants of Irish settlers were active in south Wales at the time, and 'Irish' saints could have come to the South West from Wales. Some of the

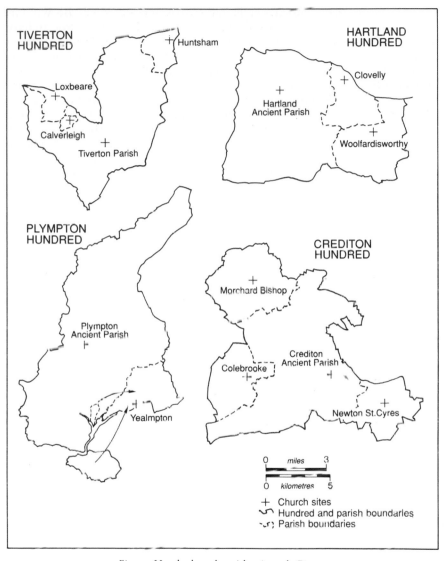

Fig. 2 Hundreds and parishes in early Devon.

or at least a zone of influence, in the two nearby hundreds of Wonford and West Budleigh.[31] Four other Devon churches have, or used to have, much larger parishes than normal, reflecting their minster origins. Tiverton still covers 17,585 acres for civil purposes, though it has been divided ecclesiastically. Hartland (with its former dependency of Welcombe) used to include 19,091 acres, and Crediton 20,971 acres, counting Kennerleigh and Sandford which belonged to it in medieval times. Largest of all was Plympton, whose priory church was also the mother parish church of the two other churches in Plympton and those of Brixton, Plymstock, Shaugh Prior and Wembury—an area which totalled 29,234 acres. Large minster parishes like these can be traced elsewhere in England, and there was, perhaps, one parallel example in Cornwall. There, the minster of St Stephen (Launceston) had jurisdiction over eight nearby churches in medieval times, including Boyton, St Giles-on-the-Heath, Laneast, North Tamerton, St Thomas, Tremaine, Tresmere and Werrington.[32] Elsewhere in Cornwall, however, the minster churches did not possess unduly large parishes in historic times, so either they never had them or else they lost them very much earlier than was the case in England.

Along with the minsters, a number of other religious sites existed from early times. There were burial grounds—perhaps pre-Christian in some cases, but assimilated to the Church once Christian funerals and prayers were said in them. South-western England contains a number of churchyards which seem to have originated as early Dumnonian cemeteries. They are roughly oval, surrounded by a bank or wall, and are higher inside than outside through the accumulation of burials. Lewannick and Sancreed are examples in Cornwall, and Lustleigh in Devon. The British place-name prefix *lan,* meaning an enclosure, often appears to indicate similar early burial grounds, and is particularly common in west Cornwall, with isolated cases further east: Landkey in north Devon, *Lantokay* now Street in Somerset and *Lanprobi* at or near Sherborne in Dorset.[33] Many of these early cemeteries and *lan* place-names later became the sites of church buildings. Other religious centres may have survived from pre-Christian times, like the holy wells so common in Cornwall and also found in Devon, the holy trees of which we hear at St Breward and St Endellion, and the holy paths associated with St Endelient and St Paul Aurelian. The fifth- and sixth-century Celtic saints established further sites in the form of shrines and oratories. Such early religious centres did not always possess buildings, however, and Christian rites may have been carried out in the open air by visiting bishops or minster priests. Theodore archbishop of Canterbury (668–690) allowed confirmations and masses to take place 'in the field', and an English writer of about 800 noted that many places in England had no church but a cross, where services were held.[34] A number of decorated stone crosses survive in the South West from the ninth and tenth centuries, chiefly in Cornwall, with a few examples in Devon such as Colyton, Copplestone and Exeter. Some stand in churchyards like those at Lanherne and Sancreed, while others such as the famous Doniert stone near St Cleer are in now-isolated places by roads or in the countryside.[35]

Eventually, church buildings were erected on many of these sites, and probably at fresh locations too. They seem to have become common in the tenth century. King Edgar's laws of 960-2 about tithes lay down that all payments shall be made to the old minster to which the parish belongs, but allows for the existence of other churches within the parish. If a lord has a church on his land with a graveyard, he may transfer to it a third of the tithe. If he has a church without a graveyard, he may only support it in addition to paying minster-tithes.[36] This indicates a transitional period in which local churches were appearing— the ancestors of modern parish churches—but had not yet gained equality with the minsters. Unfortunately, it is difficult to know when building took place in most cases. This is especially so in Devon, where early churches were probably often made of cob or timber and, being later rebuilt, have left no original traces. We may guess that Chittlehampton and St Sidwell's (Exeter) had buildings early on, because both these places housed the shrines of local saints in the later middle ages. Elsewhere, what is thought to be a Saxon crypt survives at Sidbury, and there is Saxon masonry at two ancient church sites in Exeter: St George and St Martin.[37] Documentary references to Devon churches other than the minsters do not begin until the eve of the Norman Conquest. St Michael (East Teignmouth) is mentioned in 1044 and St Olave (Exeter) in about 1050, while St Martin (Exeter) was dedicated in 1065, confirming its Saxon origins.[38]

The documentary evidence is better in Cornwall, where the existence of numerous local churches can be dated to at least the early tenth century. This emerges from a bald and apparently unpromising list of 48 saints inserted at that date into a Breton manuscript of works relating to Seneca.[39] The purpose of the list is not clear, but the writer who compiled it evidently had in his mind, as he did so, the locations of some of the places in Cornwall connected with the saints. He mentions in geographical sequence the saints of the churches around the Fal estuary (St Anthony and St Just in Roseland, Gerrans, Philleigh and probably Ruan Lanihorn), the saints of the churches of Probus and Ladock which neighbour one another further east, and (in less strict order) the saints of the cluster of parishes including St Austell, Creed, St Ewe, Mevagissey and St Mewan (*Figure 3*). All these places are later known to have had church buildings dedicated to the saints concerned, and it is reasonable to assume that they already had them by the early tenth century. Churches so close together must also have had, at least informally, parish boundaries. At first such places

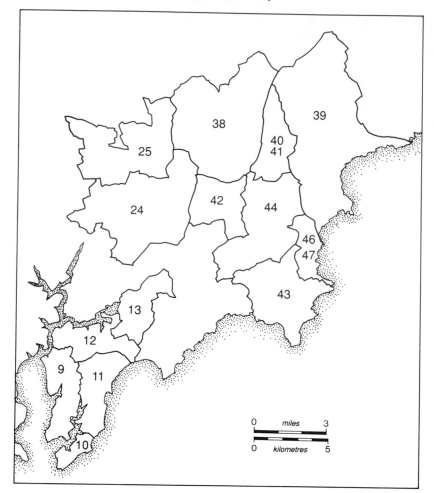

Fig. 3 Early churches in southern Cornwall.

 9 Iust (St Just)
10 Entennin (St Anthony)
11 Gerent (Gerrans)
12 Filii (Philleigh)
13 Rumon (Ruan Lanihorne)
24 Propus (Probus)
25 Latoc (Ladock)
38 Elenn (St Stephen)

39 Austoll(St Austell)
40 Megun (St Mewan)
41 Iodechall (? St Mewan)
42 Crite (Creed)
43 Guron (Gorran)
44 Euai (Ewe)
46 Memai (Mevagissey)
47 Iti (Mevagissey)

may have been served by itinerant clergy, but in the long run the tendency in both Cornwall and Devon was for the local churches (excepting very small chapels) to acquire a priest of their own. The permission for him and his church to receive a third of the minster tithes was imperceptibly increased, and in the end his church established its own parish boundaries, often coinciding with the boundary of the manor in which the church stood. This was especially the case in Devon, where many churches must have been founded by lords of manors for their tenants, so that the tenants would not attend churches and develop loyalties elsewhere. By the twelfth and thirteenth centuries the old minster parishes had become fragmented, except for a few places like Crediton and Hartland. The minster became a simple parish church, sometimes losing its surplus clergy at the same time; its parish was restricted to part of its original territory, and the rest was divided into the parishes of the newer but now equal local churches.

The Church was not only enshrined in churches and clergy, however, but in the souls and bodies of the people. Here the aristocracy played an important role from the start, bringing into the Church the ostentatious open-handedness which characterised their life outside it. They founded churches and granted them endowments. Athelstan 'the half king' (so named from his importance) was a major holder of land in Devon and Somerset, who seems to have given an estate at Brampford Speke to Glastonbury Abbey soon after 944.[40] Two other Devon magnates, Ordulf and Aethelweard, were closely involved in the foundations at Tavistock in 981 and Buckfast in 1018 respectively. When lords built local churches, they appointed the priests and acquired the power of patronage; they sometimes freed their slaves in public ceremonies, and when they died imposing monuments were raised in their memory. This leading role was to change in details, but it endured in principle right down to recent times. In contrast, the religion of lesser people is chiefly recorded in early days with regard to their duties and obligations. Already in the early eighth century King Ine was ordering his subjects to pay church scot: a payment in kind (e.g. grain) from every household once a year on St Martin's Day.[41] By 926–30, in Athelstan's reign, church scot had been joined by soul scot (a mortuary fee payable at death) and plough alms (a penny per plough-team rendered after Easter). All these had to be paid to the local minster.[42] Tithes originated as payments made at the donor's choice to pilgrims, poor people or churches, but under Edgar in 960–2 they too were appropriated to the minsters and later on to other local churches.[43] The development of tithes (one tenth of crops and young animals, paid each year) was of immense importance in Church history. It enabled the system of small local churches with resident clergy to grow up, and for the next thousand years tithes provided the main support of these clergy. The Church did not surrender them till 1936, when the crown bought

out the Church and collected the tithes to recoup itself, finally ceasing to do
so in 1977.

Tithes bound heads of households to support the Church. There came to be
heavy penalties for non-payment and much resentment among those who paid,
but it would not be right to see the laity's involvement in the Church as solely
a compulsory one. There were also voluntary lay activities, notably through
the foundation of religious associations or guilds. The earliest guild that we
hear of in the South West was founded at Exeter in the first half of the tenth
century, and had its statutes carefully written down. Its members—an unspecified number— formed their guild ostensibly 'for the love of God and for
our souls' need', but also for fellowship. They met three times a year, and must
have been important folk (probably only men), because they are mentioned
bringing retainers with them. Each member had to supply a quantity of malt
and honey, presumably to brew ale and mead for drinking. At each meeting a
priest said two masses, one for living members and one for the dead, and each
guild brother had to say or cause to be said two recitations of the psalter.
When a brother died, the others arranged for six masses or psalters to be said
for him; if anyone went on a pilgrimage 'south' (i.e. to Rome) the rest gave
5d. each, and if anyone's house was burnt, 1d. Quarrels between members
were punished with fines.[44] By the early twelfth century there were also guilds
in the countryside, as we see from the fourteen affiliated to Exeter Cathedral.
Woodbury near Exeter had no less than three of these, Colaton Raleigh two,
and various other places one each—including Halsford in Whitestone and
Nutwell in Woodbury, which were not even parishes. Three of the guilds seem
to have been restricted to twelve members, but the others admitted up to thirty,
including clergy, laymen and women. In two cases, both of guilds at Woodbury,
the statutes are quoted and specify the payment of 1d. a household at Easter
or Martinmas, and 1d. when any guild member died—arrangements very
similar to the ancient dues of church scot, plough alms and soul scot. In return
the guild members were probably prayed for by the canons of Exeter (their
names are preserved in the cathedral records), and no doubt convivial meetings
were held at least once a year, with eating and drinking together.[45]

Women were Christians too, but we hear much less about them than men.
Some of the early saints were women, but they were outnumbered by the men
and the churches dedicated to them did not become so important. One or two
noble Celtic women like Cunaide and Nonnita were commemorated on
memorial stones, and a few noble Saxon women are mentioned giving property
to churches: Sulca to Glastonbury in about 760, Aelfwynn the wife of Ordulf
to Tavistock, and Gytha the wife of Earl Godwin to St Olave (Exeter) in about
1050.[46] A small number of women were admitted to some of the guilds, but
not to all; the Exeter guild statutes speak only of brothers, and of the fourteen

rural societies ten were also confined to men, to judge from the members' names. Of the rest, Nutwell's included one woman out of twelve members, Clyst St George's two out of 29, Alwine's guild at Woodbury two out of 30, and Broadclyst's—the only one with a large group of women—ten out of 45. In all four organisations, however, the women were listed after the men. The impression given by all these sources, Celtic and Saxon, is that women took less part than men in public religion, doubtless through lack of property and status. Their contribution came in other ways: attending services and upholding religion at home, like King Alfred's mother who encouraged her children with their lessons.[47] Such support was crucial to the Church, but it was not so highly valued and was very rarely recorded.

Unity and Order

In the early days of the south-western Church in the fifth and sixth centuries, Christians were united by a common faith and religious observances rather than by laws and rulers. The first Life of St Samson portrays the saint as a bishop who came into Cornwall by chance and possessed little power to command. He was turned away from the monastery at Docco and had to win over the Christians at the idol by means of a miracle.[48] Later on, bishops became established locally with definite powers, and St Aldhelm seems to refer to the bishops (*sacerdotes*) of the Dumnonian kingdom in his letter to King Geraint of about 700.[49] The earliest Dumnonian bishop to whom we can attach a name, a place and a date is Kenstec, who had his seat in the monastery of *Dinuurrin* (possibly Bodmin) at some time between 833 and 870, when he made a promise of obedience to Archbishop Ceolnoth of Canterbury.[50] St Germans, too, may have been a bishop's seat before the Saxon conquest of Cornwall, in view of a charter of King Athelstan dated 936 which apparently restores (rather than grants) the property of the bishop there.[51] Cornwall thus acquired at least one resident bishop, possibly more, and Kenstec's submission to the archbishop of Canterbury (at about the time of Egbert's Cornish campaigns) shows Cornwall beginning to be brought into the English Church organisation.

The growth of Church authority is easier to follow in Devon. In 705 King Ine established a new bishop's seat at Sherborne, with St Aldhelm as its first occupant, to supervise the Church in the lands which the Saxons had recently conquered in Somerset, Dorset and Devon.[52] Shortly afterwards, King Geraint granted the bishop of Sherborne an estate at Maker on the Cornish side of the Tamar estuary, and in 739, as we have seen, King Aethelheard of Wessex added a large estate at Crediton, giving the bishop a base in Devon. Sherborne continued to be the seat of the bishop in charge of Devon until, in the 890s, King Alfred gave his friend the Welsh bishop Asser what Asser described as

'Exeter, with all the district (*paruchia*) belonging to it in Devon and Cornwall'. This is generally interpreted as making Asser a suffragan bishop, auxiliary to the bishop of Sherborne, with special responsibility for the area concerned, and marking a further stage of English control over the Church in Cornwall. An Anglophile Welshman was well suited to act as bishop of the two south-western counties, and in due course Asser was promoted to be bishop of Sherborne as well. When he died in 909, the South West was divided from Sherborne permanently. A new bishop's seat was founded at Crediton, under a Saxon bishop responsible for ruling Devon and perhaps Cornwall too. But if Cornwall was intended to be included, the arrangement did not last long, for in about 930 King Athelstan established or re-established a bishop's seat at St Germans, and appointed Conan, a cleric with a Celtic name, to hold the office. It has been suggested that Conan and his successors were suffragans of the bishop of Crediton, but it is possible that they were independent from the first, and this was certainly the case after 994.[53] By the end of the tenth century, both Cornwall and Devon had bishops of their own, on the standard English pattern.

The bishops carried out the spiritual direction of the Church. They confirmed children and adults, consecrated holy oil for baptising babies and anointing the sick, ordained clergy, held Church synods, and supervised the churches and clergy of their dioceses. Their effectiveness, however, owed much to royal support, and the kings of Wessex (later of England) also took a crucial part in the development of Church order. It was the kings who established the new dioceses and influenced the appointment of bishops. They took the initiative in founding minster churches on royal estates, and later on in the tenth century they supported Dunstan and Aethelwold in reviving monasticism in England. The three monasteries founded in Devon as a result, Exeter, Tavistock and Buckfast, were set up under the patronage of Edgar, Aethelred and Cnut respectively, with some assistance from local magnates. The kings, beginning with Ine in the South West, also enforced Church payments on the laity, and issued laws defining the rights of minsters and local churches. In return for all this help, the kings expected loyalty and prayers from the clergy. Athelstan, between 930 and 939, ordered the clergy of every minster to sing fifty psalms every Friday for the benefit of the king, and individual kings were prayed for at the houses they had founded or endowed: Athelstan himself at St Buryan and Exeter.[54]

Finally, the king was involved with a major reorganisation of the south-western Church in 1050.[55] At this time there were still two dioceses, with bishops' seats at Crediton and St Germans, but since 1027 they had been held in plurality by one man. Neither diocese was well endowed with revenues to support its bishop, at a time when bishops' responsibilities and expenses were

Plate 3   St Clether well-house, Cornwall
The late-medieval well-house over the spring at St Clether; the spring then passes through an
adjoining chapel.

increasing, so uniting the two was an obvious solution. Leofric, who became joint bishop of Crediton and Cornwall in 1046, was a reformer who set out to solve this and other local problems. He disliked the fact that his cathedral in Devon was at Crediton in the countryside, and wished to move it to Exeter, a city of growing importance. Cathedrals in Europe were generally in cities, and the English tradition of rural cathedrals was coming to seem anomalous. Later, in the 1070s, other English bishops were to follow Leofric's example and transfer their seats to towns like Chichester, Lincoln and Salisbury. Leofric also wanted his cathedral to be staffed by canons following a strict continental discipline, whereas the canons of Crediton were probably living a rather worldly life. It is always easier to make a fresh start on a new site. Accordingly, Leofric applied to the pope for permission to move his cathedral to Exeter (an application which reflected the growing papal involvement in English Church affairs), and the pope, Leo IX, wrote to the king of England, Edward the Confessor, ordering the move to be made. Edward agreed, but he also went further and approved the union of the two dioceses, about which the pope was not apparently consulted. Leofric selected the old minster in Exeter as his new cathedral, south-west of the present building, and Edward and his queen came personally to enthrone him there as first bishop of the new united diocese in 1050.

The union of Devon and Cornwall into the diocese of Exeter lasted until the creation of Truro diocese in 1876. The bishop of Exeter took over the property of the previous bishops of Cornwall, notably at St Germans, Lawhitton and Pawton, and subsequent bishops visited these estates from time to time, as well as staying on their various manors in Devon. Within this unity there was, from the first, a good deal of variety, which had developed during the previous 700 years or so of Christianity in the South West. There were different kinds of churches in 1050: two monasteries, over two dozen minsters staffed by canons or priests, and a large but unguessable number of local churches, some with resident clergy and some without. There were many other cult centres: chapels, crosses, burial grounds and wells. There were altars and shrines dedicated to international saints in Devon, like the Virgin Mary, St Martin, St Olave and St Peter, and to a myriad of Celtic saints in Cornwall. There were guilds of local people, also diverse in size and membership. In short, a complex mosaic was already taking shape, and much more would be added to it in later centuries.

CHAPTER TWO

From 1050 to 1307

Christopher Holdsworth

For if heaven be on this earth and ease to any soul,
It is in cloister or in school, by many skills I find,
For in cloister cometh no man to chide or to fight,
But all is buxomness there and books to read and to learn.
(Langland, *Piers Plowman*)

Cathedral and See in 1050

The installation of Leofric in the old church of St Peter's in Exeter in 1050 marks a new stage in the history of the Church in the South West.[1] A man described by a near contemporary as British *(Brytonicus)*, that is to say in modern terms either Cornish, Welsh or Breton, but who bore a noble English name, was conducted to his new *cathedra* or throne by his king (Edward the Confessor) taking his right arm with the queen (Edith) taking his left. The act neatly symbolised the close relationship between throne and Church which had developed over the centuries, more especially during the preceding century of reconstruction and reform in both institutions. But the fact that this enthronement took place with papal approval points towards something else, the beginning of a new stage in the development within the western world of the authority and influence of the bishop of Rome. This had started with the election as pope in 1049 of a Lotharingian noble who had taken the name of Leo (IX). He was, in a brief five years, to begin the process of changing an institution with little power beyond the city of Rome into one which affected the whole of the West by, for example, taking the papacy 'on the road' and holding a series of reforming Councils in France, the Empire and Italy.[2] One of the themes of this chapter will be the impact of this revived papacy over three centuries upon the diocese, where its interests were not always the same as those of the monarchy, although Exeter was not a place where their interests were so opposed that violent clashes resulted, as at Canterbury.

To Leo, writing from Reims where he was holding a great council, Exeter seemed a city much more suited to serve as a centre for the life of the Church than Crediton which he called a hamlet *(villula)*.[3] Leofric probably felt the same, yet may have put more store upon the walls which surrounded the larger place offering some defence against disorder at a time when the memory of the Vikings was still strong. Leofric may, as we have already seen, have been some kind of an Anglicised Celt, but he had experienced himself the effects of Scandinavian expansion having been forced out of England when the country was taken over by the Danes after 1013.[4] One result of his exile was to take him to Lotharingia where some of the best schools of the day were to be found. There his mind was formed in the kind of Christianised Latin learning which Carolingian scholars had developed. There, too, he seems to have been convinced that one of the best ways of ensuring order in churches served by a community was for it to follow the rule composed in the eighth century by Chrodegang, bishop of Metz within the very area where he was studying. This he determined was to be used in his cathedral. Such a concern for the maintenance of order sounds another significant theme of this period, which we shall see taking various forms. It leads us now to ask what resources Leofric had for his task in 1050.

One must admit at the start that his cathedral was fairly small, a mere 32.5 metres or so long, even though this made it larger than any other church in the city.[5] Until recently it used to be thought that the Saxon minster lay to the east of the present cathedral, but excavations in the 1970s showed that it was about 25 metres south and west of the present west front, under what became the medieval church of St Mary Major, demolished in 1971. Serving this cathedral there was a body of canons, perhaps as many as twenty-four, whose daily life was punctuated by celebrations of the services for night and day, following a pattern laid down in the eighth-century rule.[6] At their head was an archdeacon, but otherwise there was no formal division of labours between them. They probably shared the income that came to them equally, and it was derived from a part of the endowment of the bishopric, the other part going to the bishop. His wealth was considerable, derived from a widely-dispersed estate, described adequately for the first time in Domesday Book compiled in 1086.[7] This shows us that its core was in the adjacent counties of Devon and Cornwall, with outlying parts in Oxfordshire and Sussex which had been given to Leofric and his successor Osbern by the king and had been conveyed by them to the see.

In 1086 the bishop enjoyed an income which made him the sixth wealthiest bishop in England (whilst ruling over the fourth largest diocese), and placed him on a level with the 42 richest lay nobles; certainly no one within his diocese was his obvious superior. These resources were used to support a large household, like a lay lord's, but which would have included a fair number of clerics to write his letters and manage his lands. Beyond the cathedral and his household there seem to have been few other signs which we would recognise as ecclesiastical administration; the bishopric was not yet divided up into archdeaconries and rural deaneries, and little is known about the pattern of local churches.[8] Minsters and smaller churches are only clearly recorded in a few places, though probably no one lived very far from some kind of church, or place where, from time to time, preaching and the celebration of the sacraments took place, as, for example, at a cross outdoors. Within the towns, churches were probably more common: we know that Barnstaple, Kingsbridge, Kingsteignton, Lydford and Totnes had at least one each, whereas Exeter by the twelfth century had as many as 29, which put it on a par with Canterbury and above York. But the diocese in 1050 had not completed the process by which England became divided into parishes, and Leofric was not by later standards so well-furnished with means by which he might foster the life of the Church and bring it into order and unity.

Changes over Three Centuries

Between 1050 and 1307 things were to change very considerably, so that by the end something very much like the present organisation existed. Why did this happen? Let us begin by looking at the pressures operating at the 'parish level'. Everywhere in England, as indeed in western Europe, there was a fairly steady growth of population, so that there were around twice as many people at the end of these years as there were at their start.[9] This process occurred in the old centres of population, villages and towns, as well as at new places, higher up valleys for example, or where there had been woodland, as well as around the edges of towns. Alongside this growth a much more complex economy and society were coming into existence, for although most people continued to get their living directly from agriculture, total production grew and those who were able to enjoy a larger share of it, because of their position in society, were able to command products, often from places far away from the South West, which made life more comfortable. Wine, furs, the finest Flemish cloth, for example, could be afforded by a few, and a class of merchants and tradespeople developed to serve such needs. Parallel with this growth in population and expectations we can understand how it was that people who had been accustomed to travel some distance to get to the mother church of their area, decided that they wished to have a church or chapel of their own, and so the number of places where worship was regularly offered multiplied considerably.

But changes during this period were not all, as an economist might say, 'demand led'; they did not all result from the demands of laymen and women. Some of them came about as the suppliers of Christian services, the clergy, developed new ideas about what they should be doing.[10] It came to be thought, for example, that marriage was incompatible with the exercise of priestly functions, so that whereas formerly sons had often taken over churches where their fathers had served, this was now forbidden. Another force was the growth of more precise ideas about the powers exercised by priests in the eucharist. By the second half of the twelfth century the word transsubstantiation had been invented by theologians to express what happened to the bread and wine. Similar ideas led the Church to attempt, in a way it had never done before, to see that every child was baptised and confirmed, so that it could participate in the eucharist, and this involved, too, a stress upon the necessity for regular confession, since it was held that to receive communion whilst in a state of sin was itself sinful. Regular confession and communion went, therefore, together. The fading away of a priestly caste who inherited their positions also raised questions about the selection and training of clergy. Ideas like these brought about many of the changes which we shall observe in this period. Part of the drive towards them came from a series of relatively well-educated and serious-minded popes, as well as from energetic bishops and clergy below them. As a result of these pressures from below and above, something like the present parish organisation emerged by the end of the thirteenth century, and between it and the bishop intermediary levels of organisation—archdeaconries and rural deaneries—had emerged about a hundred years earlier, by which time the cathedral chapter had organised itself more elaborately too. Every person in the diocese was now near to a place where he or she could receive the sacraments, whilst the growth of institutions above parish level enabled the clergy to regulate what went on in the parishes more efficiently. Let us now look more closely at these layers for a moment, working from the centre outwards.

By the time of Bishop Brewer (1223–44), the diocese had a very much more impressive cathedral than the minster taken over by Leofric in 1050.[11] William Warelwast began to build it, in the new Romanesque style, in 1114 on a site north-east of the old church. Work had progressed sufficiently far for the clergy to move into the east end of the new building in 1133. Fifty years or so later, around 1180, when the church was finished, they had a new home almost three times the length of their old one, which would have fitted easily into the new nave. By 1225 the former somewhat amorphous body of canons was led by four great officers, the dean, precentor, chancellor and treasurer, responsible for overall discipline, music, secretarial duties and education, and church furnishings respectively.[12] To assist them there had grown up a complex body of lesser clergy, boys and young men to sing, and twenty-four vicars choral in priestly orders who deputised for the canons. There were also four archdeacons, based at the cathedral but each in charge of a separate area of the diocese: Exeter (east Devon), Cornwall, Totnes (south and west Devon), and Barnstaple (north Devon).[13]

Within each of the archdeaconries, the parishes by 1200 had been grouped into rural deaneries, of which there were eventually thirty-six. There is much about the way these divisions occurred that we can only speculate on, and it is hard to understand why, for example, places like Cadbury or Dunkeswell became the centre of a deanery. Probably very old and now obscured patterns of local life had something to do with it. There also developed a system of Church courts to supervise and discipline the clergy and laity, though within this period they have left extremely sparse records. At the parish level it is clear that by around 1300 the diocese was provided with almost as many churches as it had at the Reformation over two hundred years later: about 413 in Devon and 170 in Cornwall, plus many lesser chapels. We may note here too that the total area occupied by the diocese was almost the same as that of the two modern counties save that one parish, Thorncombe, now in Dorset, was a detached island belonging to Exeter, separated by a piece of Salisbury diocese, while Salisbury in turn possessed an island within Exeter diocese, the parish of Stockland northwest of Axminster between the Otter and Yarty valleys.[14]

Let us now examine some other aspects of life at the parish level. Every parish church had a patron responsible, in theory, for choosing the clergyman (subject to the bishop's oversight).[15] Sometimes the patron was the lord of the local manor—king, bishop, monastery, or nobleman; sometimes patronage was shared between a number of people, just as the lordship of manors was often shared. Quite often patrons gave their rights to monasteries, so that the latter came to have a significant amount of patronage. The clergyman thus appointed was called the rector, and he enjoyed the income which went with his position, or benefice: the profits of Church land or 'glebe', offerings at the church made, for example, at funerals, and, most important, tithes—a tenth of the crops and young animals produced in the village, generally by this time reckoned at a fixed amount each year. When monasteries became patrons of churches, they often decided to 'appropriate' them (making them almost wholly within their control), becoming the rectors themselves, taking most of the income, and leaving the rest to a deputy clergyman or 'vicar'. The appointment of vicars, like that of rectors, was also subject to episcopal approval, and vicars had the same rights and duties, except, of course, that they did not receive so much income. Bishops, indeed, tried to lay down minimum stipends for vicars at the time they approved appropriation, and from time to time more generally in their statutes.[16] Both rectors and vicars enjoyed tenure for life or until they resigned, and both were expected to provide church services and care for the

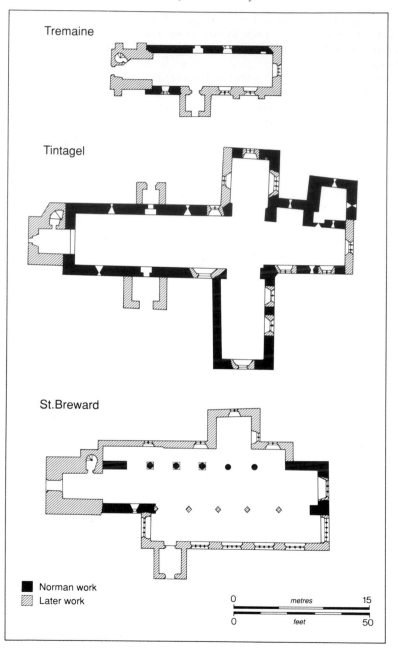

Tremaine

Tintagel

St.Breward

■ Norman work
▨ Later work

Fig. 4   Norman church plans in north Cornwall.

souls of their parishioners, either personally or through a paid curate. Because the parish system grew up gradually, rather than being planned, and was often related to the system of rural estates, parishes varied greatly in size and value. In Devon, for example, the great minster parishes of Crediton, Hartland, Plympton and Tiverton continued to include thousands of acres, whilst the tiniest ones like Dotton and Rousdon in east Devon covered only 214 and 255 acres respectively. Clergy incomes consequently varied too, from North Molton, probably underestimated at £33 a year in 1291, down to the small city parishes in Exeter worth only £1 or £2. This in turn affected the type of clergyman in each parish. Wealthy, well-connected men tended to get the rich parishes, their poorer counterparts the poor ones, and both moved to better themselves if opportunity offered. It seems and was an inequitable system, but it survived largely unchanged right through the Reformation up to the mid-nineteenth century, and clergy incomes did not become uniform until the middle of the twentieth.

In the parishes there was also a great deal of church building during the twelfth century. Unlike Saxon work which rarely survives, Norman masonry is widely traceable in churches throughout the South West, although often not much of it is left, due to later rebuilding. In this, of course, parish churches resemble the cathedral at Exeter. The simplest kind of Norman church consisted of a rectangular nave and chancel, sometimes hardly divided, as at Tremaine near Launceston (*Figure 4*). This could be amplified by adding a north aisle to the nave, as was done at St Breward and Morwenstow (Cornwall), north and south aisles as at St Mary Arches in Exeter, or transepts which are well preserved at Tintagel. We know little about the worship which went on inside these churches. Few of their fittings survive and documentary references about parish services are rare, but architecture gives some hints. The priest celebrated mass, perhaps weekly, at the high (or chief) altar in the chancel, and baptised babies in the font, usually towards the west end of the church. Aisles suggest processions, and transepts could have been used to house extra altars, images of saints, or tombs of important people. Norman church worship, however, seems to have been simpler than it became later on in the fourteenth and fifteenth centuries. The church was more open inside. Less was done to screen off the priest from the congregation at the beginning of our period, just as many priests were married, like the laity. Altars and chapels were less secluded from public contact, and there was less room for grand processions or extra, private devotions.

By the thirteenth century this was changing. Pressure was increasing on the clergy to be celibate, as we have seen, alongside the development of new ideas about what happened when the bread and wine were consecrated. Once Christ was thought to be physically present at the mass, it seemed more necessary to distance him from the congregation by screening off the chancel where mass was said and by withdrawing any lesser altars into closed chapels or behind partitions. At the same time the idea was gaining strength that if the priest prayed for the dead by name during mass, the merit of the service was transferred to relieve them in purgatory, a place where everyone feared having to spend some time being purged of their sins. By the thirteenth century there was an immense popular wish to have masses said for the dead. Poor people paid the clergy a few pence to say one or two; wealthier yeomen and townspeople formed guilds and funded priests to say regular masses for the souls of all their members, living or dead. The wealthiest clergy and aristocracy founded perpetual chantries, with endowments to pay a priest to say mass for their souls for ever at a side altar in the parish church. In consequence, not all but many churches acquired more altars and priests to do this work, especially up to the Black Death in 1349 when clergy were more plentiful and their wages were low. The simpler churches of Norman times often became bigger and more complex as a result, with screened off chancels and room for side altars, guild chapels and chantries. That is why so many were rebuilt in the later middle ages, and why relatively little Norman work survives.

The Bishops

Many of these developments could scarcely have taken place without there being competent people to carry them out, so it may be well to pause for a moment to consider what we know about the bishops in office in the 250 years after Leofric's appointment.[17] There were fourteen of them in all, enjoying mostly fairly long episcopacies, about eighteen years on average, with generally only short vacancies between. Exeter was not so wealthy a see that any king was tempted to keep it empty for long in order to take its revenues into his hands. The average vacancy from the death of one bishop to the consecration of his successor was a year and eight months. The longest gap occurred when Henry Marshal died in November 1206; his successor was not elected until April 1214 and consecrated on 5 October that year, a total vacancy of almost eight years. This protracted interlude took place, however, in exceptional circumstances when England was under a papal interdict, and vacancies at this level in the Church were not filled. Not only, however, was Exeter led by men who were at the helm for relatively long periods, but they were often men who knew the diocese before they were appointed. Most of the fourteen bishops had either held some office here or were Devon born and bred.[18] This predominance of local talent was peculiarly marked between 1245 and 1291 when Blund, Bronescombe and Quinel were natives of the county and probably born within its leading city. More local roots could almost certainly be found

Plate 4   Tintagel parish church, Cornwall

One of the region's best surviving Norman churches, on the bleak Atlantic coast, still showing much of its original chancel, nave and transepts.

if one looked hard enough. Bitton, for example, although a Gloucestershire man and someone who had risen in another diocese (Bath and Wells) before he became bishop, had a cousin among the canonesses at Canonsleigh as well as a nephew serving as prior at Plympton when he died.[19] Both of these could have gained places through his patronage, but they could just as well have been local people. In any case the fact that so many bishops knew the diocese and some of its problems before they gained the highest office in it must have given them a good start. The diocese was, on the whole, guided by people who knew a good deal about what they had to do and remained alive long enough to carry their plans through.

Yet here we must recognise that a bishop, as we shall see in other periods too, was far more than just the father of his local flock; he was a great lord and counsellor to the king too. Just how much time any bishop was away from his diocese is impossible to know until we can reconstruct itineraries with the aid of bishops' registers—the records of their activities—the first of which to survive is Bronescombe's (1258–80).[20] From the registers we can see that Bronescombe could rarely spend more than half of any year in the diocese, whilst his successor Quinel (1280–91), less involved with public business, achieved on average two-thirds of the year at home, and Grandisson (1327–69) left for business elsewhere only rarely.[21] This range of relations between 'home' and away is probably not greatly out of keeping with the situation earlier before registers were kept. William Warelwast (1107-37) who acted as ambassador for Henry I and travelled at least twice to Rome for him, or Bartholomew (1161–84), who was used frequently as a judge-delegate by the pope, may well have been nearer to Bronescombe's pattern than Grandisson's.[22] Bartholomew, indeed, may remind us that the demands of the wider Church could be just as time-consuming as those of a king. Here it is important to realise that successive bishops attended councils of the western Church with some assiduity, from William Warelwast who was one of the four English bishops at the Council of Reims in 1119, to Bronescombe who was at the Council of Lyon in 1274. The most significant council of the period, the Fourth Lateran summoned by Innocent III in 1215, was attended by the newly installed Simon of Apulia (1214–23).[23] At such ecclesiastical gatherings, or indeed at national assemblies and parliaments, bishops were brought up to date and made aware that their diocese was part of the larger unities of kingdom and Church which might, from time to time, make their own demands upon the resources of their diocese. In 1275, for example, Bronescombe attended a council held in London where the clergy agreed to give a tenth of their income to the king. Shortly afterwards the bishop called the clergy of Devon to meet in Exeter to debate and accept what had already been agreed at London.

Statutes and Standards

Can we measure the effect of these contacts upon the diocese? We can, but only in an impressionistic, rather than a statistical, way, and that only for the latter part of our period. First, we can look to see whether bishops attempted to legislate for their diocese as popes and archbishops did for their wider responsibilities, and then whether their statutes reflected the concerns of those higher prelates, after which we may ask whether their legislation had any effect. The earliest statutes for the diocese to survive come, almost certainly, from the time of Bishop Brewer (1223–44), whom we have already noticed as an organiser.[24] His statutes reflect the work of a provincial council held at Oxford in 1222, as well as statutes made by his seniors, Archbishop Langton and Bishop Richard Poore of Salisbury, all of which had been influenced by the Fourth Lateran Council. Brewer imposed the form of the Creed agreed at that assembly, for example, and copied the words in which Poore had insisted upon annual confession and communion by the lay people. Oddly enough he seems to have been less strict than the Fourth Lateran about the limits within which marriage between relatives could be permitted, only forbidding it within the fourth degree not the fifth, i.e. allowing it to fourth cousins, whereas the council only permitted it to fifth ones.

Another great set of statutes comes from a diocesan synod held at Exeter by Bishop Quinel in 1287, covering 77 pages in the modern edition, with a further 17 being occupied by his summary or *Summula*, a handbook which his statutes required every clergyman to have.[25] Quinel insisted that each parish priest should teach his parishioners the Creed, the Lord's Prayer and Ave Maria, a provision found in Brewer's statutes, but here with the addition that the Creed should be taught in the vernacular (*saltem in lingua materna*). These Quinel statutes are of the greatest interest (deserving much more attention than they can have here), and clearly show that the bishop was abreast with the work of the main English provincial councils. Apart from his statutes we can also see another reflection of the wider world when, in July 1283, he permitted a rector to be absent from his parish to study upon condition that he assigned part of his stipend to the poor in his parish 'as it was ordered in the last council at Lambeth', that is to say at the council held there in October 1271, which Quinel attended.[26] One may, incidentally, note here that almost a sixth of the institutions of clergy to parish churches which Quinel made were of men described as 'Master' in his register, and therefore probably university graduates.[27] Higher education was improving in his day, thanks to the development of the new universities.

Statutes are not, of course, the only evidence that diocesan synods met, and isolated scraps suggest that they occurred under Leofric, William Warelwast and Bronescombe, besides Brewer and Quinel.[28] But how far down into the Christian community did this legislation penetrate? A couple of anecdotes, little more, survive to suggest that bishops made formal visitations around the diocese in the twelfth century, but a hundred years later we know much more about the process.[29] Bronescombe's register shows that he visited most of the diocese, save north Devon, between August 1259 and February 1260, travelling right into Cornwall where he dedicated no less than 21 churches. Later on in 1261 he set out again, and again in 1272, but equally he never reached large parts of his diocese. There is no sign that Quinel ever attempted a general visitation, whilst for Bitton (1292–1307) the only surviving sign of this kind of activity is a set of decisions (*decreta*) made at Launceston in 1306 or 1307. We should probably not take this as evidence that this was the sum of bishops' visiting; records of visitations were far less likely to survive than, say, records about land, but it must be admitted that we know very little about visitation for most of the period 1050 to 1350.

A chink in the wall, no more, is fortunately provided by a manuscript relating to a visitation by the dean and chapter of Exeter Cathedral of a number of parishes over which they had jurisdiction in 1301–2, during the time of Bitton.[30] This was partly edited by Hingeston-Randolph in the course of his edition of the register of Stapledon (1307–26), Bitton's successor. In all, Hingeston-Randolph—the scholar to whom everyone interested in the diocese owes so much (mixed with a good deal of frustration provoked by his index-treatment of the registers)—provides the text of the visitation of 15 churches. From this it is clear that the visitors based their questions upon the legislation of Bishop Quinel, over, for example, which liturgical books and objects should be in every church. It is striking to find that in five places copies of his statutes existed (termed here *Synodus*, and in one case called Bishop Peter's, i.e. Quinel's), suggesting that legislation *was* becoming known at parish level. Even more important is the fact that the parishioners stated at nine places that their local clergy were good, whilst only one appeared to be grossly offending propriety by keeping company with a married woman. At one place, Cole-brook, parishioners complained that whereas their rector preached regularly on the gospel, he did not tell them much about the Creed, the Ten Command-ments or the mortal sins. At Colyton, on the other hand, they seemed more satisfied, reporting that their previous vicar had brought in the friars to preach for him, whilst the present one told them as much as he knew, which was enough for them. If such a picture were typical of the whole diocese—and one must recall that the sample represents less than 3 per cent (15 out of around 583) of the total number of parishes—Exeter may have been a reasonably well-served and united diocese.[31]

Monks and Nuns

Up to this point nothing has been said about one important part of the Church in the diocese, namely the religious houses (monasteries, nunneries and friaries). The reason for doing so is that although they have left far more records than the rest of the Church put together (because those who inherited their lands at the Reformation were concerned to preserve whatever privileges those lands had gained in earlier times), they probably directly affected the general religious life of the diocese relatively little. Nonetheless their indirect effects were considerable. Let us start by reminding ourselves of the chronology of monastic expansion.[32]

When Leofric became bishop there were only two active 'monastic' foundations in the diocese of Exeter, both abbeys following the Benedictine Rule, at Tavistock and Buckfast, founded between 970 and 980 and in 1018 respectively. Devon was only on the fringe of the area affected by the so-called Tenth-Century Reformation, and it will easily be appreciated how marginal Cornwall was to the movement since neither house was in that county. One hundred years later, around 1150, there were 16 monastic houses in the diocese, whilst fifty years further on again, say in 1201, the total had grown to 26, and by 1300 when the development had stopped there were 37, 35 more than there had been in 1050. These bare figures conceal a good deal, in particular how many sorts of religious life there were in this period. In fact, three types of religious life existed for a man: as a Benedictine monk, as a regular canon, or as a friar. Eighteen houses within the diocese provided the first kind of life, nine the second, and seven the third, making 34 houses in all. For women there were essentially two types of life, as a nun following the rule of Benedict, or as a canoness following the rule of Augustine. Within the diocese there was one house of the former type, Polsloe, and two of the latter, Canonsleigh and Cornworthy, bringing the total of houses to 37 (*Figure 5*, p 36; *Table 2.1*, pp 40-1). Now we need to consider for a moment the basic characteristics of these ways of life and the chronology of their development.[33]

Until the late eleventh century monastic life in western Europe generally followed the rule of Benedict of Nursia (*c*.480–550), but then began an extraordinary 'inventive' period during which various groups sought to rediscover the original meaning of that rule, or indeed to imitate the life of the first monks and hermits who had lived in the desert places of the eastern Mediterranean from the late third century onwards. Over the centuries Benedict's rule had been interpreted in many ways—this was inevitable since it failed to deal with many sides of monastic life—and each house developed its own customs. Some monasteries gained such a high reputation, Cluny in Burgundy, for example, that their way of life was widely adopted by other

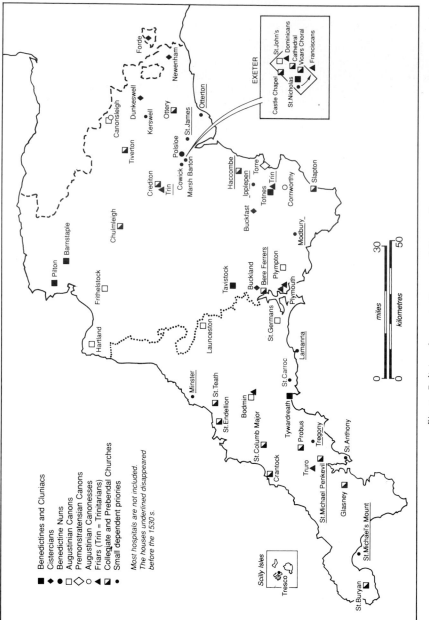

Fig. 5   Religious houses in Devon and Cornwall.

Benedictines and Cluniacs
Cistercians
Benedictine Nuns
Augustinian Canons
Premonstratensian Canons
Augustinian Canonesses
Friars (Trin = Trinitarians)
Collegiate and Prebendal Churches
Small dependent priories

■ ◆ ● □ ◇ ○ ◀ ◩ ·

Most hospitals are not included.
The houses underlined disappeared
before the 1530's.

Scilly Isles

Tresco

EXETER
St.John's
Dominicans
Cathedral
Vicars Choral
Franciscans
Castle Chapel
St.Nicholas

Forde
Newenham
Dunkeswell
Canonsleigh
Kerswell
Ottery
Tiverton
St.James
Crediton Trin
Cowick
Marsh Barton
Polsloe
Otterton
Haccombe
Ipplepen
Torre
Totnes Trin
Buckfast
Cornworthy
Slapton
Modbury
Chulmleigh
Pilton
Barnstaple
Frithelstock
Hartland
Minster
St.Teath
Launceston
Tavistock
Buckland
Bere Ferrers
Plympton
Plymouth
St.Germans
Lamanna
Bodmin
St.Carroc
St.Endellion
St.Columb Major
Tywardreath
Probus
Tregony
St.Anthony
Crantock
Truro
St.Michael Penkevil
Glasney
St.Michael's Mount
St.Buryan

miles
kilometres

0   30
0   50

houses. Barnstaple Priory, established around 1107, was the first Cluniac priory within the diocese. The most successful reform of Benedictine life occurred at Cîteaux, also in Burgundy, founded in 1098, which rapidly gained a family of hundreds of houses all over western Europe. Its first offshoot in the South West was Brightley founded in 1136. A little earlier than these Benedictine reforms, a succession of popes began to encourage clergy who worked together in large, well-endowed, churches (like the Anglo-Saxon minsters) to live in real community with each other, pooling their incomes and setting up a common dormitory and refectory, so popularising what we call regular canons. This development was all part of that attempt to improve the life of the Church which we have noted began with Leo IX, though it is often called the Gregorian Reform after Gregory VII (1073–85). In the early twelfth century these new regular canons took as their basic guide a letter which St Augustine (354–430) had originally written for a community of women. It attracted people seven centuries later because Augustine was a very revered theologian in the West, and because it was written in such general terms that it could be easily interpreted to fit a more, or a less, severe form of life, for example in provision of food and clothing, or insistence upon manual work. Here again among the canons as with the monks, the customs of some houses were adapted more widely than others. Arrouaise in Flanders was the model for the reform of the old minster at Hartland encouraged by Bishop Bartholomew in 1165-9, whilst Prémontré in north-eastern France was copied at Torre founded in 1196.[34]

It is hard for us now to see what exactly differentiated monks from canons since their lives, punctuated by night and day services, were often very similar. Most of them, too, had little pastoral contact with the population at large, although canons did sometimes undertake parish duties in some of the churches which were given to them. Early in the thirteenth century two remarkable individuals, St Francis Bernadone (1181–1226) and St Dominic Guzman (c.1170–1221), created a third kind of life, that of the friars, which centred not only on the recitation of the office in a church but on preaching and teaching ordinary people. Unlike monks or canons who were supported by extensive endowments, the new friars were encouraged to live by begging. Hence these new groups were called mendicants, from the Latin verb *mendicare*, to ask for alms. They came to Exeter diocese from about 1230 onwards. It is significant that a very high proportion of all the foundations made since Leofric's day, 20 of the 37, involved links with 'mother houses', often well outside the diocese, whose life they copied. Sometimes the mother house received regular payments from its daughter, sometimes, as with Cîteaux or Prémontré it retained significant supervisory powers to see that standards of observance remained high. Such links certainly drew those involved into an awareness of the wider world beyond the diocese.

Part of the increase in numbers of religious houses may have merely reflected
the growth in population (which was noted earlier), but the increase was larger
than this, and must be connected with a new enthusiasm for the religious life
among possible entrants which was sweeping western Europe. Some of the new
groups accepted people who could not easily become monks, or canons, because
they were too poor to provide the entry gift often demanded, or not literate
enough to take full part in the work of a choir monk. Cîteaux and Prémontré
particularly let in the poor and illiterate as lay brothers or sisters, whose main
function was to work on the lands which supported the monastery, but who
observed a simplified cycle of services based on the repetition of a few prayers,
notably the Lord's Prayer and the Hail Mary. The friars, too, admitted many
lay brothers.

It would, however, be grossly misleading to suggest that all these communities were sizeable, with, say, as many as a dozen full-time religious in
them.[35] Probably about eleven—almost a third of the total—were in fact little
more than centres for the collection of rents sent to a mother house in France,
staffed by a mere handful of religious. It is hard to see how they can have
achieved a very satisfactory life. Cowick and St James's Priory, for example,
both on the outskirts of Exeter, seem unlikely ever to have had more than four
monks in them. We should not, however, conclude that those monks did not
believe their life to have had a value, or that their prayers were not appreciated
by others, particularly those who founded them, but such houses scarcely
provided an outlet for more than a few. Houses like Tavistock, or the reformed
Buckfast, Dunkeswell, Forde, Hartland, and Torre, on the other hand, were
very different, at least until the Black Death, with relatively large numbers,
probably at least two dozen monks each, sometimes considerably more. As for
the friars, who arrived after the other kinds of religious, although they needed
very little to start their life for they depended largely upon begging, they
certainly gathered in significant numbers. In Exeter, for example, there were
36 Dominicans in 1297, and 34 Franciscans.[36] Nonetheless if one tried to arrive
at a total of monks and nuns in the diocese around 1300, when nationally this
was at its largest, one would not be far wrong in supposing that were no more
than four to five hundred of them. This makes an interesting comparison with
the number of parishes, of which there were around 583 in 1291, and in each
of which (to judge from the visitation materials) there were three or four clergy
of various grades.[37] So parish clergy were far more numerous than 'regular'
(monastic) clergy, yet the resources devoted to the regulars were very considerable and had a great impact upon the Church at large. Before examining
some sides of that impact, we need to ask why patrons and benefactors wanted
to devote some of their resources towards this relatively small group of people.

The answer is bound up with a view about the place of man in the universe which is hard for us to appreciate now.[38] Basically, it was believed that the demands of the Gospel and those presented by ordinary life were irreconcilable: there were, for example, huge tensions between attempting to observe the commandment to love one's enemies and fulfilling the duties expected of a noble warrior. Flight from the world to an enclosed community seemed the safest thing to do, but if you could not do this, then the next best thing was to support such a community which, in return, would pray regularly for you. Just as the work of the parish clergy became increasingly concentrated upon offering the mass for the dead, so monasteries were in many ways focused upon praying for those who had made their way of life possible. This sense comes across very strongly in almost every document recording a gift to a monastery, most of which were drafted in the monastery concerned. So we find, for example, Baldwin earl of Devon giving the church of Tiverton and other lands to the priory which he was setting up at St James on the southern side of Exeter 'for my soul and that of my wife Alice, and of my father Richard and my mother Alice, as well as that of the most noble king Henry'.[39] King, founder and family would all have been regularly prayed for at St James. Similar sentiments moved every donor to a monastery or community of regular canons, and even the much larger numbers who dropped their small coins into the collecting bowls of the friars.

Monastic Resources

From the point of view of patrons and benefactors a sizeable proportion of their wealth was invested in monasteries. So far the evidence has not been carefully weighed, but we know that Buckland, for example, seems to have received about a tenth of the total income available to its very wealthy foundress.[40] Records made at the time of the dissolution of the monasteries in the 1530s (which we may use for an indication of the situation around 1300, because, on the whole, houses did not make large gains, or suffer substantial losses after that) show that houses had significantly different levels of support, derived from very varied forms of estate.[41] Plympton Priory, for example, headed the list at the dissolution with a clear income of £912 a year, whereas Kerswell, the poorest monastery apart from the friaries, had about £29. In the 1530s these sums were received by 21 canons and 2 monks, respectively, say £44 each in the first case, and £15 in the second. The two houses of Augustinian canonesses show another kind of variation.[42] Canonsleigh had land in Suffolk, Dorset and Somerset, besides Devon, amounting to well over 5,600 acres, bringing in £197, whilst the small house of Cornworthy gained its income of £63 from five places nearby, most of which came from glebe land, offerings and tithes belonging to three parish churches which had come into its

Table 2.1: Major Houses of Monks, Nuns and Friars

	Date	Name and type	Dependent on
1	970–80	Tavistock Abbey (Ben.)	
2	1018	Buckfast Abbey I (Ben.)	
3	pre 1087	Otterton Priory (Ben.)	Mont St Michel
4	c.1087–91	St Michael's Mount (Ben.)	Mont St Michel
5	1087	Exeter, St Nicholas Priory (Ben.)	Battle Abbey, Sussex
6	c.1088	Totnes Priory (Ben.)	St Serge, Angers
7	c.1088	Tywardreath Priory (Ben.)	St Serge, Angers
8	c.1107	Barnstaple Priory (Cluniac)	St Martin des Champs, Paris
9	1119–29	Kerswell Priory (Cluniac)	Montacute Priory, Somerset
10	1121	Plympton Priory (Aug.)	Holy Trinity, Aldgate
11	c.1124	Bodmin Priory (Augustinian)	Merton Priory, Surrey
12	1127	Launceston Priory (Aug.)	Holy Trinity, Aldgate
13	1136	Buckfast Abbey II (Savigniac, 1147 Cist.)	Savigny, Normandy
14	1136	Brightley (Cist: 1141, Forde)	Waverley, Surrey
15	c.1140	Modbury Priory (Ben.)	St Pierre sur Dives
16	1141	Exeter, St James Priory (Cluniac)	St Martin des Champs
17	by 1144	Cowick Priory (Ben.)	Bec, Normandy
18	by 1159–60	*Polsloe Priory (Ben.)	
19	1160	Canonsleigh Priory (Aug. canons, *canonesses 1285)	Plympton
20	c.1165–9	Hartland Abbey (Aug.)	Arrouaise
21	c.1170–84	St Germans Priory (Aug.)	
22	by 1183–7	Pilton Priory (Ben.)	Malmesbury, Wilts.
23	by 1190	Minster Priory (Ben.)	St Serge, Angers
24	1196	Torre Abbey (Prem.)	Welbeck, Notts.
25	pre 1199	Trebeigh (Kn. Hosp.)	
26	c.1200	Bodmiscombe (Kn. Hosp.)	
27	1201	Dunkeswell Abbey (Cist.)	Forde
28	c.1205–38	*Cornworthy Priory (Aug.)	
29	c.1220	Frithelstock Priory (Aug.)	Hartland
30	pre 1232	Exeter Priory (Dom.)	
31	pre 1240	Exeter Priory (Franc.)	
32	1247	Newenham Abbey (Cist.)	Beaulieu, Hants.
33	pre 1259	Truro Priory (Dom.)	
34	pre 1260	Bodmin Priory (Franc.)	
35	1271	Totnes Priory (Trin.)	
36	1278	Buckland Abbey (Cist.)	Quarr, Isle of Wight
37	pre 1296	Plymouth Priory (Carm.)	

Houses of female religious are starred. Numbers with planned in brackets.
'Will' = number of pounds sterling paid by the executors of Bishop Bitton's will.

in the Diocese of Exeter, 970–1300

Founder	Numbers	Will	£ Value in 1535	
Ealdorman Ordulf	21 in 1539	20	902	1
Earl Aethelweard	see 13 below			2
King William I	(4)	2	120	3
Robert count of Mortain	3 in 1362 (13)	2	110	4
King William I	(6)	2	147	5
Juhel of Totnes	6 in 1377 (10)	2	124	6
Richard s. of Turold	6 in 1333	2	123	7
Juhel of Totnes	6 in 1279	2	123	8
Matilda Peverell	6 in c.1298	–	28	9
Bp. William Warelwast	40 in 13thc.	5	912	10
Algar & Bp. William	11 in 1381 (13)	5	270	11
Bishop William	13 in 1381	6.13.4	354	12
King Stephen	14 in 1377 (13)	5	466	13
Richard fitz Baldwin	c.60 in c.1170	6.13.4	374	14
Valletort family	?6	1	c.70	15
Baldwin de Redvers	2 in 1279 (5)	1	c.16	16
William fitz Baldwin	?4–6	2	78	17
William de Tracey ?	16 in 1347	13.6.8.	164	18
Walter de Claville;	7 in 1284: 50 in			19
1285, Matilda de Clare	1314 (40)	13.6.8.	197	
Geoffrey of Dinham	11 in 1381 (16)	10	306	20
Bp. Bartholomew	11 in 1381	10	227	21
	4 in 1534	2	56	22
Wm. de Bottreaux	max. 3	1	22	23
William Brewer I	26 (13 min.)	10	396	24
Henry de Pomerai	3 in 1338	–	60	25
	4 in 1338	–	50	26
William Brewer I	12 in 1539 (13)	5	295	27
	9 in 1377 (13)	6.13.4	63	28
Robert Beauchamp	8 in 1377 (13)	2	127	29
	36 in 1297	6.13.4		30
	34 in 1297	20		31
Reginald de Mohun	23 in 1349 (13)	13.6.8.	227	32
	11 in 1538	5		33
	9 in 1538	5		34
Local laity and Bp. Bronescombe		–	14	35
Amicia, countess of Devon	13 in 1539 (13)	5	241	36
	8 in 1297	–		37

Source: D. Knowles & R. N. Hadcock, *Medieval Religious Houses: England and Wales*, 2nd ed. (London, 1971), with additions and corrections.

possession. Such differences owed a lot to the resources controlled by the first founders, and to the degree of interest which the houses came to evoke from the wider world.

Much of the income of monastic houses came from 'appropriated' parish churches, where they installed a vicar to undertake the pastoral role for them, whom they paid relatively poorly.[43] Records drawn up in connection with a tax raised for Pope Nicholas IV in 1291 reveal how just how poor vicars were, on average receiving £2.6s.8d. a year, although Bishop Quinel thought that 5 marks, i.e. £3.6s.8d., was the minimum acceptable.[44] Parish income was also depleted when monks got exemption from paying tithe on such land as they cultivated themselves, rather than let out at rent. This was particularly significant in the case of the Cistercians, who, on the other hand, rarely accepted churches or tithes themselves, at least until around 1200. So, at Thorncombe, the parish in which Forde was founded, some 40 per cent of the titheable land paid nothing to the support of the local parish church.[45] To these ways in which parishes paid for monks and nuns, one must add the payments made from within the diocese to houses outside it. Domesday Book shows that such 'alien' houses, most of them in France, were taking £140 a year from lands and rights which they had been given in Devon and Cornwall, nearly twice the income then received by Tavistock Abbey.[46] By 1300, houses within the diocese gained some money from the world beyond (we have already noticed Canonsleigh), but the balance would seem to have lain the other way. Certainly for Cornwall the dissolution figures reveal a striking situation; in all the Church received a total of over £4083 there, of which a third (£1454) went to support monasteries and collegiate churches within the county. About the same was taken by the bishop, the dean and chapter of Exeter Cathedral and monasteries within Devon and beyond (c. £1500), leaving less than a third for all the parish clergy in the county (£1249).[47] Altogether, the Church at large, particularly in Cornwall, paid dearly for the minority who pursued salvation within a monastery.

Monastic Differences and Similarities

But to return once more to our main theme of unity and variety, let us now consider the degree to which variety in openings in the religious life within the diocese created disunity, struggle and division. We may approach this question in two ways: firstly by looking for signs of rivalry between different sorts of religious, and secondly for evidence of disputes between them and other parts of the Church. There is little sign of the former effect, although we know that the Benedictines and their reformed brothers, the Cistercians, indulged in lively controversy during the first half of the twelfth century, and that in the fourteenth century the friars argued against the way of life of the secular clergy and of monks.[48] But these controversies erupted elsewhere rather than in the South West, except in the case of rivalry between the two main kinds of friars, Franciscans and Dominicans. Between 1279-81 the Dominicans opposed the attempt of the Franciscans to move from an insalubrious site in Exeter to somewhere healthier (did they hope that their confrères would be killed by disease?), but finally they were defeated.[49] Apart from this the various kinds of monks, canons and friars subsisted in a friendly way, and one must therefore ask, why was this so? An answer may be found in the impulse which brought most of these communities into existence; they were not, with some exceptions, created by people wishing to become monks or nuns themselves, but as we have seen by people who saw in such communities assurance that they themselves would arrive in heaven soon after they died, rather than stick somewhere less entrancing. And such people were not, on the whole, ardent supporters of just one way of being prayed into the hereafter, even if those they patronised might be inclined to think that their way of doing it was better than anyone else's. Let us consider a few examples of this tendency.[50]

Early in the twelfth century William fitz Baldwin, lord of the great honour of Okehampton, gave estates on the edge of Exeter to the prestigious abbey of Bec in Normandy which came ultimately to be looked after by a small community of monks at Cowick. It was natural for him to do this since his grandfather had been involved in the establishment of Bec itself. William's younger brother Richard, on the other hand, established Cistercians upon lands near the centre of his estate at Brightley near Okehampton, the first home of the monastery which later moved to Forde. We cannot be certain about what had influenced him to do this, but it is highly likely that the example of his cousins in the 'Clare' family was significant. As another example of the same kind of dispersed largesse we may observe that great servant of the Angevins, William Brewer, who in 1196 founded a house for canons following the strict customs of Prémontré, close to where he was born at Torre. Five years later, in 1201, he also founded Dunkeswell in the eastern part of the county, for Cistercians. Here was a man whose estates and interests, like those of many a great lord, stretched far beyond the diocese, and there too he made other foundations and benefactions. He brought the Premonstratensians to Torre from Welbeck in Nottinghamshire, a house to which he had made gifts from lands he held in the Midlands, whereas his attention seems to have been drawn to the Cistercians through contact with two remarkable abbots of Forde, Baldwin and John, whom he had come across at the king's court. Thirdly, we may note Matilda Peverel who, in the 1120s, founded Kerswell, a small priory which observed the customs of Cluny, following the example of her father who had established a Cluniac priory on his lands at Lenton, near Nottingham about twenty years earlier. Her husband, on the other hand, lord of Blagdon in Somerset, made gifts to Augustinian canons at Plympton, Cistercians at Stanley in Wiltshire, as well as to other houses overseas like Tiron and Savigny. This widely spread beneficence may help to explain why, on the whole, variety did not mean rivalry. Even the friars, who to some extent were jokers in the religious pack because their needs and way of life were so different, merged into the wider religious scene through gaining the position of confessors to bishops or to communities of nuns.[51]

As for disputes between religious houses themselves, or between them and parts of the wider Church, we can certainly find some striking incidents.[52] Abbeys contested rights over local churches with lords, for example Tavistock with a layman over the chapel at Leigh near Milton, or the dean and chapter of Exeter with the mother house of St James's Priory (St Martin des Champs in Paris) about what rights the monks of St James had concerning tithe and burial of the people living near to them. Most such tugs of war, significant because they had economic as well as spiritual implications for those involved, were settled fairly quickly. Only a few such quarrels dragged on for years or had spectacular results.[53] One may cite as examples of such, the five-year-long dispute between the dean and chapter and the Dominicans over the right to hold the funeral of Sir Henry de Raleigh which lasted from 1301 to 1306, or the quarrel between Bishop Bronescombe and Forde about the church at Ottery St Mary which lasted two years, 1275–77, and involved excommunication, an appeal to Parliament, and pacification through the king. One year later in 1278 the Cistercians fell foul of Bronescombe again, when the new monks of Buckland failed to get his permission before starting their life within his diocese. He laid them under interdict and it needed the mediation of the Franciscan archbishop of Canterbury, John Pecham, and then that of Queen Eleanor, to persuade him to lift his sentence. This proved to be his last official act made on his deathbed. Yet one can not argue from these two examples that Bronescombe was an inveterate enemy of the Cistercians, for in 1270 he gave no less than 600 marks, i.e. £400, a huge sum, to those of Newenham when he dedicated their church.

Bishops indeed played over the centuries a notable part in developing and fostering the religious life in the diocese, as they had been supposed to do since the Council of Chalcedon (451).[54] William Warelwast, for example, helped to transform the old minsters at Bodmin, Launceston and Plympton into regular communities following the rule of St Augustine, whilst Bartholomew helped bring about similar changes at St Germans and Hartland. Again and again bishops made greater and lesser gifts to the very bodies which in some cases were seeking to gain from the pope exemption from their diocesan's rights over them. But all this is not to suggest that the variety created a uniform pattern

Plate 5   Forde Abbey, Thorncombe, formerly Devon
The splendid lodging built by Abbot Chard (for himself) before the abbey was dissolved in
1539: a far cry from early Cistercian austerity.

across the diocese. There were, for example, no sizeable monastic communities at all in Cornwall apart from the regular canons at Bodmin, Launceston and St Germans, and not a single house there for women who wished to follow the monastic life. North Devon too had few foundations, but this is probably not surprising when one bears in mind its terrain where, apart from the narrow coastal strip, the land was too rugged and poor to be of much use for monks.

Between 1050 and 1350, the diocese of Exeter produced few men or women who made much of a mark on the wider national or international scene. Baldwin (d. 1190), sometime archdeacon of Totnes and abbot of Forde, who became successively bishop of Worcester and archbishop of Canterbury, is one of the few exceptions to the rule.[55] Contrariwise most of the movements in the life of the Church took some root here, though one can not claim that monasticism flourished to the same extent as in Yorkshire or Lincolnshire, for example. Perhaps the land was on the whole not rich enough and too isolated to provide sufficient resources, but the situation may have owed a lot to the interests of great lords who might have patronised monasticism in directing their charity elsewhere, outside the diocese. We have already seen how some of the choices which founders made to support one group rather than another seem to have been influenced by just such links. It is possible, too, that the relative wealth of the bishop himself, combined with the resources controlled by the dean and chapter, may have used up too great a proportion of the resources of the two counties to leave many pickings for monks and nuns.

In this whole area there are many questions which need further exploration. We need to know far more about the feudal geography of the diocese, for instance, which may be part of the answer. One may suggest, for example, that the considerable size of the estate which formed the core of the earldom and later the duchy of Cornwall, may have had a lot to do with the paucity of monastic foundations within that county. Richard, earl of Cornwall, brother of Henry III, was a notable benefactor of monks, but when he decided to establish Cistercians it was at Hailes in Gloucestershire, and to it he gave lands and churches in Cornwall, just as he gave Cornish churches to the Cistercians of Beaulieu, his father's foundation in Hampshire. Other Cornish (and to a lesser degree Devon-based) landowners seem to have done the same, but we need to reexamine the evidence before we can be certain.[56]

Jews in the Diocese

In theory everybody who lived within any part of the West was a Christian, but one group conspicuously was not: the Jews.[57] On the whole their lives were not subject to the discipline of the Church, but rather to that of the ruler and his courts, although relationships between Christians and Jews did engage bishops from time to time. In England as a whole there is no evidence for a Jewish presence before the coming of the Normans, and it seems that Jewish communities within the duchy of Normandy provided the bulk of those who came. At first they were restricted to living in London, but gradually, as the twelfth century progressed they began to moved out to live in a number of larger towns: 17 by the early thirteenth century. The first mention of any Jew in Exeter occurs in 1180–1, but it is highly likely that they had arrived here some years earlier. Bishop Bartholomew wrote a treatise in the form of a dialogue against the Jews which must date from between 1180 and 1184 since he dedicated it to Baldwin, then bishop of Worcester. A chronicle being written in northern France about this time tells us that Baldwin himself had a reputation of being too friendly with Jews.[58] For such things to have happened suggests that there must have been a sizeable community in Exeter before 1180. It was, however, the only one in the South West, and seems to have been smaller and less prosperous than the Jewries of Bristol or Gloucester. There are references to individual Jews in other places, but the position of such individuals was even more precarious than that of a community. In 1271, for example, a Jew called Jacob of Norwich was found living in Honiton and had all his chattels taken into the king's hands because he was not residing in one of the places with a recognised community.[59] One would suppose that the Exeter community would have had a synagogue and cemetery, for it was organised; we hear of at least two people called 'bishops', and one as 'chaplain' and 'priest', but we do not know where their worship or burying took place. Their distinctive role was that of financiers, and Exeter, like every other town with a community, had a royal chest where financial bonds were deposited, in the charge of two Christian and two Jewish 'chirographers', i.e. makers of agreements. Jews, it may be noted, were generally literate and educated to a degree above that of most Christians. Unfortunately for them, their position was never a secure one; they were heavily taxed by the crown—sometimes under duress—and they experienced local hostility. In 1287 Bishop Quinel's synod ordered Christians not to visit Jews socially, join with them in festivities or take medicine from their doctors, all provisions which echoed those of the Council of Vienne of 1267.[60] The impulse for this order was probably the arrival in England of a letter from Pope Honorius IV addressed to the archbishop of Canterbury, ordering him to take action. Next year Henna the Jewess had stones thrown at her in South Street by a youth attending the city school, which suggests that antisemitism existed, but equally the prohibitions point to more friendly intercourse across the religious divide, and the stone-throwing was dealt with in the mayor's court.[61] We know of at least two Jews who converted to Christianity, despite the fact that if they did so the king took charge of their possessions.[62] In the end, the Jews left Exeter not through local antagonism

Plate 6 Bishop Bronescombe's tomb, Exeter Cathedral

Bishop Bronescombe, 'Walter the Good', began the rebuilding of the present Gothic cathedral in about 1275, and lies in its Lady Chapel

but a royal order of 1290, expelling them from England as a whole. They were to be absent from the South West, as a community, for the next 430 years.

A Mirror of the Diocese in 1307:
the Funeral and Will of Bishop Bitton

Some impression of the unity of the diocese despite its variety comes across in the record of what happened after the death of Thomas Bitton, fourteenth bishop of Exeter, on 21 September 1307, with which we may bring this chapter to a close.[63] Bitton was buried a few days after his death in the new choir of the cathedral, at the foot of the steps leading up to the high altar. The position was apposite for a man whose forethought had made the new choir possible, following the work of his immediate predecessors, Walter Bronescombe and Peter Quinel, who had begun the rebuilding of the cathedral into its present form in about 1270. This enormous enterprise involving the gradual emergence of a new building around the old one, took about 70 years to complete. It began, like the building of the Romanesque cathedral, at the east end, so that Bronescombe was buried on the south side of the new Lady Chapel and Quinel in its centre. Bitton was buried with a silver gilt chalice and a ring which were both found in 1763, when it was decided to remove the 'old grave slabs . . . in the Choir', and to lay them 'in the Body and Isles of the Church at such places as may want repair.' The cost of every aspect of his funeral expenses was also enumerated in the account drawn up by his executors in 1310, three years later. From this we get a remarkable picture of how the diocese must have both mourned for and profited from his end.

Those professionals of prayer, the 24 vicars choral of the cathedral and the 18 vicars of Crediton, were each paid five shillings to offer thirty masses for his requiem, a process repeated by other groups of clergy in Bath, Bristol and Wells, all places with which the bishop had close connections. The friars, both Dominicans and Franciscans, in Devon and Cornwall were also involved in spinning the rope of prayer to draw Bitton safely heavenward, a rope which cost in all a total of over £42, say roughly four times the annual income thought necessary to support the estate of knighthood at that time, or twelve times what Quinel thought was needed for a parochial vicar. Bell ringing on the day of the funeral came much cheaper: it called for people with brawn rather than brains, and so 6s 8d, half a mark, was enough to reward those who tolled the knell of the passing bishop in 34 churches and chapels in the city of Exeter. The total, one may note, was only five more than there had been at the end of the eleventh century. One prelate, the bishop of Llandaff, who came to officiate, cost a great deal more, taking £13.6s.8d. home with him for his pains, whilst his retinue of clergy, clerks, shield bearers, valets, grooms, pages and palfreymen, more than twenty in all, had to share £2.13s.10d. between them. Death brought unaccustomed largesse to 235 prisoners in Exeter gaols, who each got a penny, whilst twelve clerks locked up there and three more confined by the bishop each received a shilling. Money spilled out still wider: on the day of the funeral over ten thousand poor each had a penny, and a month later, when a memorial mass was offered, 6,348 got the same. The figures certainly astonish; could there have been so many poor in Exeter and its neighbourhood, did many of them queue up more than once, or did the executors consider that anyone who was not powerful and rich could be counted as 'poor'?

There is no end to such questions, but what we can also appreciate now is the degree to which the passing of the spiritual leader of a society was an event which had the widest repercussions, stretching from his cathedral, its city and hinterland into almost every religious house within his diocese. Among his legatees, as distinct from his mass offerers, were no less than 33 monasteries, priories and hospitals which received over £216, divided up into various sums, which express, as far as we can see, no preference for any kind of clergy. The maximum of £20 went to Tavistock, the second richest house in the diocese, whilst £1 went to each of the smallest houses of St James's (Exeter), Minster in Cornwall and Modbury. There must have been warm satisfaction in all these places when the money arrived, and we can imagine some decorous thanks-giving feast being arranged to honour their bishop. His generosity, indeed, may have set off similar reactions in communities separated by ways of life and variations in wealth, though some may have wryly reflected that 'to him that hath more will be given' if they knew about those who received twenty times more than they did.

Bitton's legacies totalled nearly £1,350, yet when they and his debts and expenses had been paid, there remained a similar sum to pay over to the dean and chapter for the fabric fund of the cathedral. The significance of this sum may be gained by realising that the *total* sum which Bitton and the dean and chapter had put into the fund from 1297 was less than £200 a year. No wonder that Bitton's successor, Walter Stapledon, gave thanks for Bitton's 'immense subventions' towards the building costs.[64] They were truly princely, though we may admit that his ability to make them depended chiefly upon incomes derived from estates given to the bishops of Exeter long before. That endowment had survived through the three centuries following Leofric's day, and upon it had been built both a cathedral and diocesan structures to organise Christian life for the many in the parishes. In addition, as we have seen, substantial resources had been found to support the few who wished to become monks or nuns. Altogether the diocese had developed a complexity and richness which Leofric would have been surprised to see.

Plate 7   St Michael's chapel, Roche, Cornwall
Medieval chapels were built everywhere: on islands, bridges, city gates and hills (as here—appropriate for an archangel).

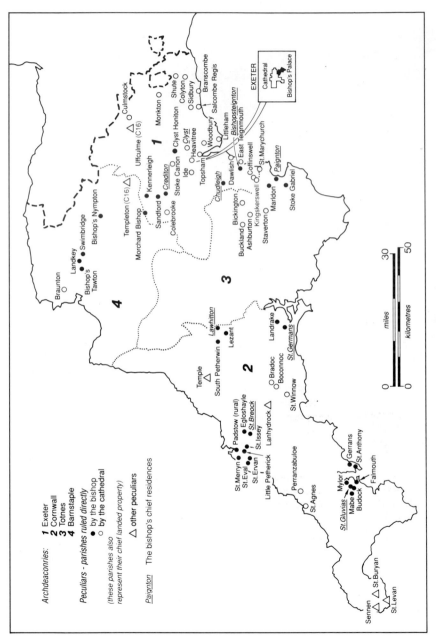

Fig. 6 Exeter diocese in 1307.

Archdeaconries: **1** Exeter
                       2 Cornwall
                       3 Totnes
                       4 Barnstaple

Peculiars - parishes ruled directly
    ● by the bishop
    ○ by the cathedral

(these parishes also
represent their chief landed property)

△ other peculiars

Paignton The bishop's chief residences

CHAPTER THREE

The Later Middle Ages and the Reformation

Nicholas Orme

And by a chapel as I came
Met I with Jesu to churchward gone,
Peter and Paul, Thomas and John,
And his disciples every one.
                    (Fifteenth-century Carol)

Diocese and Religious Houses

In the middle of November 1308 a new bishop of Exeter rode with his retinue into his diocese, along the road from Chard to Honiton. He was Walter Stapledon, the successor of Thomas Bitton, and his first business was to visit the bishop's manors and houses to see their condition and arrange for their administration. On arriving at his manor of Crediton, he found awaiting him—evidently by prearrangement—a vast crowd of clergy anxious to be ordained, and on Sunday 21 December he duly admitted them to holy orders: 273 tonsured clerks, 473 acolytes, 161 subdeacons, 81 deacons and 17 priests, 1,005 in all, their names still extant in his register.[1] This was the biggest ordination ever held in the South West, as far as we know, and no doubt reflected the fact that there had been no bishop for over a year and an inactive one, perhaps, for longer still. In a modern mind it raises questions of quality: how many of these candidates were educated or pious, and what was done to examine them beforehand? But the ordination shows, beyond doubt, the big resources of clerical manpower available to the Church around 1300. This was a time when the population of England rose to five or six million, which it was not to do again until the reign of James I. And far more of the male population, for whatever reason, were becoming clergy than have ever become so since.

This large recruitment of clergy is a testimony to the growth of the Church
in the South West since Anglo-Saxon times, a growth accompanied, as we have
seen, by sophisticated forms of government. By the early fourteenth century
the diocese had developed an organisation similar to that in England elsewhere.
The bishop was helped to rule by one or more deputy administrators called
vicars-general, four archdeacons, 35 rural deans, a bishop's consistory court
and four archdeacons' courts.[2] From time to time there were also suffragan
bishops, not permanent but employed as they were needed, rather like curates
in parishes. The diocese was not as neat and simple to organise, however, as
the list of archdeaconries and rural deaneries might suggest. Some of the
important religious houses had acquired exemption from the bishop's control,
and lay like islands independent of his jurisdiction. These included the five
Cistercian abbeys, the Premonstratensian house at Torre and the six friaries.
Four other places—the church of St Buryan (Cornwall), the priory of St
Michael's Mount, Tavistock Abbey, and the parish of Temple (Cornwall)
belonging to the Knights Templar, later the Knights of St John—also claimed
exemption, though in their cases the claims led to disputes and were not always
successful. Just to complicate matters more, about 52 parishes had been taken
out of the archdeaconries and rural deaneries since the thirteenth century, and
now constituted 'peculiars', 24 of them belonging to Exeter Cathedral and 28
to the bishop himself (*Figure 6*). They had separate arrangements made to
govern them. Add to this the fact that the bishop was never an absolute ruler.
He had to respect the wishes of the nobility and gentry who were patrons of
monasteries and parish churches, and to give way to the pope and the king
who frequently interfered with Church appointments and taxation in the
diocese. Even parish priests, once ordained and instituted to their livings, were
hard to discipline, and lay people even harder still. We often romanticise the
middle ages as ages of faith; medieval Church leaders were more prone to
lament the wickedness of the times.

Sixteen bishops ruled the diocese from Stapledon in 1308 to Veysey at the
time of the Reformation.[3] All were 'secular' clergy, i.e. not members of religious
orders, except for Richard Redman (1495–1501), a Premonstratensian canon,
and all apart from him and Thomas Brantingham (1370–94) had been to
university. In theory, every bishop up to 1327 was elected by the 24 canons of
the cathedral. From 1327 till the Reformation they were directly appointed or
'provided' by the pope, and after the Reformation the right returned to the
canons, who still possess it today. In practice, almost all appointments since
1050 have been royal ones, the crown informing the pope or canons whom it
wished to have, and generally getting its way. The main exception was in 1327
when Pope John XXII appointed John Grandisson, at a time when Edward II
had just been deposed, Edward III was young, and the crown was weak. Most

of the bishops between 1308 and 1530 were therefore king's men, and had usually been civil servants or royal chaplains who received the bishopric as a reward for faithful and efficient service. A few—Stapledon, Brantingham, Stafford and Nevill—remained in London as great officers of state (chancellors and treasurers of England) even after becoming bishops, and ruled the diocese through deputies. All were important men, whose lives were chiefly spent in administering the property of the see, the affairs of the diocese and the king's business, but they had the intelligence and the money to take an interest in other things as well. Some were builders, such as Stapledon who continued the rebuilding of the cathedral and Grandisson who reconstructed the church of Ottery St Mary. Others supported religious cults, like Grandisson who encouraged devotion to the Virgin, St Boniface and St Sidwell, while Lacy introduced the festival of the Archangel Raphael. Most liked music, maintained a choir of men and boys in their household, and patronised composers. And some were benefactors of education, founding two Oxford colleges and improving the resources of six grammar schools in Devon or elsewhere in England.[4]

The one monastic bishop in the list reminds us that the later middle ages were not a great era of monasticism. By 1308 the expansion of monks, friars and nuns in Exeter diocese was virtually over. The last new monastery was Buckland (Devon) in 1278, and the last friary (save one) was the Carmelite priory at Plymouth in the 1290s. Instead, in the thirteenth century, wealthy people had begun to found chantries and collegiate churches. A chantry was an endowment to pay a priest to pray and celebrate mass every day with intercessions for the soul of the founder, thereby lessening the pains that might be suffered in purgatory. Chantry priests were generally poor chaplains who said their prayers at altars in parish churches or chapels of ease, and between the thirteenth and early sixteenth centuries several hundred such chantries were established in the diocese, mostly temporary but some permanent, employing one, two or three clergy.[5] In a few cases, larger communities of chantry priests were founded, forming what are called colleges or collegiate churches. Three of these, St Michael Penkevil (Cornwall, 1320), Bere Ferrers (Devon, 1334), and Haccombe (Devon, 1337), were founded by local knights for four, six and six clergy each.[6] Three others, Glasney near Penryn (Cornwall, 1265), Exeter College (Oxford, for west-country students, 1314), and Ottery St Mary (Devon, 1337), were created by bishops: Bronescombe, Stapledon and Grandisson respectively. These were bigger still, Glasney being founded for 26 clergy, Exeter College for 13 and Ottery for 41.[7]

The foundation of the chantries and collegiate churches reflected both the economics and the ideas of the day. They were cheaper to set up than monasteries: generally using parish churches for their worship (sometimes rebuilding them, as at Ottery), and providing only simple accommodation and low wages for the rank-and-file chaplains who served them. With so many clergy being ordained, the rate that each could ask for his work was correspondingly low. Chantry foundations also show a shift of interest away from the cloister. In the twelfth century, the old minsters had seemed worldly and corrupt compared with monasteries; now, in the thirteenth, the new chantry colleges were reviving the minster tradition of churches served by clergy similar to parish clergy. Indeed, Bishop Bronescombe who founded Glasney also spent much time and money reforming and enlarging the minster church at Crediton.[8] This was the time when the universities were developing in England, initially for the non-monastic clergy; when the friars began working in the world; and when writers like Jean de Meung in his famous poem *The Romance of the Rose* were praising the spirituality of ordinary lay people as sometimes better than that of the clergy.[9] It no longer seemed odd to have institutions like chantries and colleges whose clergy lived in separate rooms or houses, continued to possess their own property, and walked about the world like other folk.

Even the foundation of collegiate churches, however, was affected in 1348-9 when the Black Death struck the South West. Its immediate impact was severe: we know that at Bodmin Priory all but two of the canons (about thirteen) were killed, at the hospital for infirm priests at Clyst Gabriel east of Exeter nine out of the eleven inmates died, and at Newenham Abbey twenty out of the twenty-three monks.[10] The losses among the parish clergy were smaller, but their number, like that of the whole population, fell by about a third. Henceforward, most religious houses were half full and the poorer ones were even emptier, because new clergy could choose from the best and ask for higher wages than before. It became more expensive to employ clergy, and although chantries of a single priest or two went on being founded, the only new religious houses to appear in the diocese after 1349 were two more small chantry colleges at Slapton (Devon, 1370) and at St Columb Major (Cornwall, 1427), and one last friary, a Franciscan one at Plymouth in 1383. This was more than matched by the disappearance of ten of the earlier houses. The three small collegiate churches at Bere Ferrers, Haccombe and St Michael Penkevil collapsed after 1349, unable to recruit clergy. Five of the 'alien priories', the small monasteries looking after the lands of French abbeys in the South West, fell victim to the hostility of the English and French in the Hundred Years War, were closed and had their lands given to other foundations. The two small Trinitarian friaries at Crediton and Totnes also disappeared between 1410 and 1509.[11] By 1450 there were slightly fewer houses than there had been a century earlier, and fewer clergy in them.

The houses that remained settled down to an era of peaceful and rather undistinguished history, which lasted till the dissolution of the monasteries in the 1530s. The controversies caused by the Cistercians in the twelfth and thirteenth centuries through depopulating villages and closing churches were over, due to changes in the ways of farming land. The friars' wrangles with the parish clergy about preaching, confessions and funeral dues were largely settled, thanks to regulations laid down by the popes. Up to 1300 the different religious orders had had a dynamic and sometimes unsettling effect on the Church. Now they were quiescent, and their variety was historic and familiar, not new and challenging. They were also more insular. The old ties of the Cistercian, Cluniac and Premonstratensian monasteries with their mother houses in France relaxed, under the pressures of the Hundred Years War. The 'alien priories' either disappeared or became independent English houses. The chantries and collegiate churches had never been much influenced by foreign institutions. Glasney and Ottery took an English church as their model, Exeter Cathedral, as the architecture of Ottery still shows. In literature, the fourteenth century was to see a great revival of English, led by Chaucer, and in architecture the development of an English perpendicular style. In the Church, too, local developments became more important than initiatives from popes, councils and religious organisations overseas, and this would remain the case until the Reformation.

Parishes and Churches

After 1307, as before, the religious houses of Devon and Cornwall contained only a few hundred inmates. For most people, clergy and laity, their unit of religious life was the parish, and by 1300 virtually everywhere in England lay in a definite parish and had long done so.[12] In principle, the parish system encouraged uniformity rather than variety. Each person had duties in the parish where he lived. You had to go to your parish priest on all the chief spiritual occasions of life: baptism, confession, communion, marriage, churching after childbirth, anointing of the sick, and burial. You were expected to worship in your parish church on Sundays and festivals, and you had (if an adult) to pay your priest tithes and offerings. Everyone, in whatever parish, had to accept the Church's dogmas as expressed in the creeds, together with its moral code and its regulations about fasting on Fridays and in Lent. If you did not, you could be disciplined by your priest or by the Church courts of the archdeacons and the bishop. The records of these courts rarely survive from Exeter diocese until the sixteenth century, but we know from dioceses where they exist, like Canterbury and London, that people were summoned from time to time for failing to attend church, pay tithes, obey the moral code or follow the rules about food.[13] A legal framework thus existed for enforcing the Church's laws on the individual Christian, and it was backed up by sermons and popular literature which urged compliance and warned of the spiritual dangers in store for nonconformists.

This is the strict code which we often assume the medieval Church to have imposed. In practice, it was often ineffective. Parishes were different from one another. In small ones, where the church stood in a compact village, the priest and the parish leaders could wield a good deal of power. In larger parishes with an isolated church and a scattered population living in farms and hamlets, people must have been harder to control. The character of the clergyman was another factor. He might be negligent, elderly, or too unpopular to be effective. Some clergy were absentees, represented by poorly-paid curates less able to compel parishioners to attend to their duties. We have no figures for church attendance in the middle ages, but moralists and Church leaders felt it was low rather than high, due to various competing distractions.[14] Some lay people spent their Sundays working; four Cornish churches still possess medieval paintings of a wounded Christ surrounded by the tools of the Sabbath breakers.[15] Others traded, erecting their stalls even in churchyards, tempting the congregation away from worship and disturbing the service. Others amused themselves—dicing, singing and dancing, wrestling or attending taverns—and others, having got drunk the night before, pleaded hangovers. Some people probably stayed away, as they do today, from mere indifference. There is a telling remark about Crediton made by Bishop Veysey in 1523, that the major part of the people was scarcely present four times a year at the principal Sunday mass.[16] The reason, he was told, was that the service was too long—suggesting that then as now people had to be coaxed to church by shorter forms of worship.

You could assert yourself illegally, therefore, by staying away from church, but you could also express your identity by going there, for late-medieval churches offered you a good deal of scope in how you prayed. The 'medieval churches' that survive today in Devon and Cornwall are mostly late medieval, the result of a great rebuilding which took place in the fifteenth and early sixteenth centuries. These rebuilt churches—Ashburton (*Figure 7*) is a good example—were usually larger and more complex than the buildings they replaced. The chancel where the clergy said the services, and the nave where the congregation sat or stood, were now divided by a wooden screen with windows in it. More churches now had aisles where processions could take place, and transepts or side chapels containing altars and images, so that the building had several centres of devotional activity. The chief centre remained the chancel where each Sunday the parish priest would say mattins followed by a procession and mass (the communion service) in the morning, and evensong in the mid-afternoon. The services were in Latin, and were said by

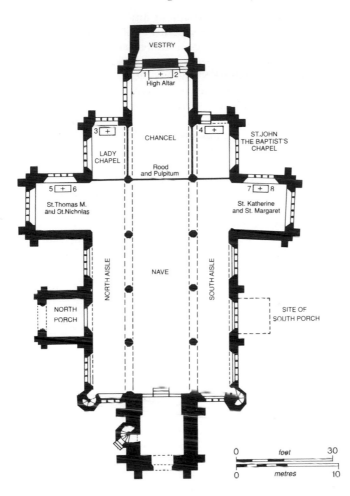

Fig. 7 Ashburton parish church in the early 16th century.
Images: 1 St Andrew, 2 St Mary, 3 St Mary in the north aisle, 5 St Thomas Martyr, 6 St Nicholas, 7 St Katherine, 8 St Margaret. Other probable images, sites not known, included: St Christopher, St Eramus, St George, St Julian, St Mary at the font, St Nectan, St Roche, and possibly St Clement, St James, St Eligius, St Mary Magdalene, St Peter and St William.
Parish stores: Green Torches, High Cross, Hogners (or St Mary in the north aisle), St Andrew, SS Katherine and Margaret, St Clement, St George, SS James and Eligius, St John Baptist, St Julian, St Mary at the font, St Mary Magdalene, SS Nicholas and Thomas, St Peter, St William, Wives, Yellow Torches, Young Men, and Young Men on the land.

the priest and his clerk in dialogue without any oral responses from the laity on the other side of the screen. The separation of the clergy and laity was not absolute, of course, since the laity could take part spiritually, rather like the audience at a concert. During the mass there was a point at which the priest came through the screen and asked the people to pray for particular causes; sometimes he made announcements or preached a sermon. At the supreme moment, the holding up of the consecrated bread by the priest, the laity took off their hats. And although they only received communion once a year at Easter, they were given substitutes on ordinary Sundays: the pax to kiss (a small disc bearing an image of Christ, taken round by the clerk) and holy bread after the service.

Nevertheless, for most of their worship the two sides—clergy and laity—pursued a different path. The latter were left to their own devices, a situation amazing to us. While the service went on behind the screen, they prayed extempore or said aloud the basic prayers which everybody knew (Paternoster, Ave Maria and Creed). Those who were prosperous and literate might take to church the simplified prayer-book known as the office (or hours) of Our Lady, and read it—also aloud. An Italian visitor to London in about 1500 noted, with a foreigner's exaggeration, 'they all attend mass every day, and say many paternosters in public, the women carrying long rosaries in their hands, and any who can read taking the office of Our Lady with them, and with some companion reading it in the church verse by verse, in a low voice, after the manner of churchmen'.[17] The most ambitious might use a copy of the same book that the priest had, for the wills of medieval noblemen and merchants sometimes mention 'my psalter' or 'my missal'. Some people also came to church, according to satirical writers and Church court records, who were drunk, noisy, irreverent or violent. There was, in short, a range of behaviour, wider than that in a modern service, for not only could you think but speak as you wished, provided you did so with decorum. You did not have to speak in time with the priest or your neighbours, as you have to do now.

Medieval parishioners could also choose if they wished to supplement these services with other pious activities. We must not assume that everybody did so, but there is evidence that many people took part in devotions extra to those required. The Church had approved a number of good works which people could do to gain merit or carry out penances: repetitive prayer with a rosary, reading devotional books, fasts, pilgrimages, charity to the poor or other deserving causes, offerings of money in return for indulgences.[18] Even in the countryside, where religious institutions were thinnest on the ground, there was scope for individual piety. Most churches, as has been said, contained images of Christ and the saints at which you could pray by yourself or in a group. Churchwardens' accounts, which begin to survive in the fifteenth century, often mention them. Iddesleigh, a rural parish in mid Devon, had five images or shrines in 1536: St Mary of Iddesleigh, St Mary in the chancel, St Mary of Pity, St Nicholas and All Saints.[19] Morebath, on the Devon-Somerset border, has left us similar evidence of its saint cults in the 1520s and 1530s. The high altar was dedicated to St George and the altar in the north aisle to St Sidwell, each with an image; there were other images of Mary, Anne, Anthony and Dominic. The church had lights as well: one, the almslight, apparently kept for the souls of dead parishioners, and others burning in front of images.[20] We know that the images at Iddesleigh and Morebath attracted devotees because the accounts refer to the image 'stores', i.e. their capital from monetary offerings, fund raisings and donations (often in the form of sheep). Clearly, people in these places were promoting the cults economically and probably therefore devotionally, though we do not know exactly who belonged to each cult and whether they subscribed to more than one.

Churchwardens' accounts exist from about 28 parishes in Devon and Cornwall before the Reformation of parish churches in the 1540s, and many mention stores attached to particular saint cults.[21] In some cases, the word 'store' is accompanied or replaced by 'guild' or 'fraternity', indicating that support for the cults not only existed but took an organised social form. Guilds—societies of people with religious and other purposes—had first appeared in the South West in late Saxon times.[22] We think of them primarily in towns, where they were often formed by craftsmen, but they were common everywhere even in country parishes. Joanna Mattingly, who has studied them in Cornwall, has found in the early sixteenth century mentions of four guilds in each of the churches of Liskeard, Poughill and South Petherwin, seven at Golant and ten each at Anthony and Camborne, suggesting that the fours are examples not totals.[23] Like the stores, the guilds supported a saint cult, probably through maintaining an image and burning a light, but more fully than the stores they were social organisations with officers, members and meetings—even if they met only once a year to remember their saint with a mass and a feast. In some rural parishes we also hear of groups defined by age and gender: the young men, the maidens and the wives, who also chose officers, collected money and maintained a light or other object in the church. We saw that the guilds of the Exeter area in 1100 were dominated by adult men; if this was so later on, it would explain why these other groups were prompted to form their own societies.

A late medieval country church in the South West, therefore, allowed diversity; it gave its members latitude to express their piety through a variety of images, devotions and guilds. But not all religious life was based in the church, even in rural parishes. During the middle ages there was a proliferation of chapels all over Devon and Cornwall, in countryside and town: a first great

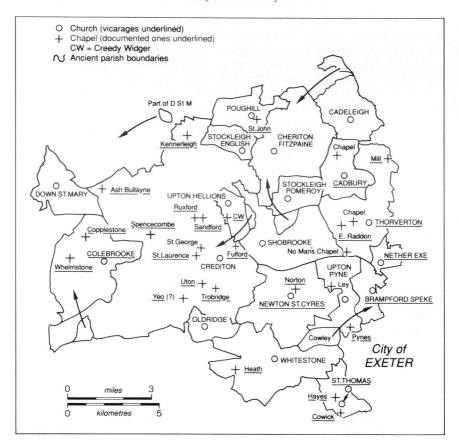

○ Church (vicarages underlined)
+ Chapel (documented ones underlined)
CW = Creedy Widger
∿ Ancient parish boundaries

Part of D St M

POUGHILL
St.John

CADELEIGH

STOCKLEIGH
ENGLISH
Kennerleigh

CHERITON
FITZPAINE

Chapel

Mill

DOWN ST.MARY   Ash Bullayne

UPTON HELLIONS
Ruxford

STOCKLEIGH
POMEROY

CADBURY

Chapel

THORVERTON

Copplestone

Spencecombe

Sandford

CW

E. Raddon

COLEBROOKE

St.George

SHOBROOKE
No Man's Chapel

NETHER EXE

Whelmstone

St.Laurence

Fulford

CREDITON

UPTON
PYNE

Uton

Norton

Ley

BRAMPFORD SPEKE

Yeo (?)

Trobridge

NEWTON ST.CYRES

OLDRIDGE

Cowley   Pynes

City of
EXETER

Heath

WHITESTONE

ST.THOMAS

Hayes

Cowick

0   *miles*   3

0   *kilometres*   5

Fig. 8   Parishes and chapels in mid Devon.

age of such buildings, preceding the second, nonconformist one which began in the seventeenth century (*Figure 8*). Chapels were another development of Saxon times, one of the oldest being St Michael's (East Teignmouth), mentioned as early as 1044.[24] They fell into three main categories. First, there were domestic chapels, very common by the fourteenth and fifteenth centuries in the houses of the nobility, gentry and some clergy and citizens—partly for status, partly for convenience. Taking examples from houses which still exist, we hear of chapels at Boconnoc in 1397, Chambercombe (Ilfracombe) 1439, Cotehele (Calstock) 1411, Fulford (Dunsford) 1402, Pynes (Upton Pyne) 1400, Sand (Sidbury) 1419, Trerice (Newlyn East) 1410, and very many others.[25] Next, there were 'chapels of ease' of a more public kind, for larger communities of people who lived at a distance from their parish churches. Some served hamlets like Kennerleigh in Crediton parish or Culm Davey in Hemyock, others villages like Newton Poppleford (Aylesbeare), Sandford (Crediton) and South Zeal (South Tawton), and yet others towns (especially in Cornwall) like Callington in South Hill parish, Camelford in Lanteglos and Lostwithiel in Lanlivery. Several of these developed into parish churches in later times. The third kind of chapel was a cult chapel, housing the image or relics of a particular saint and tending to attract its worshippers from a wide area. Such chapels were sometimes built in places of topographical significance: islands such as St Nicholas chapel on Drake's Island, rocks like St Michael's chapel at Roche or springs as at the well chapel of Madron near Penzance. Others were quite close to parish churches, like the chapels which actually stood in churchyards at Cheriton Bishop and Nymet Tracy.

By the fourteenth century the bishops were regulating the foundation of chapels by granting licences for them. Bishop Stapledon's register lists 27 grants, Grandisson's 82, Brantingham's 452, Stafford's 326 and Lacy's 383—a total of about 1,270 over the period 1308 to 1455.[26] These figures need refining. Some licences allow an unspecified number of chapels; in other cases several licences may refer to the same chapel. There were also chapels in use for which no licence survives. The real number was undoubtedly large, however, for bishops do not seem to have minded licensing chapels in principle, provided that no threat was offered to the local parish church and its clergy. Those who built chapels had to maintain them and pay for the assistance of a clergyman, while continuing to pay tithes and contribute to the upkeep of the parish church. Services in chapels were often restricted to weekdays or to saints' days, so as not to compete with parish Sunday worship, and fonts and burial grounds were usually prohibited. Finally, all monetary offerings in the chapel had to be surrendered to the parish priest. It may seem odd, with such restrictions, that there was any interest in founding chapels, but the large number recorded proves the opposite.

Many of these rural chapels have disappeared, and it is easy to underestimate their significance. No doubt some were lowly buildings, with small congregations and infrequent services. The chapel of St Bridget, Wembworthy, was licensed in 1421 for mass just once a year,[27] and a chapel on the boundary of Thorverton and Upton Pyne (not yet traced in a document) was known in later times as 'No Man's Chapel'. Nevertheless, such chapels represent an area of growth in late medieval religion, and some became important pilgrimage centres like Buxton (Derbyshire), Catwade (Suffolk) and Muswell (Middlesex).[28] This was also the case in the South West of England. The image of the Holy Trinity at St Day's chapel (Gwennap), first mentioned in the thirteenth century, was much resorted to by pilgrims and attracted bequests in Cornish wills almost as often as St Michael's Mount, the premier Cornish shrine. The chapel of Our Lady in the Park (Liskeard) was noted by the antiquary John Leland in the 1540s as a place of 'great pilgrimage', and the image of Our Lady of Loretta in a chapel at Pilton attracted lucrative offerings as late as the 1530s.[29] Cults like these reveal a shift of interest from the relics of saints, so popular in previous centuries, to images of saints which were easier to procure yet no less capable of miracles. There is also much about medieval chapels that anticipates their nonconformist successors. Often located away from the parish church, sometimes on parish boundaries, they catered for small groups of people who had withdrawn to some extent from the parish church, and sometimes they even fostered an element of religious revivalism. One of the earliest heretical Wycliffite groups in England met in the chapel of St John the Baptist (Leicester) in 1382, while the visions of Elizabeth Barton, 'the mad nun of Kent' in 1527, centred on the roadside chapel of Court-at-Street near Lympne.

The range of religious outlets was greater still in the towns, where there were more people, more money and more leisure for piety. At Ashburton in 1517, for example, there were thirteen stores in the church, each with its wardens, and three other groups of the wives, young men and 'young men upon land' (i.e. from the rural part of the parish). There was also a separate chapel of St Lawrence, with its own guild, priest and regular services.[30] In larger towns there was often a religious house or two, providing more elaborate worship (such as a sequence of daily masses) which local folk were welcome to attend. Launceston, Truro and Plympton each had one such house, and Barnstaple-Pilton, Bodmin, Plymouth and Totnes each had two, besides their parish churches and one or more parish chapels. The best recorded town in this respect is Bodmin, with the Augustinian priory of St Petrock (containing the saint's own shrine), a parish church and six parochial chapels—one (St Thomas) in the churchyard, and the rest in the town. We can get a rare view of people's religious allegiances from the financial records of the rebuilding of Bodmin church, which survive from 1469 to 1472.[31] These show a community

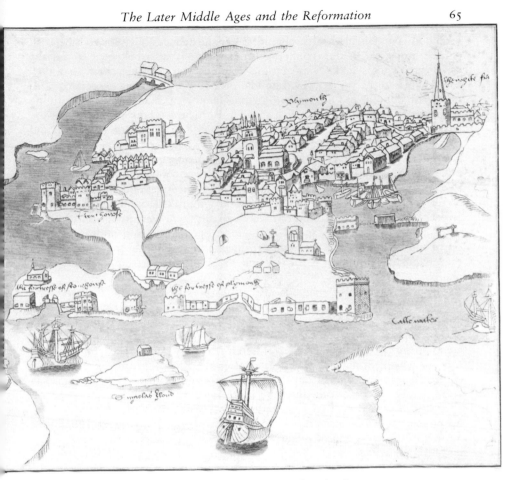

Plate 8   Early-Tudor Plymouth and its churches
An early 16th-century plan, revealing Plymouth dominated by the parish church of St Andrew
(centre) and the Carmelite friary (right). The humbler Franciscan friary stands in front of St
Andrew's, and three chapels are also shown: St Laurence, Stonehouse (left), St Nicholas on
Drake's Island (foreground), and St Katherine on the Hoe (centre right).

both united and divided in its religion. Everyone had an obligation to the parish church and gave to the rebuilding fund, but they also belonged to a large number of guilds and 'congregations', and it was through these that they contributed to the project. Two guilds, probably more, were associated with the parish church, and fifteen with the parochial chapels including six with the chapel of St Leonard alone, which stood in Bore Street. Four other guilds were based on local trades: St Petrock's (the skinners and glovers), SS Dunstan and Eloy (the smiths), St Benedict Anianus (the cordwainers or shoemakers) and St Martin (the millers). These guilds were probably mainly or wholly male, but as in Morebath and Ashburton there were a congregation of wives and two organisations of maidens, one centred on Fore Street and another on Bore Street, besides two further 'neighbourhood' guilds: All Saints, based in Pole Street and St David, based in Fore Street. In all, there were about thirty guilds in Bodmin, variously organised by gender, occupation and address. People opted out of the parish community to meet and worship in these groups, yet they retained a common parochial link and continued to support the parish church.

The widest range of religious affiliations was to be found in Exeter, the leading city of the region. As county town of Devon, diocesan centre of Devon and Cornwall, and chief market and distribution centre of the region, it acted as a provincial capital not unlike Norwich and York. The population of some 3,000 in the later middle ages was catered for by twenty-two parish churches (one of which, St James, disappeared after the Black Death), but there was enough surplus devotion from the inhabitants and from visitors to support a large number of other religious activities. The city housed, besides its parish churches, a cathedral, two Benedictine monasteries, two friaries and a large hospital, all of which attracted lay people for worship. The cathedral contained an important collection of relics and the shrines of Bishop Berkeley (d. 1327) and Bishop Lacy (d. 1455), all visited by pilgrims.[32] Exeter people also attended the cathedral for daily worship. Workers came to the Bratton masses in the nave at dawn, and leisured citizens to a succession of later masses during the mid-morning. In 1472 a very late mass was instituted at 10.00 am, just before dinner time, for the most laggard risers. Cathedral records mention the laity present on Sundays and such festivals as Christmas, Ash Wednesday, Holy Week and Easter Day; there were even a breviary and a psalter chained in the choir 'to serve the people'. Lay support for the other religious houses is also apparent. The Franciscan friary had a ten o'clock mass by 1436, and both it and the Dominican house attracted gifts in wills and were chosen by citizens as places of burial. The Benedictine priory of Cowick had its own saint, Walter, whose shrine received donations in the fifteenth century, and St Nicholas Priory in the city, on being dissolved in 1536, was the scene of a riot by local women who were used to worshipping in the monks' church.[33] The hospital of St John was a further popular place for burials, and must have been resorted to for prayer by the families of those interred.

Chapels also made their appearance in Exeter. By about 1250 the city and its immediate surroundings contained some thirteen open to the public, of which five later disappeared. The remaining eight were supplemented between the thirteenth and the early sixteenth centuries by about another thirteen, making about twenty-one in the 1530s, besides at least a dozen private chapels in people's houses.[34] Of the twenty-one public chapels, one—St George in the guildhall—belonged to the city chamber (or corporation), whose members formed its guild of supporters, and two or three were associated with craft guilds: the cordwainers, weavers and (for a short period) the skinners. The social basis of the others is not clear, but several of them were dedicated to the new cults popular in the later middle ages like St Anne, St Clair, St Loye, St Roche and the Assumption of Our Lady. One or two of these cults were connected with cures for disease, St Clair being patron of eye disorders and St Roche of plague victims, while Bishop Lacy in the cathedral was believed to intercede for people and their animals with ailments of the limbs. The altar of St Apollonia, patroness of toothache, in St Mary Major church, and the image of St Erasmus, patron of intestinal disorders, in St Petrock may have had similar functions.

Opting Out

Why were there so many places of worship in the South West, before the Reformation? At first sight, worshipping away from your parish church had little attraction. Most southern English churches followed the form of services used at Salisbury Cathedral, the Use of Sarum; all services were therefore similar, but where, by whom and for whom they were done could make a difference. Worshipping away from your parish church enabled you to leave your priest and fellow parishioners, whom you might not like, and join your neighbours, fellow workers or fellow cult-devotees in a service taken by a monk, friar or parish priest whose ministry you preferred. You could arrange to have prayers said specifically for you or the guild to which you belonged, or for your ancestors or patron saint. Masses were often dedicated to cults: Our Lady, the Cross, the Holy Spirit, or the dead. You could worship at times which might not be available in your own church, and (if you went to the cathedral, a religious house, or even a large parish church with several clergy) the service would be done with more elaboration, perhaps with polyphonic anthems to vary the plainsong. Larger churches, especially friaries, offered other

Plate 9   Ashton parish church, Devon

It typifies the rebuilt 15th-century churches so common in Devon, with their aisles and great screens separating nave and chancel.

amenities: sermons, confessions and spiritual counsel, of a higher standard than you would get from many parish clergy.

Religious choice in the later middle ages, however, differed from choice today in being tied to certain inescapable duties. Nowadays we can choose whichever church we like, or none, and have no duty to any. Before the Reformation, people could worship at different places provided they also observed their responsibilities to their parish church, which meant that they all retained a common compulsory allegiance. Sometimes the two allegiances— the voluntary and the compulsory—coexisted peacefully as they seem to have done in Bodmin in 1469-72. Sometimes they did not. Competition could arise between the parish church and its parochial chapels. The strain of supporting two places of worship could be burdensome, and chapel congregations sometimes withdrew from their parish churches to what the authorities regarded as an unacceptable degree. The register of Bishop Lacy of Exeter (1420–1455) mentions several confrontations of this kind.[35] At Polruan near Fowey in 1434 three men were charged with trying to gain parochial rights for an undedicated chapel which lay in the parish of Lanteglos-by-Fowey. It was alleged that they forced the Polruan chaplain to bless the chapel, bid prayers from the pulpit, distribute holy bread on Sundays and make wills for sick people—all attributes of an independent church. At Plympton in 1437 the parishioners of St Mary's church—technically a parochial chapel—refused to go to the parish church (the Augustinian priory) for Palm Sunday services. At Sandford in the same year, the inhabitants who had recently been licensed to worship in their own chapel, virtually stopped attending the mother church at Crediton. At Templeton in 1439, local people egged on by the Knights of St John (the lords of the manor) brought in a friar-bishop to consecrate a chapel and cemetery, where baptisms and burials took place against the rights of the mother church of Witheridge. Lacy took vigorous action on behalf of the parish church in every case, and the attempts to secede were frustrated, but not the desires. Templeton managed to gain its independence in about the 1530s, and Sandford later on.

As well as efforts by communities to withdraw from the parochial system, there must have been many attempts to do so by individuals. If we had consistory court records for the fourteenth and fifteenth centuries, they would doubtless feature people accused of not attending services, observing Fridays and Lents or paying tithes and offerings, as records show in other dioceses.[36] But in the South West, nonconformity of this kind was criminal rather than heretical, if that distinction can be made. During the fourteenth century Bishop Grandisson dealt with one or two intellectual dissenters, but they seem to have been untypical eccentrics.[37] There was a brief attempt to preach the heresies of Wycliffe in Cornwall in 1382 by his disciple Laurence Stephen, an Oxford master of arts, but when Stephen was called before the bishop to explain himself, he immediately recanted and later became a respectable rector of Lifton near Launceston.[38] No Wycliffites (or Lollards as they were called) occur in Cornwall or Devon during the fifteenth century, though they appear quite often in the counties further east. Even in the early sixteenth only three men—John Atwyll of Walkhampton in 1506, Otto Corbyn of Exeter in 1515 and William Strowde of Axminster in the late 1520s—are mentioned as being in trouble for holding Lollard or early Protestant views.[39] The first heretic to be burnt in Exeter diocese, Thomas Benet in 1532, was an incomer from Cambridge, and the second, Agnes Prest of Launceston in 1558, was also the last. In the 1520s there was little sign, in either county, of the religious changes which were about to take place. True, printed books were beginning to circulate and some chantry priests were coming to teach schools as well as saying masses. But bishops were still issuing indulgences, people were still offering money for them, and pilgrimages still went on to a number of local shrines and images (*Figure 9*).[40]

The Reformation

We have now seen how the Church in the later middle ages tried to maintain unity in respect of belief and parochial membership, while allowing the individual a range of extra ways in which to worship. The Reformation, starting in the 1520s, changed this situation.[41] One of its first and most significant statements was Luther's famous phrase of 1520, 'we are justified (or saved) by faith alone', and in that word 'alone'—the emphasis on one thing—Luther helped to shape the nature of religious change in the sixteenth century. Religion became more dogmatic, it laid more emphasis on uniformity—on everyone in a kingdom or diocese or parish believing and doing the same, and it reduced variety. This was especially the case among Protestants, but also with Catholics. We can see the change beginning in England under Henry VIII. In 1534 the king was made head of the Church of England, and papal authority was abolished. Two years later, in 1536, the crown began to dissolve first the smaller monasteries, then the friaries, then the greater monasteries and finally the collegiate churches—a twelve-year process ending in 1548. At the same time the bishop was made to surrender much of his property, and became less wealthy and powerful. This lessened the variety in the Church, for it abolished all the different kinds of clergy save for those in the parishes and a few at the cathedrals, and it cut down the number of places where people could worship. Even the parish chapels were hit in 1538 when pilgrimages were forbidden, and images attracting veneration were ordered to be removed.[42] Meanwhile, in 1536 the number of saints' days began to be reduced, and it was eventually forbidden for groups like bakers, brewers and smiths to keep such days as

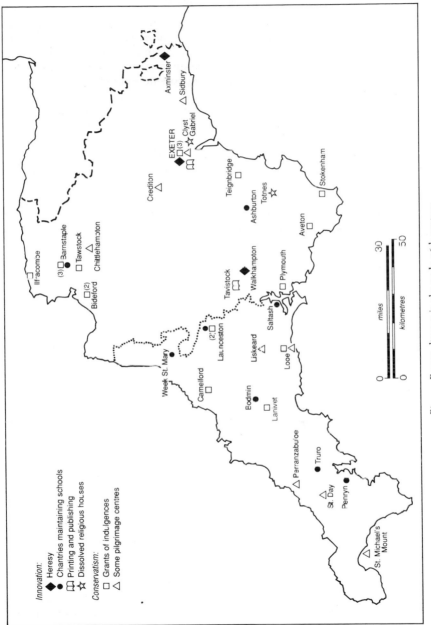

Innovation:
◆ Heresy
● ㊟ Chantries maintaining schools
㊟ Printing and publishing
☆ Dissolved religious houses

Conservatism:
□ Grants of indulgences
△ Some pilgrimage centres

Illfracombe □
(3) □ Barnstaple
□ Tawstock
△ Chittlehampton

Crediton △

□ (2)
Bideford

Axminster ◆
△ Sidbury

EXETER ◆
□ (3)
△ ㊟ ☆ Clyst
Gabriel

Teignbridge □

Stokenham □

Ashburton ●
Totnes ☆
Aveton △

Week St. Mary ●

Camelford □

Launceston ●
(2) □

Liskeard □
△

Tavistock □
Walkhampton ◆
Saltash ●
Plymouth □
Loe □ △

Bodmin □
Lanivet □

Paranzabuloe △
Truro ●
St. Day △
Penryn ●

St. Michael's
Mount △

miles
0   30
kilometres
0   50

Fig. 9   Exeter diocese in the early 16th century.

private holidays.[43] Indulgences, crusades and hermits and anchorites were not abolished formally, but faded away at the same time. On the other hand, Henry allowed the reading of the Bible in English for the first time in 1536,[44] and Bible reading became the one new Reformation activity to which the individual would be recommended to supplement his worship in church.

The simplifying process continued after Henry died in 1547 and the kingdom became officially Protestant under his young son Edward VI. In 1548 the royal government dissolved the chantries (the endowments supporting priests who prayed for the dead), thus removing the extra clergy who had staffed some parish churches—up to as many as four at Cullompton and South Molton, and five at Tiverton.[45] Henceforward, in virtually every parish, there was only a single clergyman. The same year saw the suppression of religious guilds, both the larger ones which had maintained their own chapels and priests, and the smaller ones supporting images and lights in the parish churches. In 1549 the Latin services were abolished and replaced by English ones, in the shape of the so-called first prayer book of Edward VI. The parliamentary statute which sanctioned this was called significantly 'An Act for the Uniformity of Common Prayer'. It imposed one prayer book on the whole of England, abolishing the local variations in services which had been used in the dioceses of Bangor, Hereford, Lincoln and York, and making all worship more simple. The daily services were abridged from eight to two, the day-to-day variations in the prayers and readings were much reduced, and the number of holy days observed each year fell from over 200 to about thirty-eight. At about the same time, the furnishings of churches were also simplified, through the prohibition of images in 1547-8 and altars in 1550.[46] Although this process was reversed for a few years under Mary I (1553–8), the Protestant Reformation was re-established under Elizabeth I in 1559, incorporating most of the changes under Edward VI. A few disputed points of doctrine and practice were left undefined in 1559, but in general the Elizabethan Church followed a more uniform and simple kind of worship than before 1530, and a narrower range of religious activities.

These changes were received by most of the parish clergy and their parishioners without resistance. Churchwardens' accounts show the purchase of Bibles and prayer books, the removal of images, the restoration of Catholic worship under Mary and its fresh destruction under Elizabeth, all taking place in due succession. Sometimes the churches took a little time to respond to changes, but it is difficult to know if the reason was positive dislike of them or merely laziness and inefficiency. It was dangerous to oppose the changes in public, and rare to comment on them in church records as Christopher Trychay, vicar of Morebath, did in 1555. When his parishioners brought back to the church the Catholic ornaments which they had preserved from destruction in Edward VI's reign, Trychay wrote that 'they dyd lyke good catholyke men'.[47]

There was, however, one major outbreak of religious protest in 1549, the so-called 'Prayer-Book Rebellion', set off by the introduction of the book on Whitsunday, 9 June (*Figure 10*, p 74).[48] Disturbances broke out at Bodmin on the 6th before it had even been used, and at Sampford Courtenay (Devon) on the 10th after the congregation had experienced it once. Two separate county risings soon developed, involving several thousand people led by a few gentry, clergy and yeomen. Towards the end of June, the Cornishmen joined the Devonians near Exeter and the two forces made a powerful attack on the city, beginning on 2 July and lasting for over four weeks. But the city held out, its fear of rebellion and disorder outweighing its dislike of religious change.

The rebels drew up their demands under fifteen headings for submission to the king, several of the sections beginning with the robust words 'we will have'. Virtually all the topics concerned religion, testifying to the annoyance which the Reformation had caused in a conservative society. The demands included the abolition of the whole new Protestant worship of Edward VI 'because it is but lyke a Christmas game', the handling of religious matters in English reminding the rebels of the semi-farcical morality plays performed at holiday times. Evidently the prayer-book's virtues were less obvious at first than they are to its supporters nowadays! But the prayer-book was not the only issue, and the rebels went some way towards dissenting from the Reformation of Henry VIII as well. They wanted the holders of monastic lands to give back half to re-establish two abbeys in each county, and Cardinal Pole to be recalled from Rome —surely a step towards the resumption of links with the pope. It may seem that to champion the old religion was to support variety against uniformity, but the rebel demands were actually characterised by intolerance. They asked for the English Bibles to be called in, the heresy laws to be restored, and those who refused to worship the communion bread to 'dye lyke heretykes against the holy Catholyque fayth'.[49] Clearly, the rebels had absorbed the new dogmatism of the age. They were also prepared to kill and die for their cause. Two stiff battles took place at Fenny Bridges and Clyst St Mary before the king's forces lifted the siege of Exeter on 6 August, and only after a further struggle at Sampford Courtenay on the 17th was the rebels' spirit finally broken. The government was equally determined, and the captured leaders suffered execution, the vicar of St Thomas (Exeter) being hanged in his mass-vestments from the top of his own church tower.

The Reformation therefore triumphed, and with it came a greater emphasis on the parish-church community at the expense of the individual. In the first place, the alternative places of worship which people had used were nearly all removed. The dissolution of the monasteries deprived Barnstaple, Bodmin, Launceston, Plymouth, Plympton, Totnes and Truro of their distinctive facilities. In Exeter five houses disappeared—the two friaries, two priories and

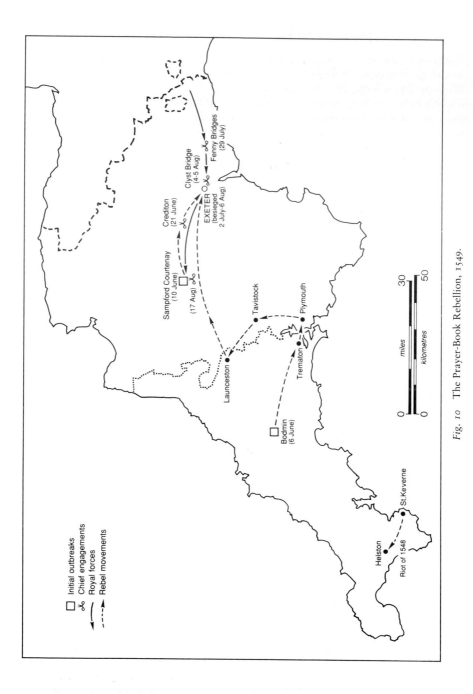

Fig. 10 The Prayer-Book Rebellion, 1549.

the large hospital—all of them previously frequented by lay people. Only the cathedral remained. Parochial chapels were not formally dissolved, but most of them were doomed under the new order. The abolition of chantry priests and guild priests left fewer clergy to serve them; their special saint-cults and pilgrimages were forbidden, and the authorities did not encourage small coteries of people to worship separately after the 1540s. Some domestic chapels may have stayed in use for family prayers and some chapels of ease went on serving fairly large communities like Newton Poppleford and Okehampton, but these were a minority. In Exeter two of the twenty-one chapels survived as parish churches (St David and St Sidwell), two were taken over as almshouse chapels (St Anne and Livery Dole), and the rest were demolished (like the cathedral charnel chapel) or converted to other purposes (like those in the guildhall and the weavers' and tuckers' guild). Some of those which still exist in Devon and Cornwall generally, like No Man's Chapel (now in Crediton cemetery) and Trethevey near Tintagel, were rescued by Victorian or modern antiquaries from the barns and cottages into which they had been turned. They have not had a continuous use since the Reformation.

The worshipper in search of variety was therefore foiled, and even his parish church provided less choice than before. The new Protestant services on Sundays and festivals were a modified version of the medieval ones. They normally consisted of mattins, the litany and the ante-communion (the first half of the communion service) in the morning, and evensong in the mid-afternoon. The full communion service (the old mass) now took place only three or four times a year. But other kinds of worship—processions, masses in side chapels and devotions before images—were no longer allowed. It followed that the church building, which had previously had various centres of devotional activity, now had only one.[50] The clergyman and clerk were brought out of the chancel and placed in desks alongside the congregation in the nave; the pulpit for preaching was also there. The chancel usually contained the communion table, replacing the old altar, but this was only used for the rare communion services and then merely to consecrate and sometimes to communicate the bread and wine. Most even of a communion service took place in the nave. The outer parts of the church—aisles, transepts and side chapels—had no separate role, and often became redundant. Sometimes they were integrated with the nave, and filled with seating. Sometimes they were converted to other uses: schools (as in the Lady chapel at Crediton), aristocratic burials (as at Colyton and Tawstock), or vestries (as in some of the smaller chapels of Exeter Cathedral). Parish worship was therefore consolidated; everyone was brought together, there were no alternatives and those who tried to escape continued to be liable for punishments. The Church's own penalties were reinforced by new ones from the government. The Second Act of

Uniformity of 1552 imposed six months imprisonment on anyone attending any other kind of service (i.e. Catholic ones), with a year for a second offence and life for a third. During Elizabeth I's reign, when Catholic nonconformity became a problem, these penalties were increased.

Moreover, when you attended the new services, it was more difficult to distance yourself from them and follow your own devotions. Instead of watching a Latin service conducted by a priest on the other side of a screen, you now had a service in English carried out by a clergyman closer at hand. The congregation did not contribute much more to the saying of the new service than they had done to the old; most of the prayers were still said by the clergyman or his clerk. But there was no opportunity now to pray aloud on your own, while the service was going on. Everyone was expected to follow the service and do the same thing, not worship privately and individually.[51] Going to church after the Reformation was rather like going to school. The surroundings were now often plain and whitewashed. In place of the old images there were written texts on the walls: the Lord's Prayer, the Ten Commandments, the prohibited degrees of marriage. The clergyman held forth from a reading desk or pulpit not unlike a schoolmaster's high seat, and his discourse contained a good deal of instruction via prayers, Bible readings and sermons or homilies. Under his eye sat the congregation, stationary on benches or in pews. Not that the Reformers introduced seating to churches; it had come in already, during the last decades of the pre-Reformation Church, as the Catholic symbols of the Passion testify on many old bench-ends. Rather, the Reformers capitalised on a trend they found and developed it, for there are two sides to the Reformation. It broke with the past in some respects, while in others it inherited and continued what had been happening in late-medieval Catholicism.

It was easier to enact uniformity than to enforce it. Churches varied in their fittings, clergy in their ministries, and congregations in their spirituality. There went on being uncooperative people who did not attend church, observe the Church's laws or pay church tithes and dues. From 1559 onwards there was, for the first time in the South West, an organised body of religious dissenters: the Roman Catholics. They were not very numerous, but they included a handful of gentry families like the Arundells of Chideock (Dorset) and Lanherne (Cornwall), the Chichesters of Arlington (north Devon) and two Roscarrocks of St Endellion (Cornwall). These and later Catholic families gave protection to missionary priests, and in the eighteenth century their houses became bases from which public churches were eventually established in some of the towns. Still, despite these difficulties, uniformity remained the policy of the crown and the Church authorities, and strenuous attempts were made to impose it, first on Catholics and later on Protestant dissenters. The Reformation ushered in a new era of religious enforcement and resistance to it, which did not begin to subside until the end of the seventeenth century.

Old and New

Elizabeth I succeeded Mary in November 1558, and in the following spring a Parliament dominated by Protestants re-established the Reformation by a number of statutes nowadays known as 'the Elizabethan Church Settlement'. The Settlement restored a Protestant Church of England under royal control with prayer-book services, on what turned out to be a permanent basis. The dissolution of the religious houses was confirmed, and so was the abolition of saint cults, masses, public prayers for the dead and indulgences, though saint cults lingered on, especially in the recourse to holy wells for healing in Cornwall. Much else remained unaltered; indeed, perhaps less changed than stayed unchanged. The Settlement left bishops, dioceses, Church courts, peculiar jurisdictions, parishes, the patronage of benefices, the parish clergy, church buildings, churchwardens and tithes, all virtually as before. Even some of the changes were not as great as they seemed, or seem today. The assertion of royal control over the Church only proclaimed what, to a large extent, had always been true. Church services, although no longer masses, were still conducted by a clergyman and made up of set prayers. Even the Puritans, who began to come to prominence after 1559 with strict views on personal morality and Sunday observance, were the successors, in these opinions, of medieval preachers and reformers.

The Elizabethan Church, however, was much more than the old Church shorn of monasteries and certain kinds of worship. New ideas and institutions were growing up, which made it different from the Church of fifty years before. In the first place, it was much less insular. As in the twelfth century, what was written and done on the continent was important in shaping religious affairs in England. Calvin's writings were widely read by scholars, and committed Protestants looked for inspiration to the Church that he had founded at Geneva. The pope was much in people's minds, usually as an enemy, especially after Pius V declared Elizabeth deposed in 1570, and the Jesuit Order was important in training Catholic missionaries to reconvert the English. The crown and the Church authorities, fearful of Catholics and sometimes of Calvinists too, were more vigilant about the opinions of clergy and laity than in earlier, more easy-going times. Preaching by clergy outside their own churches was carefully licensed, censorship of books was enforced, and education came under more scrutiny. Before the Reformation there were plenty of schools in Devon and Cornwall, but they were not (as people sometimes assume) 'Church schools' in a conscious sense. The bishop and his officers did not inspect them or lay down what they should do. It could be taken for granted that they were Catholic, for what else could they be? The Reformation modified this situation. Schools became strategic places to implant the Protestant religion in the rising generations (or the Catholic religion under Mary), and the authorities woke up to their importance. In 1538–40 Henry VIII issued a uniform Latin grammar to be used in all schools—anticipating Edward VI's uniform prayer-book, and in 1554 Mary ordered schoolmasters to be examined and licensed before they taught, deputing the task to the bishops. Although this was a Catholic initiative, it was so in tune with the times that it was kept in force under Elizabeth, and the bishops remained in charge of vetting and controlling schools for the next 200 years. Education thus became more closely involved with Church leaders and their policies.[52]

Social welfare was another sphere of change. The medieval Church had urged the laity to support the poor and sick, and this was done informally by wealthy people and religious houses with gifts of food and money. During the middle of the sixteenth century, however, the crown gave the Church the task of organising charity, as well as encouraging it. A series of Acts of Parliament beginning in 1536 ordered the churchwardens of each parish to gather alms, relieve the poor, sick and disabled, and compel 'sturdy vagabonds and valiant beggars' to work. By 1598 the wardens were supplemented by four overseers of the poor, voluntary contributions were replaced by compulsory rates, and poor relief was extended to apprenticing poor children and providing work for the unemployed, as well as supporting the sick. Other Acts bound the parishes to appoint surveyors of highways to maintain the local roads.[53] The parish now became a unit of secular as well as ecclesiastical government. Take Ashburton. In 1578–9 its wardens paid out 8d. to a poor blind man, 8d. for hose and shoes for a bastard child, 5s. to find an orphan girl a place as a servant, 3s. 4d. for a shroud for a pauper's funeral, a fine of 4s. 2d. for not repairing the highways, and various sums of money for arms for the local militia.[54] For the next three hundred years, until the creation of parish councils in 1894, clergy and wardens, like the bishops, became enmeshed in public affairs with new responsibilities. It is a paradox that the Reformation gave Church officers powers they had not previously held, as well as taking wealth and power away.

There was also new activity in scholarship and literature. The changes in religion moved theologians to write controversial books about them, and historians to record the things which had passed away like monasteries and shrines. A notable pair of such men from the South West were Thomas Harding (1516–72) and John Jewel (1522–71): born in north Devon, scholars at Barnstaple school (though not together), and eventually Catholic and Protestant respectively. Jewel became bishop of Salisbury in 1559 and published *An*

Plate 10 The choir screen, Exeter Cathedral

Here looking very much as the Reformers left it in 1559: bare of the images and altars which once stood on and beneath it.

Apology for the Church of England in 1562, the first important work in its defence. Harding, by then a Catholic exile at Louvain, replied with a *Confutation* (1565) and other works of attack. Then there were the Hookers: John (*c.* 1526–1601) and his nephew Richard (1554–1600), who was helped to university by Jewel. John, a city officer in Exeter, was a pioneer local historian, writing accounts of the city, the county of Devon, the bishops and the Prayer-Book Rebellion, in which he took a strongly Protestant line while dealing justly with Catholics as individuals. Richard, born at Heavitree and educated in Exeter before moving away from Devon, was the outstanding champion of the Church of England in his day. His *Laws of Ecclesiastical Polity* (1593–7), written in Wiltshire and Kent, ably justified the Church's constitution and worship against Puritan attacks, doing so on the grounds of reason and accordance with God's laws. Finally, there were the Cornishmen: Richard Carew (1555–1620), whose description of the county, *The Survey of Cornwall* (1602), handled the Catholic past with Protestant irony, and Nicholas Roscarrock (*c.* 1550–1633) whose *Lives of the Saints* responded by retelling Cornwall's saintly legends and recording the last memories of Catholic worship there. Works like these form part of the positive achievement of the Reformation. They helped to compensate for the destruction of so much art and learning in the 1530s and 40s.[55]

CHAPTER FOUR

The Seventeenth and Eighteenth Centuries

Jonathan Barry

> The world's turned upside down, from bad to worse,
> Quite out of frame, the cart before the horse.
> The felt-maker and saucy stable groom
> Will dare to perch into the preacher's room;
> Each, ignorant, do of the Spirit boast,
> And prating fools brag of the Holy Ghost.
> (John Taylor, *Mad Fashions*, 1642)

Divisions and Dissent

The late sixteenth and early seventeenth centuries, as Hooker and his fellow-writers show, were new in another respect: in their controversies. The Church of Elizabeth I, inherited by James I and Charles I, with its mixture of Catholic and Protestant organisation, worship and theology, suited the crown and satisfied some people, but was irksome to others. A residue of Catholics, not very many in the South West, dissented inwardly and sometimes outwardly. A much bigger number of anti-Catholics (stimulated by Catholic political threats from Spain, France and Ireland) wanted the Reformation to be carried further, with a more thorough purge of Catholic institutions and a more evangelical kind of religion.[1] Such people were known to their contemporaries, and have come down in history, as Puritans. Throughout the seventeenth century and well into the eighteenth, the presence of Catholics and Puritans (or their successors) caused disturbances in the Church, with many consequences. Let us remind ourselves of how events unfolded.

Most Puritans under Elizabeth I and the early Stuarts were Anglicans, anxious to reform the Church of England from within, rather than separatists trying to break away. The crown and the Church authorities, however, wished to maintain the Elizabethan Settlement, and this caused friction with the Puritan activists. Friction increased in the 1620s with the growth of Arminianism,

81

a high-church movement within the Church of England. Arminians were Anglicans as well, but their views on theology and worship often differed, seeming (to Puritans) to emphasise the clergy, Church ceremonial, saint cults and even pilgrimage and monasticism in ways reminiscent of Catholicism. Thanks to the patronage of Charles I, most of the bishops were Arminians by the end of the 1630s, and the strains in the Church grew greater. The next milestone was the outbreak of the Civil War in 1642, which disrupted the power of the crown and the Church authorities for the first time since the Reformation. The Puritans, who dominated the side that won the war, were able at last to embark on reforming the Church as they wished. But they did not agree how to do it. One party, the Presbyterians, wanted to keep a well-organised national body to which everyone had to belong, replacing the bishops and archdeacons by the Calvinist system of synods and presbyteries. Others, the so-called Independents or Congregationalists, favoured a looser Church in which each parish congregation ran its own affairs. The confusion of the Civil War also allowed other groups to emerge, notably the Baptists and the Quakers, with their own distinctive beliefs and practices. By 1650, when the Civil Wars were over and a republic had been set up, the religious situation was far more complicated than it had been ten years previously. There were still traditional Anglicans, but their bishops had no authority and the Elizabethan prayer-book services were not supposed to be held. Some of the former Anglican clergy and their congregations had become Presbyterians, others Congregationalists and even Baptists, and yet other Baptist and radical groups had organised themselves and set up meetings away from the parish churches. There was a good deal of hostility between these various parties—especially towards the Quakers, whose missionaries entered the South West in 1654 and whose views on religion and society were considered to be particularly subversive and egalitarian.

In 1660 the monarchy was restored, and so was the traditional Church of the Elizabethan Settlement. Two years later, the Anglicans in Parliament pushed through an Act of Uniformity which revived the requirements which Puritans had formerly found hard to accept about the Church. Hundreds of clergy felt unable to conform and left their parish churches, followed by many laity, augmenting the groups who had already departed from the Church in the 1640s and 1650s. Presbyterians, Congregationalists, Baptists and Quakers were now all separated from the Church of England, and the Anglican establishment began a protracted struggle to suppress them and bring everyone back into the national Church. The nonconformists, or dissenters as they were usually called, experienced recurrent, if intermittent, legal and physical harrassment under both common and ecclesiastical law, for their absenteeism from parish services and for attending what became known as 'conventicles'—religious meetings conducted outside the authority of the Church of England. During this period of persecution, which lasted until 1687, the dissenters also continued their rivalries with one another. But their common experience also drove them together, forging a nonconformist identity which was strengthened when, in 1689, Parliament passed a Toleration Act which finally allowed them to set up their own places of worship. This toleration was limited, however, since it did not give dissenters the right to hold public offices (which remained confined to Anglicans), and it was not extended to Catholics. They too had been frequently persecuted up to the 1680s, and their activities only gradually came to be tolerated during the eighteenth century. Full civil rights for dissenters and Catholics were not conceded until well into the nineteenth.

The right to attend their own places of worship offered to Protestant dissenters in 1689 remained controversial for several decades, as Anglicans of the Tory party, claiming that the established Church was in danger, sought to limit or even reverse the position of religious pluralism. After 1715 such conflicts became less intense, not least because the dissenting threat to the Church of England grew manifestly less severe, as nonconformist numbers stabilised. The Whig bishops stressed their common cause with other Protestants against Jacobite Catholicism. Furthermore doctrinal divisions began to weaken the dissenters. The question of the Trinity triggered a dispute in Exeter (1716–20), which then provoked a nationwide split within Presbyterian and Congregational ranks. But from the 1740s the Church faced a new challenge in the shape of the evangelical revival which gave birth to Methodism. In its initial phase, at least, this revival affected all denominations and its leaders strove to portray their efforts as intended, not to establish new Churches, but to encourage spiritual renewal within every Church, perhaps as a prelude to Protestant reunification. Certainly the movement had strong clerical and lay roots within the Church of England, particularly in the South West, but in the end establishment hostility forced Methodists to look outside the national Church and to follow the dissenters into setting up separate congregations. They did so with success, especially in Cornwall, where Methodism came to supplant the Church of England as the majority religion of the people. The decades around 1800 also saw other nonconformist groups displaying renewed vigour in many areas, and once more challenging the position of the Church of England. The twin pressures of the Napoleonic Wars and massive social and economic upheaval injected a new bitterness into religious antagonisms.

Such conflicts require explanation, but there are dangers in offering an account of Church history too rooted in the denominational divisions which had resulted by the nineteenth century. The aim of this chapter is to explore not just varieties of belief and practice, but also deep-seated uniformities of character and aim, amongst the Protestant Churches of the region. The Reformation established an enduring tradition of assumptions about the essence

Plate 11   Loughwood Baptist chapel, Dalwood, Devon

of Church life, and about the need for religious unity within the community, which lasted well beyond the onset of nonconformity. At the same time the Reformation did little to eradicate the varieties of Church conditions created by jurisdictional, geographic and social variations within Devon and Cornwall. Arguably the diversities of Church experience which these produced, within the Church of England and other Churches as much as between them, were as important as the denominational differences which have so monopolised the attention of historians.

The Regional Setting

Compared to many parts of the country, the continuity of the diocese of Exeter through the Reformation changes, and its coincidence with the counties of Devon and Cornwall, offered a promising basis for Anglican uniformity. But, if alternative centres of power like monasteries and parish guilds had gone, the diocesan and parochial system remained full of anomalies. Although the bishops and other leading officials of the diocese were generally active and mounted an unusually thorough effort to coordinate diocesan affairs through archdeaconries and rural deaneries, their struggle was often fruitless.[2] The parochial patronage system after the Reformation gave the wealthier laity power to nominate clergy to most benefices. They acquired the old monastic patronage, and their power over the clergy was extended, as we shall see, by changing financial circumstances. Legal anomalies continued to frustrate the work of the bishop and his officers, not only through the overlap of jurisdictions on Devon's eastern boundary, but through the peculiar jurisdiction or patronage rights of bishops and chapters such as those of Salisbury and Windsor in the area. Divided jurisdictional rights almost always produced other types of religious variety. In December 1663 Bishop Ward wrote to Archbishop Sheldon noting two parts of his diocese

> especially wch are disorderly and troublesome. One is the Easterne part wch borders upon Somerset and Dorset shires, wch being the border of 3 Dioceses as wel as of 3 Counties gives great opportunitie to the Sectaries to play their tricks and escape. The other part is in the South-Hams . . . And for the disorders there, I may in great measure impute them to the *Church of Windsor* . . . Some of the most populous and considerable places within my Diocese (impropriated churches belonging to Windsor) have stood void ever since Aug. 24. 62. [the day when nonconformist ministers were ejected] and there is hardly one parish (within my diocese belonging to that church) where I have not mett with complaint either that they have no minister or a pitifull ignorant one, or the min[iste]r hath complained for want of sufficient maintenance.

As examples he named two boroughs, St Germans and Plympton Maurice, and the 'populous sea towne' of Brixham, which were 'wholely destitute' of clergy.[3] As Ward also noted, however, the diocesan capital itself was the scene of frequent disputes (notably between the cathedral and civic authorities) and of religious pluralism.[4] How much chance, therefore, did the diocesan leaders have of controlling affairs in distant parts of Cornwall and north Devon?

Significantly, it was not just the Anglican establishment that found it hard to maintain a uniform strength across the region, or even to identify our two counties as a single unit. By 1600 the Roman Catholic presence had shrunk to a few areas close to the homes of leading recusant gentry and did not grow again until the very end of this period.[5] Historians who have identified Puritan ministers and laymen within the Church of England before 1640 (and there were only a handful of separatists at this stage) have also insisted on their concentration in certain districts, such as Exeter and south-east Devon, the north Devon coast, and the area of Devon and Cornwall around Plymouth, together with parts of the South Hams. Most of these areas later became nonconformist strongholds.[6] Many of the nonconformist efforts at regional organisation in this period sought to integrate Devon, and to a lesser extent Cornwall, within a wider south-western grouping, always including Dorset and Somerset and sometimes stretching up to Bristol, Gloucestershire and Wiltshire (for example the Baptist Western Association of the 1650s, which excluded Cornwall).[7] Even the so-called Exeter Assembly, officially consisting of Presbyterian and Congregational ministers of Devon and Cornwall, which met during the 1650s and again from 1691, regularly attracted a contingent of west Somerset and Dorset ministers, often exceeding the Cornish representation.[8]

In part this reflected the apparent divergence of the Cornish experience of nonconformity from that of the other three counties. Devon, Somerset and Dorset were centres of so-called 'old dissent', that is Presbyterian, Congregational and to a lesser extent Baptist churches dating from the mid- to late seventeenth century. The Presbyterian presence was matched only in north-west England. By contrast all these groups were strongly underrepresented, by national standards, in Cornwall (see *Tables 4.1* and *4.2*).[9] Daniel Defoe's description of early eighteenth-century Liskeard mentioned 'something rare, for the county of Cornwall, a large new built meeting-house for the dissenters, which I name because there was but three more and these very inconsiderable in all the county of Cornwall; whereas in Devonshire which is the next county there are reckoned about seventy, some of which are exceeding large and fine'.[10] Only the Quakers managed to attract as many followers in Cornwall as in other south-western counties, and even this was at a low level by national standards.[11] By contrast the Methodist movement, famously so strong in Cornwall, or west Cornwall at least, made very little headway in the other

Table 4.1: Estimates of dissenting numbers in the South West c.1715

		England	Cornwall	Devon	Dorset	Somerset*
Estimated pop.		5441670	116970	253150	89550	201090
Presby- terian	congregs.	637	11	57	20	48
	hearers	179350	1190	18220	5090	13630
	% of pop.	3.30	1.02	7.20	5.68	5.78
Indep- endent	congregs.	203	1	7	2	2
	hearers	59940	350	3580	880	500
	% of pop.	1.10	0.30	1.41	0.98	0.25
Partic- ular Baptist	congregs.	206	2	12	3	9
	hearers	40520	450	3170	660	1470
	% of pop.	0.74	0.41	1.25	0.74	0.73
General Baptist	congregs.	122	0	0	2	3
	hearers	18800	0	0	310	940
	% of pop.	0.33	0	0	0.35	0.47
Quaker	congregs.	172	12	14	23	35
	hearers	39510	410	640	350	740
	% of pop.	0.73	0.35	0.25	0.39	0.37

*Somerset figures here exclude Bristol.
Source: M. Watts, *The Dissenters* (Oxford, 1978) p. 509.

Table 4.2: Estimates of dissenting strength (excluding Quakers) 1772–3

	England	Cornwall	Devon	Dorset	Somerset*
Places petitioning for statutory relief, 1772	807	6	47	21	39
Presbyterian or Indep- endent congregations	706	5	43	23	36
Presbyterian or Indep- endent ministers	699	5	38	23	33
Baptist congregations	374	3	15	2	14
Baptist ministers	353	1	13	2	13
Wesleyan preachers	131	7	4	0	4
Wesleyan society membership	33839	1994	425	0	1360

*Somerset figures here include Bristol; all the Wesleyan figures for Somerset
are included in the Bristol circuit.
Source: based on figures in *Transactions of the Congregational History
Society* 5 (1911–12), pp. 379-80, 385.

three counties before 1800 save in a few urban areas. Even in these areas, which were often centres of old dissent as well, the Methodists never stood out as they did in Cornwall.[12]

When considering geographical unity and variety we also need to look, of course, below county level. Different types of Church arrangements, both Anglican and nonconformist, can be associated with different types of settlement. Perhaps the most obvious and important was the rural-urban contrast. Given the increasingly urban concentration of old dissent, at least in Devon, the weaker urban structure of Cornwall may help to explain the difference between the two counties. But we also need to consider varieties within the countryside, for example between the more densely populated arable regions, well supplied with villages or small market towns, and the pastoral areas of thin and dispersed settlements. How far did the established Church have a pattern of churches appropriate to the changing pattern of settlement? How far could nonconformist Churches meet the demands, either of concentrated populations via urban churches, or of scattered rural groups via itinerant ministry? Did the cloth trade of Devon bring town and countryside together, allowing towns to act as centres for rural dissenting (or Anglican) congregations? By contrast, did the new concentrations of population outside the traditional urban framework created by the growing tin industry of West Cornwall sow the seeds for evangelical revival? Equally, did the Plymouth conurbation's rapid growth overstretch the Church of England, despite Admiralty efforts to discourage dissent?[13]

It would be wrong, as we shall see, to adopt any simple geographical determinism to explain the variety of Church experiences, but access to an appropriate church was certainly an important factor. Many of the efforts of both Anglican and nonconformist authorities in this period were centred on the matter, based in part on the sense that they were in competition to provide a service to customers who might well turn to another church if they failed to get the provision they needed. In this competition the Anglicans had the advantage, of course, of a universal parochial network, whose funding was relatively secure, whereas nonconformist provision depended far more on the support and resources of the specific community. On the other hand the Anglicans lacked the flexibility of the other groups in responding to new requirements. Regional and national arrangements to support the education and maintenance of the ministers of old dissent were matched and indeed exceeded by the central direction of itinerant preachers amongst the Quakers and Methodists.

Denominational Similarities and Differences

The labels of Anglican and nonconformist, together with the various denominational terms such as Presbyterian, Congregational, Baptist, Quaker and Methodist, have been used so far, for convenience. There are in fact many problems with assuming that each of these represents a unified Church that can obviously be distinguished from the others. If we consider the Churches under the three headings of worship, doctrine and ecclesiastical government, we may be struck as much by the variety within particular Churches and the similarities between them as by clear-cut denominational differences, especially concerning worship and doctrine.

If we examine worship first, the unifying factor across all the Churches is the post-Reformation emphasis on preaching as the heart of the service, and hence on the congregation as 'hearers'. The Church of England before the Civil War had gradually managed to create a preaching ministry. By 1603, 223 of the 604 parishes in Exeter diocese had preaching clergy, of whom only 29 were non-graduates, and later bishops ensured that they ordained an overwhelmingly graduate, and hence preaching, clergy.[14] Bishop Hall, defending his episcopal record against Puritan criticism in the 1640s, wrote that

> As well might we complain of too many stars in the sky, as too many orthodox preachers in the Church . . . Can they check me with a lazy silence in my place? With infrequence of preaching? Let the populous auditories where I have lived witness, whether, having furnished all the churches near me with able preachers, I took not all opportunities of supplying such courses [i.e. of sermons], as I could get, in my cathedral.[15]

The sermon remained the centrepiece of both Anglican and nonconformist worship thereafter well into the nineteenth century. It is true that there was some revival of Anglican sacramentalism, but this was a patchy affair and we should not forget that the celebration of communion was taken just as seriously (but no more frequently) by all the dissenting groups save the Quakers.[16] More generally, despite well-aired controversies over issues such as bowing at the name of Jesus, there is little evidence that liturgical divergences lay behind the different types of Church. Puritan deviations from Anglican norms in performing the liturgy remained as prevalent within the Church after the Civil War as before, and most Anglican services remained very simple by later standards. The elaborate rituals of Exeter Cathedral were as different from most Anglican services as the silent meetings of the Quakers; the average parish service shared many more characteristics with a nonconformist meeting.[17] Even the cathedral, however, emphasised its provision of an elaborate succession of sermons as well as a sequence of morning, evening, weekday and holy day services. In this respect it took to an extreme the general contrast between urban and rural provision. Town churches were much more likely to provide a full range of services and monthly communions; rural churches, whether Anglican or dissenting, could rarely sustain such services.[18] One other distinguishing characteristic of the cathedral was of course its musical provision. Here too it was untypical, and the spread of music in church services during the eighteenth century was a cross-denominational trend, partly spurred, it seems, by competition between churches and always most advanced in towns. A leading Devon advocate was John Newte, rector of Tiverton, and his defence of the lawfulness of organs in 1696 stirred quite a controversy, since such provision was distrusted by many, both Anglicans and nonconformists, as smacking of popery.[19]

For the laity, different Protestant churches, whilst no doubt offering variety, nevertheless would have contained much that was familiar, and this may help to explain the uneasy sense shared by Anglican and dissenting ministers that the laity were always ready to go off to attend another church if for any reason their usual church did not offer the wonted services. Hence Ward's anger at the failure of the Windsor chapter to fill vacant livings, particularly because, at Brixham, this had given an ejected minister an excuse for resuming his ministry:

> at length finding that no man was putt in his stead, and that the people went off, Some to Atheisme and debauchery others to Sectarisme (for he is a Presbyterian) he resolved to adventure to gather his flocke again. And he had gathered as I am told a flock of 1500 or 2000 upon Sunday last . . .

What drew the flock to new pastors was satisfactory preaching. In December 1614 Bishop Cotton had summoned the clergy of his diocese to order them to tell parishioners not to go to other preachers with 'better gifts than their own pastors'; one such example, taken from the next decade, is provided by a man living three miles from Exeter who recalled that 'there being a mean preacher in that place we went every Lord's Day into the city where were many famous preachers of the word of God'. In the first decades of the next century John Bond of Sheepwash went to his parish church on Sunday morning, but attended the Hatherleigh Presbyterian meeting in the evening, there being no second sermon at Sheepwash.[20]

This fluidity was assisted by the lack of clear doctrinal differences between the Churches. With the exception of the Quakers, distinguished chiefly by their rejection of *all* doctrinally based versions of Christianity, there was no clear-cut theological division, either between Anglicans and nonconformists or among the nonconformists during this period. When the Act of Toleration of

1689 restricted toleration to Churches that conformed to the doctrines of the Thirty-Nine Articles (the Calvinist and Trinitarian orthodoxy of the Protestant Reformation), this caused no problems for the great majority of south-western dissenters. Even the Baptist stress on adult baptism was a disagreement about means rather than fundamentals and did not prevent extensive movement both of individual Baptists and of Baptist congregations in and out of other dissenting Churches. Whilst popery, Unitarianism and Quaker beliefs were beyond the pale, there was otherwise a recognition of the other Churches as legitimate Churches of Christ, divided on Church government rather than doctrine.

Matters did change in the eighteenth century with the collapse of Calvinism and the spread of Arminian and especially Unitarian doctrines, indelibly associated with Exeter Presbyterianism because of the famous controversies that broke out there in the late 1710s.[21] Churches did indeed now divide on doctrinal issues, and statements of doctrine became a feature of newly established churches. But this was a protracted and infinitely complex process— only around 1800 could one clearly distinguish two new wings of dissent—one formed from Congregational and Baptist Trinitarians and incorporating many former Presbyterian congregations, and another smaller grouping based on Presbyterian and occasionally Baptist churches that had adopted Unitarianism, or at least refused to impose a Trinitarian orthodoxy. Furthermore the Church of England had itself been equally affected, though less visibly divided. Then as now it was home to many types of ministry, some sharing the refined moralism of the Unitarians, but others the Trinitarian evangelicalism of the Congregationalists. Until the Methodist movement finally separated fully from the Church in the 1780s and 1790s, its ministers added to this complex doctrinal position. Many have quoted the famous remark of Dr Wright (rector of St Mary Arches, Exeter) in November 1739 that Wesley's preaching was 'not guarded. It is dangerous. It may lead people into enthusiasm or despair.' They less often quote the previous sentences: 'I allow all that you [Wesley] have said to be true. And it is the doctrine of the Church of England.'[22]

In his comment on this in his Journal, Wesley noted that 'by a religious man is commonly meant one that is honest, just and fair in his dealings, that is constantly at church and sacrament and that gives much alms or (as it is usually termed) does much good'. Against this he wished to set a much higher standard: that of the converted saint striving for perfection. In seeking this goal, Wesley saw no alternative but to override the existing forms of Anglican provision, with its settled and ordained ministry, through the use not just of itinerant field-preachers but of lay preachers and lay-directed Methodist societies. The dangers of this were apparent not just to Dr Wright, but also to that highly evangelical clergyman, Samuel Walker of Truro. The clerical opponents of Wesley and Whitefield are often portrayed as thoughtless conservatives

unwilling to adjust their methods to obvious needs. But Walker was a model
minister, whose spiritual aims were identical to Wesley's. Moreover he sought
to fulfil them through the establishment of religious societies, both of local
clergy and of pious lay people. But he refused to endorse Wesley's use of
itinerant lay-preachers. Lay preaching was illegal and dangerous, though lay
participation in reading-groups or the like was highly desirable, provided they
remained under clerical direction. Above all, itinerant preachers were literally
illegal. The Toleration Act of 1689 had only offered legal immunity to
nonconformist worship conducted within licensed meeting-houses, while the
1604 Canons of the Church of England forbade lay-preaching. Since Walker
insisted that the Church of England was defined by its legal position, *not* by
any distinctive form of doctrine or worship, so this use of lay-preachers was
bound to lead to separatism. And so it was to prove, of course, despite Wesley's
desires, by the 1780s and 1790s.[23]

This brings us to the third area of unity and variety—Church government.
Here surely we have firm grounds for difference, as Walker implied. But even
here the picture is complex. We can distinguish quite sharply between those
(especially Anglicans) who believed in the desirability of a national, established
Church, and those, like Quakers, Baptists and Congregationalists, for whom
the national Church was at best the sum of many gathered churches, each
established by particular congregations of believers and responsible only to
God. Unfortunately this neat distinction excludes the largest single group of
original south-western dissenters—the Presbyterians. They only shifted reluctantly, first under the pressures of ejection and persecution and then with the
offer of toleration, away from hopes of a Presbyterian national Church towards
a congregational view. As a halfway house they established voluntary associations of ministers to try to coordinate aspects of their Church life. In the latter
respect they were copied by other dissenting groups, most notably the Quakers.
In practice eighteenth-century Quakerdom was a considerably more centralised
body than the Church of England, with individual meetings subject to monthly
meetings of their district, quarterly meetings for the county and national
meetings both in Bristol (for the South West) and in London, from whence
came a stream of directives and literature regulating every aspect of Church
life.

As hinted at the start, the Church of England was in practice a very complex
body, subject only indirectly to national control or even diocesan management.
Control of the individual parish lay in no single pair of hands but was divided
between the Church authorities, the patron of the living, the incumbent (who
in most cases had tenure for life), the churchwardens and vestry of the parish,
and the mass of the congregation (see *Table 4.3* for the patronage position in
the 1780s). As we shall see, there is no simple formula to determine the balance

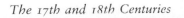

Plate 12   Lancelot Blackburn, bishop of Exeter
Bishop from 1717 to 1724, and then promoted as archbishop of York, he conveys the restrained
dignity of official Anglicanism.

of power between these various forces. Since the Reformation they had resulted in a Church highly resistant to central authority, save through the ultimate weapon of the ejection of ministers. During the mid-seventeenth century this occurred twice, namely in the mid-1640s and in 1662, affecting first royalist and then nonconformist clergy in over half the south-western parishes, yet precisely the same problems of control persisted throughout the period. The problems facing Bishop Trelawney and his successors in the eighteenth century were similar to those encountered by Bishop Hall and his predecessor Cotton; neither Cotton's authoritarian stance nor Hall's tireless diplomacy could ensure that the bishop got his way.[24]

The Search for Unity

There are, therefore, many problems in defining unity and variety in the early modern Church. We can, however, learn much about the Churches in this period by examining the underlying issues which produced these complications. One of the most important of these was the widespread belief that Church unity was not only desirable but essential. One could find all sorts of expressions of this, but the essence is captured by a lengthy quotation from the minutes of the Exeter Assembly, that gathering of ministers, mainly Presbyterian but including some Congregationalists, whose official title was the United Brethren of Devon and Cornwall. In 1713 they replied to a letter from Robert Ham, rector of Stockleigh English, in which he complained that one of their number had denied the apostolic nature of the Church of England, so producing 'an increase of our discord and animosities and of our unhappy divisions (which eat out the very heart of all true religion and indanger our best interests)'. The Assembly replied that it was their

> settled purpose to do what in us lies towards the restoring and preserving peace, unity and love; and for the healing of breaches. We are satisfied that the Particular Churches of England according to the National Establishment are true Christian Churches and that their Presbyters are Ministers of Christ,

though they dissented regarding the terms of communion, discipline and officers of those churches. They continued by saying that they wanted

> to manage our dissent with as much Christian temper and peace as possible . . . And we should heartily rejoice to find you, and your brethren entertaining the same charitable sentiments with relation to us and our congregations; which, in a great measure, would prevent these ill consequences of our unhappy differences which may otherwise eat out the heart of true religion and indanger all our best interests.[25]

Throughout the Assembly's deliberations the conviction that unity and peace must be sought, between ministers, between churches, within congregations, forms a constant theme, leading both to condemnations of slanderers, backbiters and sowers of discord and to efforts to arbitrate. The whole mood is summed up in some lines in an epitaph for the leading Dartmouth minister John Flavel (1630–91), entered in the Assembly minute-book:

> Fraternal strifes long grieved him which were ended,
> Triumphing in their union he attended;
> The Synod's councils he did moderate
> Then fled with angels to associate.[26]

Yet, as this example suggests, this unity-seeking was as much inward-looking as outward, and tensions always existed between reinforcing the unity of the group and establishing union with the outside world. The distinction is clearest in the case of the gathered churches. These Baptist and Congregational congregations comprised those who had rejected the inclusive membership implied by the parish church, preferring to form unions of the godly who covenanted together to establish a higher union than mere co-existence in the same community. The Taunton church covenant of 1654 conveys the feeling well:

> We will converse together in spirituall and Church communion with all charity, purity, and humility—preferringe one another and thinking one another better than ourselves; whereto we have determined we will walk together unanimously by the same rule, in other things of lesser concernment and inferiour allay we will bear with one another and make our moderation known to all men; we will not make our brethren's difference from us or concurrence with us, in such things as these, the grounds and measure of our love or dislike; that there may be noe [s]chisme in the body we will love the truth.[27]

The basis of unity was here a voluntary one of equals, as the Quakers' proper title, the Society of Friends, suggests, but the emphasis was less on individualism than on community.

In this respect dissenters shared the conventional wisdom that religion was a, probably *the*, fundamental basis for community within society, without which peace and harmony and the good society would be unattainable. At the Reformation the threat of a breach in this unity had led to a strengthening of the provisions to ensure uniformity at the parish level, as Nicholas Orme has demonstrated in Chapter Three, and the success of this campaign was to convince almost everybody by 1640 that Protestant unity of worship was an essential foundation-stone of community. The subsequent collapse of this unity created a long-lasting tension between a continuing adherence to religion as the sole foundation for true unity and its actual tendency to generate divisions and prove a focus for conflict. A tiny minority of nonconformists adopted the solution of opting out of the wider community, creating their own self-sufficient society and seeking only to be left alone. At the other extreme, a much larger body of Anglicans sought to eradicate religious dissent as an inevitable threat to communal unity: as the Devon Quarter Sessions of 1681 put it in an order that was to be read in all Anglican churches: 'whilst faction and schism is allowed and permitted in the church we can never expect peace and quiet in the state'.[28]

Between 1660 and 1720 a complex struggle ensued between three groups in the South West: the two mentioned above and the larger middle group of low-church Anglicans and mainstream nonconformists who sought to establish a place for the dissenters, either back within the fold of a broader Church, or as a loyal and accepted ally in the Protestant fight against popery, regrettably unable to unite on some matters but fundamentally in unity. For example John Sowter's *The Way to be Wise and Wealthy* (Exeter, 1716) contained a short preface 'persuading all Protestants to lay aside party-prejudices, and to unite and love one another'. There is no space here to go into this theme in detail, but it has been admirably covered recently in Peter Jackson's study, which shows how the period of persecution of dissenters between 1660 and 1687 was characterised, not just by physical and financial struggles (though these should not be downplayed), but as much by a propaganda battle. On the one hand the persecutors sought to portray the dissenters as the breakers of unity, quintessential outsiders. Take for example William Gould's 1672 cathedral sermon attacking 'the peddling sectarists of the nation (those mushrooms of Christianity, that so suddenly sprung up in the late night of confusion)'. He could not see how the Church and state 'should make any account of any other interest in them than a man makes of the vermin that breed out of his excrementitious sweat'. On the other hand the opponents of persecution portrayed persecution itself as the destroyer of unity and community values, stressing the values of neighbourliness and Protestant solidarity and emphasising the legal rights of the dissenters. After 1689, the battle continued, both over whether the granting of toleration had been correct and in the broader context of the party struggle of Whigs and Tories.[29]

This in its turn raised a further dilemma about religion and unity: how far were religious differences breeding faction and party, or were parties taking advantage of the cloak of religion to promote their own divisive interests? John Fox's mid-eighteenth-century memoirs of west Devon dissenters were intended 'to show how difficult it is to be an honest man in any party of religion as a party and how few can be said to deserve that title of whom such a party is composed'. The fear of this ensured that periods of political tension, whether or not they were generated by specifically religious issues, were always times when religious divisions looked dangerous. The coincidence of the Wesleys' first major campaign in Cornwall with war against the French and the Jacobite threat in the 1740s was responsible for much of the early hostility to Methodists, based on claims that they were 'popish incendiaries' aiming at 'bringing in the Pretender'.[30] The situation recurred in subsequent periods of war, notably in the 1790s when many other dissenting groups also came under renewed suspicion. At a local level, elections tended to bring out religious antagonisms. Defoe's comment on early eighteenth-century Dorchester has interesting implications for other towns. He thought it 'a pleasant agreeable town to live in, and where I thought the people seemed less divided into factions and parties than in other places; for though here are divisions and people are not all of one mind, either as to religion or politics, yet they did not seem to separate with so much animosity as at other places. Here I saw the Church of England clergyman and the Dissenting minister or preacher drinking tea together, and conversing with civility and good neighbourhood, like catholic Christians and men of a catholic and extensive charity'.[31]

Church and Community: Ministers, Buildings and Congregations

Many other examples could be given, both of animosity and reconciliation. To understand both sentiments we need to consider why the Churches were such focuses of interest in communal unity and in particular how far the respective positions of the minister, the church building and the congregation helped to create our complex web of unity and variety. The main reason, it may be suggested, why the Church seemed the natural focus of community was that there were no alternative associations within the average community that could fulfil the role. The Churches provided the intellectual leadership, the physical space, the communal meeting-place and time, when there were no rivals save other Churches. Moreover, through the institution of the parish, local and Church government were totally intertwined. In the countryside, at least in areas where the parish church was at the centre of the rural community, it was hard for any rival Church to survive in this period.

Within the towns, rival centres of community could much more easily coexist, not necessarily because the Anglican Church was weak, but because there was room for more. Defoe comments about Bideford:

> Here, as is to be seen in almost all the market towns of Devonshire, is a very large, well-built and well-finished meeting-house and, by the multitude of people which I saw coming out of it, and the appearance of them, I thought all the town

Plate 13 St George's parish church, Tiverton

A new church for a growing town, built 1714–33, to plans by the London architect John James. The west gallery was added in 1842.

had gone thither, and began to enquire for the church. But when I came to the church, I found that also large, spacious and well filled too, and that with people of the best fashion.[32]

Another such town was Tiverton, where the Presbyterian meeting, supported by many of the leading clothiers, defeated the parish church in the struggle for local power in the early eighteenth century. Many south-western towns were the centres of chronic factionalism on religious lines during this period.[33] No wonder that the mayor of Tiverton in 1752, faced already with a bewildering array of religious sensibilities to satisfy, responded thus to the arrival of Methodism:

> What little room there is for any new religion in Tiverton? another way of going to Heaven when there are so many? You know sir there is the old church and the new church, that is one religion, then there is Parson Kiddell's at the Pitt Meeting House [Presbyterian], Parson Westcott's at St Peter Street [Congregational], and the old parson Terry's at the Meeting in Newport Street. Four ways of going to Heaven already. Enough in conscience I think. And if they won't go to Heaven by one or other of these ways, by God they shan't go to Heaven at all herefrom, whilst I am mayor of Tiverton.[34]

The irate mayor's description identifies the three main ingredients of those alternative ways to heaven, namely the minister, the meeting house and the congregation. In each case a complex of social and cultural considerations, rather than a simple denominational label, determined the uniformity, or lack of it, in the nature of churches.

It is right that we should start with the ministers for, despite our assumptions about Protestantism, the century after 1540 was in many ways the period when the clerical profession established a higher status within English society. There were far fewer clerics, but those there were became overwhelmingly university or higher education trained, set apart from their congregation or, as they are so often called, their 'hearers' or their 'people'. Reliance on the preaching power of the clergy was as much the hallmark of most dissenters as it was of both Puritans and reforming bishops within the Anglican Church. For example, the Axminster *Ecclesiastica*, the record of a Congregational church in the late seventeenth century, constantly places the ministers centre-stage.[35] Even within supposedly lay ministries, such as those of the Baptists and Quakers, informal elites of local and itinerant ministers not only brought the churches into existence but remained powerful. In a closely parallel way the Methodist movement, despite its lay-preaching aspect, was dominated by rival associations of preachers, and it was their decisions that ultimately determined the movement's future. All the churches shared a number of common problems arising out of this dependence on ministers. The first was the problem of maintaining a full-time ministry, at least at the standards of remuneration expected by a learned man. The problem was greatest for the nonconformists, and it was undoubtedly the burden of trying to support, let alone train, a learned clergy, which eventually overwhelmed many small congregations, leaving the ministers clustered in the towns, where they could also supplement their incomes most easily.[36] The established Church had the advantage of Church wealth and compulsory taxation, through tithes, to raise clerical income. But the Anglican Church's parochial structure had not been devised with this in mind and never proved ideally suited to the task, despite repeated efforts which ensured by the late eighteenth century that most livings were worth more than the £50 minimum seen as necessary (see *Table 4.3*). Even to achieve this the Church had to accept pluralism and performance of other duties, such as schoolmastering or medicine.[37]

Clergymen also had to depend on voluntary contributions from the congregation as well as tithes and Church property. The problem was often most acute in the towns, where tithes had become meaningless and churches often lacked even the parsonage houses that subsidised rural livings. Bishop Ward noted in 1666 that one clergyman had been promised £100 a year by his parishioners, then a substantial income, to minister in Exeter, but commented that it would 'never be well, till such men shall cease to depend upon voluntary contribution; to such purpose the late act for the union of churches signifies nothing at all in this city where the legall dues of all the parishes wil hardly raise a good maintenance for one good man'. This financial problem had led to the establishment of lectureships by many towns in the early seventeenth century, for without such civic initiatives, it was hard for such communities to obtain leading preachers. Diocesan opposition to these arrangements seemed perverse to Puritans keen to strengthen Protestant evangelism, yet such lecturers, though not necessarily anti-establishment, were notoriously independent of diocesan control and keen to court lay popularity. After 1660 lectureships were rare, although in some places the congregation or town council owned the right of appointing the clergyman or at least appointing to a chapelry. This was the case in Devon towns such as Plymouth, Dartmouth and Crediton, while in 1688, 51 parishioners of Stockland clubbed together to purchase the advowson (and the tithes) of their parish.[38]

Usually it was only gentry families amongst the laity who had such power of presentation. Nonetheless, the power of the purse gave humbler lay people a hold over their clergy. Nicholas Orme's observations on the power of the late medieval laity are recalled in this quotation from the Cornish antiquarian, William Hals, about Truro in his time, the mid-eighteenth century:

Table 4.3: Reputed value of Anglican livings in 1782: Devon and Cornwall

Annual Value	Not known	Up to £50	£51-75	£76-100	£101-200	£201-300	Over £300	Total Devon	C'wall	% of Total
Type of Living (1)										
Livings held by rectors	11	13	36	82	129	42	11	246	78	53.8
% of rectorial livings	3.4	4.0	11.1	25.3	39.8	13.0	3.4	76.0	24.0	
Livings held by vicars	11	6	29	90	67	12	1	132	84	35.9
% of vicarial livings	5.1	2.8	13.4	41.7	31.0	5.6	0.5	61.1	38.9	
Livings held by curates	39	12	7	4	–	–	–	41	21	10.3
% of curatial livings	62.9	19.4	11.3	6.4	–	–	–	66.1	33.9	
Total number of livings	61	31	72	176	196	54	12	419	183	
% of livings in total	10.1	5.1	12.0	29.2	32.6	9.0	2.0	69.6	30.4	
Patron of living (2)										
Bishop of Exeter	1	–	1	17	17	4	–	15	25	6.4
Exeter Cathedral	5	1	12	16	16	4	1	42	13	8.9
Extra-diocesan church bodies	9	1	5	6	4	–	–	23	2	4.0
Oxford and Cambridge	2	–	–	1	4	3	2	6	6	1.9
Incumbent himself	1	2	4	9	13	4	1	33	1	5.5
Other clergymen	2	–	3	12	14	2	–	21	12	5.3
Ecclesiastical sub-total	20	4	25	61	68	17	4	140	59	32.0
Crown	7	6	5	29	16	5	–	38	30	11.0
Aristocracy	6	2	5	11	28	8	4	41	23	10.3
Gentry, esquires and knights	17	14	28	59	71	18	5	144	69	34.2
Other individuals	3	3	7	8	15	5	–	33	8	6.6
Recusants	1	1	3	2	2	–	–	9	–	1.4
Lay corporations	–	–	–	7	3	1	–	11	–	1.8
Lay sub-total	34	26	48	116	135	37	9	276	130	65.3
Not known	12	2	–	3	–	–	–	9	8	2.7

1. Figures record 'reputed value' of each living, *not* the incumbent's total income, as he may have held several livings.

2. Where several types of patron shared a living, dual entries have been made; hence the totals exceed the number of livings.

Source: Thesaurus Ecclesiasticus Provincialis, Or A Survey of the Diocese of Exeter (Exeter, 1782).

As when it was a free chapel and the minister subsisted on the oblations and subventions of the altar, so now, comparatively, on the piety and charity of his hearers by voluntary subscriptions from whence it may be presumed that the rector must demean himself well and labour hard in his vocation to get a competent maintenance at least he must walk with such upright and wary conduct as that he went barefoot upon the edge of a very sharp knife and did not hurt his feet; since he must converse with, and have to do with, men of diverse principles and opinions on religion in this place, as of old his predecessors had with monks, Dominican and Franciscan friars who were sharers or pealers of his profits.[39]

As this extract suggests, it was the power of the laity that worried the clerical profession. Walker of Truro, who was in fact only vicar to an absentee rector, hated the annual collection he had to make from door to door to supplement his income. In theory he should have shared this equally with the clerical rector, but Walker knew that people would not give him a proper sum if they thought half the money was going to somebody else, and so arranged a flat sum payment to the rector. When, to ease his dependence, he successfully applied for a gift to Lord Dartmouth, as a patron sympathetic to evangelicals, he urged Dartmouth to keep it secret, for his congregation would have been jealous of a rival patron. When Walker died his successor, a non-evangelical, reaped the fruits of dependence on public opinion. Many of his flock disliked his preaching and left the church, joining up with the remnants of the Presbyterian church to form a new dissenting chapel.[40]

But the dissenting clergy were equally averse to falling dependent on their congregations. The historian Finberg has noted with characteristic insight that the Exeter Assembly was in one sense a clerical union, in which the ministers united to ensure that they exercised spiritual power that outweighed the local power of their congregations. The titles of two Assembly sermons later printed, John Walrond's *The Dignity of the Ministry* (London, 1707) and John Kiddell's *The Dignity of the Ministerial Character and the Means of Supporting It* (London, 1747), illustrate the point. Wesley, again from the ministerial perspective, noted the same tensions within his movement, observing of the Redruth Methodist society in 1788 that they were 'apt to despise and very willing to govern their preachers'.[41] For the relationship between congregation and minister, like any highly charged relationship, was a love-hate one. The minister was the single most important ingredient of any church, and in a sense his interests were those of the church. John Fox, who had been trained for the dissenting ministry, noted the power of the clergy and their ruthless use of it, in his opinion, to feather their nests and render their followers their allies in their political battles. According to Fox, Jacob Sanderbrook of Tavistock:

had in him very much of the wisdom of the serpent, and so thoroughly understood the temper of his people that he knew how to govern them absolutely and to please them at the same time . . . He took great care to tell his people that he was one of Christ's ambassadors and was vastly displeased at anything said or done to deprive 'em of the power and respect which they ought to have . . . By this art these ministers in general maintained the respect which was paid them . . . He was likewise very often consulted in politics, for he was able to direct the votes of most of his hearers in time of an election.[42]

Yet their interests were also different. Clergy might have several churches to care for—itinerancy and pluralism were required in many areas—yet this would generate lay self-sufficiency and break the pastoral tie. The clergy might also prove unsatisfactory. Not every clergyman could be a John Wesley, and even Wesley said that, if he served a single congregation for a year, 'I should preach both myself and most of my congregation asleep'.[43] Wesley's high-intensity evangelical preaching was hardly compatible with a long-term relationship with one flock—but this was what faced most churches. No wonder that the choice of a new minister, where either Anglican or dissenting groups had the choice, provoked endless disputes. This frequently led to the break-up and re-formation of dissenting churches.[44] Anglicans lacked this option, but they could go to hear other ministers in neighbouring parishes, as we know many did from reiterated official complaints.

A growing problem moreover was not just whether a preacher was 'popular', in the phrase so often used at the time, but also with whom in his congregation he was popular. Could the same style of preaching appeal to all classes in the community and satisfy both sophisticated townsfolk and country people? As the ministers absorbed the latest learning, such as Unitarian notions, could they carry their unlearned congregations who then, as today, might distrust theological speculation? But if the minister played safe and avoided all controversy, would he be as interesting? During the recurrent crises of the seventeenth and early eighteenth centuries, while the Protestant Reformation seemed to both clergy and congregations to be in danger, their respective fears and aspirations never diverged too widely. By the late eighteenth century, however, there were fewer educated ministers who shared the dramatic world-view of many ordinary Devonians, still full of beliefs about the millennium, witches and radical change. Increasingly such language could only be heard from lay preachers. The intense sufferings of the Napoleonic Wars brought forth such expression of popular religious fervour as Primitive Methodism, the Bible Christians and Devon's own prophetess, Joanna Southcott.[45]

Intimately associated with these questions about the minister were issues about the church, meeting-house, or preaching-house as it was often called. Again it is clear that, like a minister, a building provided a vital unifying force for which congregations yearned, but equally clear that buildings also divided. The sheer cost of a building dedicated to worship put it beyond the reach of many rural areas, where scattered congregations had to rely on itinerants preaching in private houses. Former monastic or guild chapels were pressed into service by nonconformists, one example being the Abbey Chapel at Tavistock.[46] Despite official funding, Anglican churches were often neglected. In Cornwall and large parts of Devon the parish church was located far from many parishioners, even if the 'church-town', or settlement which contained the parish church, was the leading hamlet. Often the Anglican clergy recognised the problem. In a letter of 1733 Lewis Southcomb, himself rector of Rose Ash, explained that he had reopened the medieval Trinity Chapel near Honiton Barton in South Molton parish:

> As this place is two miles from the same parish church [i.e. South Molton's] and there is yet another mile in the same parish beyond it . . . It must always be tedious, if not impracticable, to attend the church as they ought, especially in the winter-time, and not without abundance of trouble at any season of servants, women, children . . .[47]

The construction and maintenance of a nonconformist chapel tended to divide the congregation. Not only was the location contentious, but the process brought the better-off to the fore and gave them power, as owners or trustees, over the rest of the laity, similar to that of churchwardens and vestry in many Anglican parishes.[48] Furthermore within both churches and chapels the physical layout was used to express the hierarchies and divisions within the community, as well as to unite them in worship. Men and women might be separated; the rich sat in the best pews and the poor at the back, as the plan of Honiton parish church in 1755 (*Figure 11*) illustrates. The practice of financing dissenting chapels by differentiated seat-prices made such discrimination as much a feature of Methodist tabernacles and Baptist chapels as of Anglican churches, generating endless conflicts in all sorts of churches.[49] Although the Reformation had, in some respects, lessened the notion of the church as a sacred space, it is clear that most people wanted some regular association of building and worship, even if it was now within the whitewashed schoolroom atmosphere of the Protestant church. Ironically the Act of Toleration, far from lessening this tendency, actually reinforced it. Dissenters, who had been forced to meet in private or even outdoors to avoid persecution between 1662 and 1687, now saw the opening of their own place of worship as the symbol of their

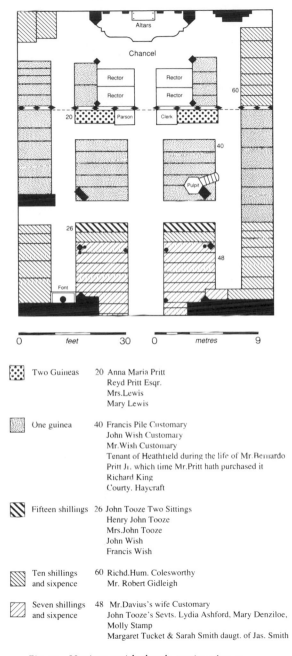

Two Guineas   20 Anna Maria Pritt
                 Reyd Pritt Esqr.
                 Mrs.Lewis
                 Mary Lewis

One guinea   40 Francis Pile Customary
                 John Wish Customary
                 Mr.Wish Customary
                 Tenant of Heathfield during the life of Mr.Bernardo
                 Pritt Jr. which time Mr.Pritt hath purchased it
                 Richard King
                 Courty. Haycraft

Fifteen shillings 26 John Tooze Two Sittings
                 Henry John Tooze
                 Mrs.John Tooze
                 John Wish
                 Francis Wish

Ten shillings 60 Richd.Hum. Colesworthy
and sixpence   Mr. Robert Gidleigh

Seven shillings 48 Mr.Davius's wife Customary
and sixpence   John Tooze's Sevts. Lydia Ashford, Mary Denziloe,
                  Molly Stamp
                  Margaret Tucket & Sarah Smith daugt. of Jas. Smith

Fig. 11   Honiton parish church, seating plan, 1755.

emancipation. Indeed it was only by worshipping in a licensed place of meeting that they qualified for toleration—not attending *any* religious building on Sunday was still a legal offence until the nineteenth century, although a largely unenforceable rule.[50] The outdoor evangelism of the sects in the mid-seventeenth century gave way to a chapel-bound worship which, while uniting the already converted, did little to convert others. Or so one may conclude from the stagnation, if not decline, in old dissent in the early eighteenth century, evident in our region as well as nationally.[51]

It was in this context that the Methodist revival of field-preaching was such a shock to both dissenting and Anglican communities, although ultimately it was the former that benefited. Even here, however, it is noticeable how the power of church buildings soon re-established itself. Many clearly found the novelty of public meetings and itinerant preachers exciting, and this reached an audience, especially in Cornwall, unaccustomed to attending church. Nonetheless the people who joined Methodist societies and persisted were usually attenders at their parish church or a dissenting meeting.[52] In Wesley's time they were encouraged to continue such attendance. Then, as Methodists gradually drifted away to form a separate denomination, their members' instinct was to build their own chapels and recreate the same type of society. Tensions about these issues were to surface in the nineteenth-century divisions between mainstream Wesleyans, with their substantial chapels, and Primitive Methodists or Bible Christians, meeting in private houses or make-shift meeting-places.[53]

This leads us to the congregation. What function did it play in running affairs, and can we distinguish clearly between the social composition of the various churches? On the surface the differences are obvious. The parish church embraced the whole community, yet had a clearly defined hierarchy of power which left the congregation little formal control. By contrast dissenting churches are seen as more select but democratic, although their social profile is often thought to have varied, with Presbyterians attracting the better-off and the other groups more of the poor. Methodism, it is widely assumed, found its supporters amongst the poorest. All of these assumptions are, as John Triffitt has shown, at best half-truths. Within every type of church, Anglican and nonconformist, we find a number of rings of involvement. Within the Anglican setting we can distinguish the vestrymen, the communicants, the regular congregation and the occasional attenders. Within most dissenting bodies we can do the same, with meeting-house trustees and regular subscribers as the inner ring, members or communicants as the next ring, regular hearers and then occasional hearers. In September 1709 the Exeter Assembly heard from two meetings. Hatherleigh 'say they have about 150 hearers, near 50 communicants', able to raise £15 p.a. themselves, while Penzance 'raise about £30 per annum . . . about 150 or 200 hearers, 30 communicants'. There were genuine differences about how far different denominations could reach to the top of the social scale; initially at least Presbyterians could attract gentry support lacking for other dissenters, for example. Yet it seems clear that most churches attracted hearers from across the social spectrum of the community within which they were based, but drew their membership more narrowly from the middling sort, and their inner ring from the better-off of their community, who alone could afford the time and offer the financial support. Once again, the variety of religious experience lay within each church, rather than between churches.[54]

This brings us back to the question of the social geography of dissent. The distribution of Anglicanism and nonconformity found before 1800 in the South West does not fit easily with some of the models developed for the nineteenth century, to be discussed by Bruce Coleman in Chapter Six. These explain the pattern of religious allegiance by distinguishing between arable and pastoral regions or open and closed parishes.[55] Many reasons might be given for the discrepancy between these models and the situation in the South West during the seventeenth and eighteenth centuries. The widespread distribution of the Devon cloth industry and the pattern of tin-mining made south-western social patterns distinctive. More fundamentally, before the growth of population and transport facilities, and during an age when it was the middling groups who sustained all kinds of Churches, the key consideration in our period is not the total society but the existence within an area of a critical mass of potential middling supporters. Communities without these groupings could not sustain nonconformity on a large scale (that is with minister, meeting-place and public congregation) or in the long term. Survival in those conditions depended on combining a national or international support network with an intense tradition of family loyalty, which was the means by which both Roman Catholics and Quakers perpetuated themselves.[56] Had it not been for the Church of England's parish and tithe system, it, like mainstream dissenting groups, would have found difficulty (or, rather, even more difficulty) supporting itself across the country.

Two hypotheses are suggested by this. First, in the case of old dissent at least, we should not expect an inverse relation between Anglican strength and dissenting strength. Both were frequently strongest in the same areas, notably the towns and the populous and wealthy clothmaking districts. The clashes which draw our attention to the power of dissent in those areas reflected the power of both sides, while the weakness of dissent in remote country districts of Devon and in much of Cornwall does not in itself prove that Anglicanism held a strong hold over the people, as evangelicals of every type recognised. Yet in eighteenth-century conditions evangelicals found it hard to affect much permanent change; only at the very end of the century can we begin to see a new basis for dissenting and in particular Methodist expansion, tapping new populations and developing types of church organisation which could use the considerable collective wealth and labour of the lower classes. In this respect the strengths and weaknesses of the early modern Churches seem to have more in common with the medieval pattern, described in earlier chapters, than with the Victorian story told below.

Conclusion

The traditional reading of Church history in this period, so influenced by denominational assumptions and nineteenth-century attitudes, is dominated by the story of conflicts between Church and chapel. It can easily be assumed, therefore, that unity was little sought after in this period and that denominational groups expressed inevitable and deep-seated varieties in types of religious community. This chapter has demonstrated that there were indeed inbuilt forces in the social and cultural position of the Churches in this period that generated great variety. However it has laid equal stress on the perhaps unexpected uniformities of aspiration and experience across the Churches. It was the fundamental *similarities* of character and aims, the unity of aim of pious and respectable members of the community to use their Church to express their values (of which aspirations to unity and the expression of social distinctions were equally a part) which lent to the Church conflicts of this period the particular intensity that comes from fraternal struggles, whilst ensuring that they did not, ultimately, overthrow the establishment.

CHAPTER FIVE

The Nineteenth Century: The Church of England

John Thurmer

> Onward, Christian soldiers,
> Marching as to war,
> With the Cross of Jesus
> Going on before.
> (Sabine Baring-Gould, 1864)

The Constitutional Revolution

Between the years 1828 and 1835 Great Britain underwent a 'constitutional revolution', to use Professor Geoffrey Best's term.[1] This was both a revolution in the constitution and a revolution achieved by constitutional means —notably by acts of Parliament. From the Church's point of view it was comparable in importance to the Reformation legislation of Henry VIII and Elizabeth I exactly three hundred years before. Until 1828 Britain was a Church-state in which citizenship and churchmanship were identical. There were qualifications, dispensations, and gaps between theory and practice. But the principle still existed, inherited from the conversion of the Roman Empire, of an established Church which everyone belonged to and had to support, notably through paying tithes. After 1689 you could worship away from the Church, but if you did so you lost your civil rights, and no one could be king, or hold any public office or go to University without affirming the beliefs and following the practices of the Church of England. To the modern student this appears to favour the Anglican denomination unduly and unfairly. But in their own day, Anglicans did not see it like that. The Church of England was not a favoured denomination. It was the people of England, the community of the realm performing its religious duty to God, the monarch and the neighbour, and

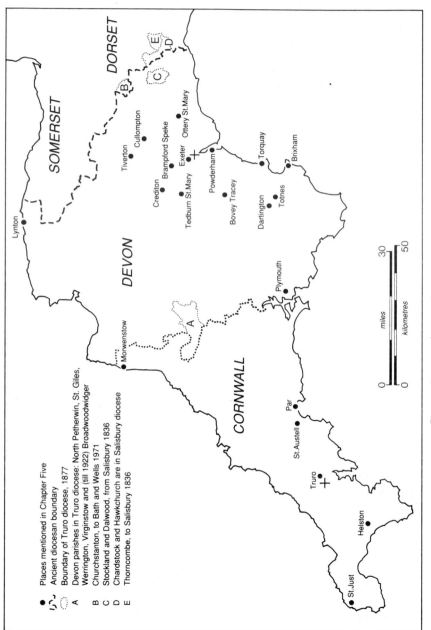

Places mentioned in Chapter Five

Ancient diocesan boundary

Boundary of Truro diocese, 1877

A   Devon parishes in Truro diocese: North Petherwin, St. Giles,
     Werrington, Virginstow and (till 1922) Broadwoodwidger

B   Churchstanton, to Bath and Wells 1971

C   Stockland and Dalwood, from Salisbury 1836

D   Chardstock and Hawkchurch are in Salisbury diocese

E   Thorncombe, to Salisbury 1836

Fig. 12   Exeter and Truro dioceses since 1876.

those who were not of the Church of England were not fully part of the civil community either.

The revolution began in 1828 when Parliament repealed the seventeenth-century Test and Corporation Acts, thereby in principle opening full citizenship to the Protestant nonconformists. The government of the day—that of Wellington and Peel—was, as we would say, 'conservative' and committed to the old constitution, but it acquiesced in the change. A number of prominent churchmen feared that the law encouraged people to receive holy communion simply to qualify for civil office, and felt that the legislation was better repealed. A much more controversial change took place in 1829 with the Roman Catholic Relief Act. Roman Catholics had been the main enemies of the constitution from the time of Elizabeth I to the French Revolution, and were subject to many restrictions. They had been given freedom to worship and organise in 1791 but were denied full civil rights. They were rare in England and Wales but in a majority in Ireland. William Pitt intended that the constitutional union with Ireland in 1801 would include Roman Catholic emancipation, but he was unable to overcome George III's opposition, and emancipation remained unachieved and controversial. In 1829 Wellington and Peel, faced with civil war in Ireland, reversed their policy and forced an emancipation act on an unwilling nation and an unwilling George IV. Next year the Wellington government fell and the revolution proceeded apace.

Its effect on the South West was not markedly different from the rest of the country. But it left a mark on the leadership of the Church in the South West. One of Wellington's closest ecclesiastical advisers was a clergyman called Henry Phillpotts, a strong opponent of Roman Catholic emancipation. But when the government changed its policy Phillpotts changed with it, and one of the government's last acts in 1830 was to recommend Phillpotts for the see of Exeter. To high Tories he was a traitor; to liberals an insincere convert. Both might think he had betrayed his ideals for gain. A few years later the Oxford Tractarians were propounding their view that bishops and other clergymen derived their unique authority by the succession of laying on of hands in ordination originating with the apostles. Canon Sydney Smith, asked if he believed this doctrine, replied, 'I must believe in the Apostolic succession, there being no other way of accounting for the descent of the Bishop of Exeter from Judas Iscariot'.[2]

Diocese and Leaders

The diocese which Phillpotts inherited in controversy and was to rule with pugnacity for nearly forty years was the whole of Devon and Cornwall, its boundaries unchanged since Saxon times (*Figure 12*). He favoured a separate bishopric for Cornwall, but it did not come in his day. It is clear that the Church of England operated much less effectively in Cornwall than in Devon. At the beginning of the nineteenth century Devon had 463 parishes, and Cornwall 212—well under half as many.[3] This was not the proportion of the population. In 1851 Devon had 567,098, and Cornwall 355,558, or 62.7 per cent. Pluralism and non-residence affected the counties about equally in proportion to the number of parishes, and it is not easy to say exactly how many active resident clergymen there were. Probably it was about the same as the number of parishes, but of course there was no one-to-one correlation. If then it is true that the Cornish were much worse off for clergymen and churches than Devonians, this is strikingly confirmed by the figures of the national religious census in 1851. In Devon 40.1 per cent of the population attended Church of England services, well above the national average; in Cornwall only 19.2 per cent. In Devon Anglican worshippers were 56.9 per cent of the total who worshipped; in Cornwall 27.2 per cent. However limited our reliance on the census figures, they surely confirm the Anglican poverty of Cornwall and the growth of Methodism. In this respect, as Bruce Coleman says, 'there was nothing in the rest of southern England like Cornwall'.[4]

The Church Reform Act of 1836 paid special attention to the industrial areas of Yorkshire and Lancashire, but did not revive the see of Cornwall. The only recognition of the problems of the South West was in the Cathedrals Act of 1840, when cathedral establishments were generally cut down to a dean and four canons. Exeter was allowed five in view of the vast area of the see. The see of Truro was founded in 1876, when Disraeli was prime minister, and the first bishop was Edward White Benson, a rare example of a high churchman whom Queen Victoria liked—or rather disliked less than she generally disliked bishops. Benson, whom other high churchmen were apt to think quirky, had ability and imagination, and he gave Cornish churchmanship a flair and a focus. He initiated the building of the cathedral at Truro, the first new cathedral built for a new see since Saxon times. Pearson's great church is the finest of the period in the South West. Two other high-church bishops followed Benson, George Howard Wilkinson and John Gott, giving Truro the most consistent high-church diocesan tradition in the country, and illustrating the Anglican tendency to react against the dominant denomination in any particular place.

In 1882 Gladstone persuaded the Queen that Benson should go to Canterbury, and more than anyone else he gave the primacy its modern character, ceremonious and patriarchal—'pope of another world' as Urban II called Anselm just eight centuries before. When Benson died in 1896, during morning prayer at Hawarden Church while on a visit to the Gladstones, he was followed at Canterbury by Phillpotts's successor at Exeter, Frederick Temple. Temple was the last bishop of Exeter but one to be translated to another see—he had moved to London in 1885—and the only bishop of Exeter to become archbishop, though two deans, Pole and Wake, had done so. The episcopate at the turn of the century was one of the most distinguished in English history, inviting comparison with the colleagues of Thomas Becket in the twelfth century and the bench of Charles II in the seventeenth. It was presided over by two archbishops from the South West. Temple had not only been bishop of Exeter but had a Cornish mother, spent his boyhood in Devon and was educated at Blundells. It was said that he retained a Devon accent all his life.

The first suffragan bishop in the South West since the Reformation was Robert Edward Trefusis, reviving the Crediton title in 1897. And lest it should be thought (as some modern churchmen do think) that the Victorian Church was unduly dominated by the clergy, we may note a prominent example of lay leadership. In 1869 Charley Wood, second Viscount Halifax, friend of the Prince of Wales and president and patriarch of the English Church Union, married Lady Agnes Courtenay, only daughter of the eleventh earl of Devon. It was a union as fruitful for the Church as that twelve years earlier of the future prime minister and third marquess of Salisbury with Georgiana Alderson. Friends thought that when Halifax got despondent about the Church of England, as high churchmen did, it was his wife who stiffened his resolve, drawing perhaps on the long Courtenay experience of the art of survival.[5]

Henry Phillpotts

This glance at the structure and leadership of the Church of England in the South West has taken us to the end of the period. It is time to go back to the constitutional revolution and see how the South West experienced it. The fears of churchmen at that time seem to us exaggerated; but then we live under the shadow of the Victorian Church, so vigorous and creative, which came out of the constitutional revolution. They could not know what was ahead. They looked back to the French Revolution a generation before, and saw what happened when the French Church was disestablished. And the constitutional revolution was, for the Church of England, a measure of disestablishment, and more was to come; henceforth it would seem, as Keble said bitterly, 'one sect among many'.[6] In spite of this, the Church's unique legal connection with the crown in Parliament remained. There would be conflicting voices urging the direction the Church should take, and the clash of these voices forms much of the Church's public history.

Early in 1831, however, the South West acquired a bishop who himself had the firmest of views as to the way forward. Henry Phillpotts's mind had been formed at Oxford by Martin Joseph Routh,[7] the patriarchal president of Magdalen, and his young manhood was the time when the British Church-state was the only defence against godless revolution and military dictatorship. For him as bishop of Exeter after 1830, Roman Catholics and nonconformists with their new legal freedom could be ignored provided they did not get too big for their boots. Let the Church of England tighten its discipline and increase its energy. Everything, in Phillpotts's view, was already there in principle. Its doctrine, liturgy and discipline were perfect. They just needed to be applied and obeyed. The bishop and the law were there to see that they were. His episcopate, therefore, has two sides. There is controversy, dramatic and well-known, with those the bishop thought were breaking the law. But there was also a vigorous raising of standards and extension of the institutional Church—44 new parishes in Devon and 33 in Cornwall, chapels of ease, schools, a college for schoolmasters in 1839 and a theological seminary in 1862. The college, later known as St Luke's, lasted until it was merged with Exeter University in 1978. The seminary survives only as a trust fund administered by the dean and chapter of Exeter Cathedral.

During Phillpotts's time the Church underwent a liturgical revolution hardly less significant than the constitutional revolution. In 1821 Bishop Carey's visitation returns in Exeter diocese show a uniformity of liturgical practice. Sunday morning service (that is, mattins, litany and ante-communion) was at 10.30 or 11 am. Evening prayer was at 2.30 or 3 pm. Holy communion was quarterly, except in sizeable towns where it was monthly. Only in the cathedral was it weekly. The early communion service was unknown, and only three parishes in Devon and none in Cornwall admitted to having a second, or late evensong at 6.30 or 7 pm—probably an indication of the presence of evangelical enthusiasm. By 1869, Phillpotts's last year, communion at least weekly, with or without the early service, was widespread, and so was the 6.30 evening service, often in addition to the old hour of 3 pm with its baptisms and catechising.[8] Early communion before mattins was technically illegal until the Act of Uniformity Amendment Act of 1872, but there is no record of Phillpotts attacking it. Nor apparently did he object to the Victorian innovation of surpliced choirs in parish churches, singing psalms, responses and canticles—a change often associated with the late evensong. Bishop Blomfield of London objected, but not Phillpotts.

There were changes also in jurisdiction and temporalities. In the early nineteenth century there were still 'peculiar' parishes, not subject to the ordinary jurisdiction of the archdeacon and the bishop. Subdivision of parishes had raised the total to 71, of which 35 belonged to the bishop's own peculiar and 28 to the dean and chapter of Exeter. Five other peculiar jurisdictions accounted for the rest. Parochial peculiars had few friends in the age of reform and their rights were whittled away by legislation. An Act of 1836 gave the Ecclesiastical Commission power to prepare schemes, to be given effect by

Plate 14   Henry Phillpotts, bishop of Exeter
Bishop from 1830 to 1869, Henry of Exeter ruled with energy, firmness and controversy; he is
buried at St Marychurch, Torquay.

Order-in-Council, for transferring jurisdiction to the bishop, and parochial peculiars in the South West were extinguished between 1845 and 1850, when a special Act of Parliament abolished the deanery of St Buryan, which comprised three parishes at the west end of Cornwall. The last case in the peculiar court of the dean and chapter was one of defamation, also in 1850. The only peculiar to survive was that of the dean and chapter itself in the exercise of its ordinary jurisdiction over the cathedral.

The shape of the chapter itself was changed by an Act of 1840, the most important piece of legislation in the whole history of English cathedrals. All non-residentiary emoluments were abolished, and the residentiary canonries reduced from eight to five (and to four after the founding of the see of Truro). The confiscated assets went (to the chagrin of the cathedral body) to the Ecclesiastical Commission's parochial fund. The ancient dignities: dean, precentor, chancellor, treasurer and sub-dean, lost their individual status and property. The deanery became unequivocally a crown appointment; the others henceforth titles conferred at will by the bishop. The subsidiary corporation known as the Custos and College of the Vicars Choral (with rectorial rights and peculiar jurisdiction over the parish of Woodbury), though under threat, survived until 1933, but its houses between the deanery and St Mary Major decayed and were demolished in the 1850s and 1860s. Following an enabling Act of 1850, the see of Exeter also handed over its property in the South West piece-meal to the Ecclesiastical Commission, in return for a cash payment limited to the amount the bishop was now allowed to earn. The dean and chapter, already milked by the 1840 act for the benefit of the parishes, transferred their surviving estates and appropriated parishes to the commission in 1862, in return for an annual payment. These elements of extension, rationalisation and indeed revolution over which Phillpotts presided need to be remembered along with the conservatism and the famous controversies.

Evangelicals

Evangelical enthusiasm had preceded Phillpotts to the South West by two generations, and a complex relationship existed between the Church of England and the strong Methodist movements of Cornwall and west Devon. Those touched by eighteenth-century revivalism but remaining within the structure of the Church of England were called evangelicals. According to *The Oxford English Dictionary*, the adjective of this meaning is first found in 1791, the year of John Wesley's death; the noun in 1804. Authority, academic and episcopal, was often unsympathetic to evangelicals, and they looked for means of preserving their minority outlook. The constitutional revolution provided a means. Borough councils were self-perpetuating bodies, not significantly changed by the repeal of the Test and Corporation Acts, because they continued to co-opt only Anglicans. They were reformed by the Municipal Corporations Act of 1835, which gave ratepayers the right to elect councillors without religious test. Borough councils often held ecclesiastical patronage, and because of their new pluralistic character Parliament, after a bitter dispute, made them sell their patronage. Advowsons, the right to appoint the parish priest, could be bought and sold until the reform of 1933, and evangelicals took advantage of the patronage available after 1835. Municipal patronage was not prominent in Devon and Cornwall. Exeter, where parochial patronage was dominated by the dean and chapter had one such church (St Edmund) and Plymouth two (St Andrew and Charles Church). The Church Patronage Trust duly acquired the advowson of St Andrew from the borough, and other evangelical strongholds were added later: Cullompton by the Church Pastoral Aid Society in 1876 and two of the Tiverton churches, St Peter and St Paul, by the Peache Trustees in 1909. St Leonard in Exeter also fell to the Church Pastoral Aid Society, but not until 1930.

In the middle years of the century crown patronage favoured moderate evangelicals, partly because Palmerston, that old worldling, relied heavily in Church matters on his kinsman the evangelical philanthropist Lord Shaftesbury. Later, when Gladstone and Salisbury dominated crown appointments, care was taken to give the various sorts of churchmanship due share without regard to secular party politics. Evangelical prelates in the South West included Archibald Boyd, dean of Exeter from 1867 to 1883, and Edward Henry Bickersteth, bishop of Exeter from 1885 to 1900. Bickersteth had edited in 1870 *The Hymnal Companion to the Book of Common Prayer*, a not very successful attempt to limit the sway of *Hymns Ancient and Modern*, then considered dangerously high-church. After the storms of Phillpotts and the vigour of Temple, Bickersteth's episcopate is fittingly summed up by the opening words of his own popular hymn *Peace, perfect peace*.

One evangelical ministry in the South West was not marked by peace, and brought into sharp relief the question of patronage. Phillpotts's biographer accuses him of 'bitter opposition towards the Evangelicals',[9] but this is inexact. Phillpotts was not opposed to evangelicals as such. He got on very well, for example, with Henry Francis Lyte, the evangelical hymn writer and vicar of Lower Brixham. What roused Phillpotts's ire was Calvinism. Belief in pre-destination meant that a man could take a critical and superior attitude to the sacraments and discipline of the visible church, because all depended on whether one was a member of the invisible church of the elect.[10] Most evangelicals of the day were not Calvinists, and the philosophical question of predestination was not prominent, though it had been up to the eighteenth century, when it caused the rift between George Whitefield and the Wesleys.

Plate 15   George Cornelius Gorham, vicar of Brampford Speke, Devon
Phillpott's adversary, whose attempt to move from St-Just-in-Penwith to Brampford Speke
caused the great dispute of 1847–50.

Early in 1846 the lord chancellor presented to the living of St Just in Penwith an elderly learned Calvinist, George Cornelius Gorham. Phillpotts made no objection, but soon after the institution he rebuked Gorham for party spirit. Gorham was not happy with 8,000 tin miners at the west tip of Cornwall, and in 1847 the new lord chancellor responded to his complaints by offering him the living of Brampford Speke, thereby making a household word of a hitherto unknown Devon village. Phillpotts announced that he would not institute Gorham to Brampford Speke until he was assured that his doctrine was sound, and submitted him to an oral examination lasting in all 52 hours. The question at issue was baptismal regeneration. At baptism was a child made automatically 'a member of Christ, the child of God, and an inheritor of the kingdom of heaven', or was this, as Gorham said, dependent on 'an act of prevenient grace': that is, on whether he was one of the elect, a fact which might be demonstrated by actual faith before, during or after baptism? Phillpotts found Gorham unsound and refused institution. Gorham prosecuted Phillpotts for this refusal, unsuccessfully in the Court of the Arches in 1848, but successfully, on appeal to the Privy Council in 1850. Phillpotts was obliged to allow Gorham to take possession of his vicarage. He died in 1857 after a measure of reconciliation with the bishop, and his grave may be seen in Brampford Speke churchyard.[11]

Was the right of patronage—in this case, crown patronage administered by the lord chancellor—absolute, or was it qualified by conscience, individual or corporate? If so qualified, who determined the qualification? If Gorham had been excluded, many evangelical clergymen might be in difficulty, and the acquisition of patronage by the trusts would not have provided the security they expected. Again, when he lost the legal battle, hotheads urged Phillpotts to appoint a rival parish priest or to direct the congregation to worship elsewhere. A similar dispute over patronage and the appointment of rival ministers had produced schism in the Church of Scotland in 1843. All through Christian history rival structures of the ordained ministry have consolidated schism. Phillpotts refused to take this step, though he warned Gorham that if he preached his heresies from the pulpit of Brampford Speke, the bishop could prosecute him. Schism nevertheless there was, but not the founding of a separate religious body. Some high churchmen felt that the Privy Council decision involved the Church of England in heresy, and they followed the example of John Henry Newman five years earlier and joined the Church of Rome. Phillpotts's own chaplain William Maskell did this, and later in the year the renascent Roman Catholic body founded the bishopric of Plymouth within his diocese and jurisdiction. This and the other Roman bishoprics brought home to the nation the reality, even the unpalatable reality, of the constitutional revolution. The traumatic year 1850 pushed the Church of England towards defining its identity and authority independently of the crown in Parliament.

Phillpotts summoned the first diocesan synod of modern times in 1851, and pressure from him and others breathed life back into the dormant Convocation of Canterbury.

High churchmen generally attacked the Privy Council decision, and the Privy Council, as a secular body intruding into Church affairs. But supremacy in Church affairs had belonged to the crown since 1533. The exercise of the crown's supremacy through the Judicial Committee of the Privy Council instead of the old High Court of Delegates was an administrative change during the constitutional revolution, a change not at that time thought significant. The 1850 judgment was skilful and subtle, and the attacks on it sometimes give the impression that the attackers have not read it. The Committee was faced with an unsatisfactory case and an argument drawn too narrowly to be theologically illuminating. It argued whether regeneration invariably took place without asking the Coleridgean question 'what, in the case of infants, does regeneration mean?'[12] They therefore gave Gorham the benefit of the doubt, allowing that

> the grace is not necessarily tied to the rite; but that it ought to be earnestly and devoutly prayed for, in order that it may then, or when God pleases, be present to make the rite beneficial.[13]

Nobody was required to believe Gorham's doctrine, and there was no criticism of Phillpotts's doctrine. It was a judgment of toleration, the crown using its ecclesiastical supremacy to require the bishop and Church of the South West to accept a degree of variety they did not want.

High Churchmen

If evangelical enthusiasm preceded the constitutional revolution, the Oxford or Tractarian movement arose out of it as the most dramatic attempt to give the Church of England a new direction. The movement was in part a lament for the past, as in John Keble's Oxford Assize sermon of 1833; in part a radical vision of a pure Church untainted by parliaments, worldlings and heretics. The radical vision came first from a Devonian, Richard Hurrell Froude, son of Robert Froude, rector of Dartington and archdeacon of Totnes. Froude's desire to 'give up a national church and have a real one'[14] was what his friend Newman would have called 'a wild notion'.[15] But Froude's direct influence in the South West was small, partly because his sphere was Oxford, where he was a fellow of Oriel, partly because of his early death in 1836 at Dartington parsonage. There is a bleak memorial and gravestone in the old churchyard nearby, without any outward sign of the movement he affected so much by his life and death.

A far-reaching change came over Church life early in Victoria's reign, and we can date it 1840 without serious misrepresentation. Its enemies called it 'ritualism', but that is an inadequate term for a reappraisal of the relation of the inward and the outward in Church life. Before 1840 it was almost unknown, even among the Tractarians; after 1840 it was everywhere, cautious or extreme. There was the eccentric Robert Stephen Hawker, at Morwenstow, with early, if not the earliest, harvest festivals. Charles Leslie Courtenay, son of the tenth earl of Devon and uncle of Lady Agnes, became vicar of Bovey Tracey in 1849. He built the daughter church of St John, where there was advanced ritual, and assigned the patronage to Keble College Oxford which could be relied on to maintain the tradition.[16] The ritualist clergy had to watch their step with Phillpotts, whose own outlook and practice was completely pre-ritualist, like Newman's, throughout his Anglican days. Phillpotts heartily approved of pastoral zeal, multiplication of services and church restoration but none of these things excused breaking the law. His first excursion into this hazardous area was indeed an attempt at legal conformity. One of the rare variations in the court-room atmosphere of churches before 1840 was whether the preachers wore a surplice or a black gown. The use of the surplice on other occasions was not now controversial as it had been in Elizabethan and Stuart times. But early nineteenth-century piety still regarded the sermon as the main thing, with the service, or 'prayers' as they called it, simply a preliminary; and in some places the preacher was expected to wear a gown, either a graduate's gown or the so-called Genevan gown with gathered sleeves. If he had read prayers in a surplice, he changed to preach.

In 1844 the parishioners of Helston complained of their priest, Walter Blunt, for preaching in a surplice and other misdemeanours. Blunt, who was aptly named—he had sacked the singers in the organ-loft for eating apples during the service and introduced a boys' choir in the chancel—said that in the matter of this surplice he was only following the parish custom. This was an example of the principle that what one man can get away with, another makes the occasion for strife.[17] Phillpotts found in Blunt a man after his own heart. He not only supported him but issued a general order requiring the surplice for preaching. This created an extraordinary outburst of indignation far beyond the diocese. At that time of the crisis of the Oxford movement it was seen as a high Tory and Tractarian threat to the liberties of England and the Protestant religion. Phillpotts, whose aim was to take the question of vesture out of party controversy, had misjudged the situation, and he had to withdraw the order, leaving use to be decided by local custom. But even after this, early in 1845 there were riots at St Sidwell's Exeter, because the priest, Francis Courtenay, a minor member of the Powderham clan, preached in a surplice. It was his predecessor who had introduced it, but Courtenay got the blame. At the mayor's request an ungracious Phillpotts asked Courtenay to desist.[18]

Three years later the surplice was again controversial at St Sidwell's at the newly-introduced evening service. Otherwise the surplice controversy sank without trace; perhaps because other things even more divisive took its place. Phillpotts himself encountered some of those things in 1847. He usually lived not in the bishop's palace at Exeter but at Bishopstow (Torquay) and often worshipped nearby at St John's. Approaching the altar to celebrate holy communion on Easter day, he found it surmounted by a wooden cross entwined with flowers and leaves, and with two small glass vases of flowers on the table. He pushed one of these off, but it was attached by string and hung in mid-air, spilling flowers and water. He berated the vicar, William George Parks Smith, 'Flowerpot Smith' as he was called in consequence, and appointed a court of enquiry which confirmed his initial reaction that neither cross nor flowers were legal ornaments of the holy table.[19]

More important than this hopeless attempt to stem the tide of Victorian piety were the developments in Plymouth. In 1848 Phillpotts appointed George Rundle Prynne, from Par in Cornwall, to be vicar of St Peter's Plymouth, where he remained until his death in 1903. The appointment was probably a deliberate attempt by the bishop to offset Plymouth's evangelical ascendancy. It certainly made St Peter's a pioneer ritualist parish, later to be the first with perpetual reservation of the sacrament. In the same year Phillpotts made a 'Church urban' appeal to counter the spiritual destitution of the three towns: Plymouth, Devonport and Stonehouse. A response came from the daughter of a naval officer, Priscilla Lydia Sellon, who with the bishop's permission established 'The Church of England Sisterhood of Mercy of Devonport and Plymouth', the first religious order for women in Devon since the Reformation. It was not quite the first Anglican sisterhood, which had started in London three years earlier, but in 1856 it actually absorbed the first sisterhood. After heroic work at Devonport, five of the sisters there joined Florence Nightingale's party which went in 1854 to the Barrack Hospital on the Asian shore of the Bosphorus, receiving the wounded from the Crimea. Mother Lydia's own life and labours have an epic quality which matches Florence herself. They had the same courage, strong will and powers of organisation.[20] Her community gradually withdrew from Plymouth. Anglican religious orders have often not found it easy to prolong their life after the demise of the founder's own disciples. Others, however, took their place. The Community of St Wilfrid, 1866, was the first religious community in Exeter since the dissolution of the monasteries.[21] And the Community of the Epiphany, Truro, 1883, was the first to be founded by the diocesan bishop, in this case the second bishop of Truro, George Howard Wilkinson.[22]

Plate 16   St Michael's church, Exeter
A Tractarian church for a poor district, built in 1865–8, with a souring spire recalling Salisbury
Cathedral.

Phillpotts never had a legal conflict with his cathedral—a surprising abstinence, in view of a persistent theme of English Church history. Prynne and Plymouth did, however, occasion a fierce personal controversy between the bishop and the dean. On the sensitive question of auricular confession the difference between Prynne and Phillpotts was a difference of emphasis rather than of principle. But in 1852 the dean, Thomas Hill Lowe, preached in the cathedral an attack on auricular confession in the Church of Rome and its 'apish imitators' in the Church of England. Phillpotts published an open letter, castigating Lowe with savage sarcasm. 'There is very little danger' the bishop concluded, 'that . . . there will be any excessive tendency to seek the benefit of absolution. There is much more danger of its not being sought, even when . . . it would be most useful . . . The man who in these days warns his neighbour against the usurpations of priestly power in England must be one who would, with equal wisdom, have cried Fire Fire! at the Deluge.'[23]

Phillpotts did, however, succeed in having a posthumous controversy with his cathedral through the person of the eldest of his eighteen children, William John Phillpotts, archdeacon of Cornwall and vicar-general of the diocese, and the controversy concerned ritualistic ornaments. In 1874, in the course of Gilbert Scott's restoration of the cathedral, the dean and chapter commissioned a new altar reredos with sculptured panels representing New Testament scenes. The archdeacon, presiding in the bishop's Consistory Court, had ruled that a crucifix with the figures of St Mary and St John on the rood screen at Lynton were illegal, and he thought the cathedral should conform with the law as he understood it. But the cathedral was not subject to the bishop's ordinary jurisdiction, so he proceeded by means of a Visitation Court, at which Bishop Temple, on the advice of an assessor, reluctantly ruled that the reredos was illegal. The reredos, which can now be seen in full glory in Heavitree Parish Church, had been approved by a conservative chapter, an evangelical dean and a liberal bishop. But this consensus carried no weight with Phillpotts, for whom the letter of the law was everything. In great indignation the dean and chapter appealed against the decision of the Visitation Court, and the appeal was upheld, both by the Court of the Arches and by the Privy Council. The case was tantamount to legislation, for Phillpotts had the letter of the Reformation statutes on his side. But they had not been consistently obeyed, and most churchmen now did not desire that they should be. The legality in church of sculptured ornament, not superstitious in content or use, was established.[24] When Temple was bishop of London the Church Association prosecuted the dean and chapter of St Paul's for the great crucifix in Bodley's reredos. Temple now had the power under the Public Worship Regulation Act to veto the prosecution, and he did so, saying that the matter had been decided in the Exeter case. The Public Worship Regulation Act of 1874, described by Disraeli as a bill to put down ritualism, had the opposite effect, because it gave the bishops the right to veto ritual prosecutions, and they used it in a way that the Act did not expect, to protect ritual which was technically illegal. Thus in 1886 there was a move to prosecute the ritualist rector of Tedburn St Mary, Charles William Tothill, but the evangelical Bishop Bickersteth, true to his peaceable nature, forbade the prosecution.[25]

Liberals

Scepticism and rationalism did not produce, before 1869, a controversy in the diocese like those occasioned by evangelicalism or ritualism. In 1860 the volume *Essays and Reviews* introduced an outraged Church and community to biology and German biblical criticism. The chief offender, Rowland Williams, was vicar of Broad Chalke in Wiltshire. Had he been beneficed in Devon or Cornwall, Phillpotts would have shown more zest in upholding the inerrancy of scripture and the eternity of punishment than did his brother of Salisbury, the devout Walter Kerr Hamilton, who prosecuted reluctantly and from a sense of duty. As with Gorham, only the Privy Council preserved Williams from the wrath of the majority of vocal churchmen. It fell to Cornwall to provide the 1860s with its sceptical honest-to-God bishop, John William Colenso from St Austell; but he ministered, not in Cornwall but in Natal, which for a time experienced actual schism and rival bishops, and caused a crisis for the world-wide Anglican communion.[26] At the same time Devon, short on saints in earlier times, produced the martyr John Coleridge Patteson, first bishop of Melanesia, in 1871. Scott designed the pulpit in the cathedral nave in memory of him.

But the South West had its liberal controversy nevertheless. When Phillpotts at last went to his rest in St Marychurch, Gladstone nominated Frederick Temple as his successor, and Temple had written the first contribution in *Essays and Reviews*. A man is known by the company he keeps, and the essay itself, *The Education of the World*, would be shown to have liberal tendencies. The ancient custom, given force of law by Henry VIII, was that the cathedral chapter elected as bishop the crown's nominee.[27] Would they elect Temple in 1869? The chapter at Hereford had shown signs of resistance to Hampden, the Tractarian *bête-noire*, in 1847,[28] and in 1839 the Exeter chapter, advised by their astute clerk Ralph Barnes, successfully rejected crown nominees for the deanery.[29] The chapter on 11 November 1869 which received the *congé d'élire* and the royal letter missive must have been a tense one, but the Chapter Acts are uninformative, largely limited to transcribing official documents, the text of which would easily be available elsewhere. They do not record the six prebendaries who voted against Temple, but mention the four who did not

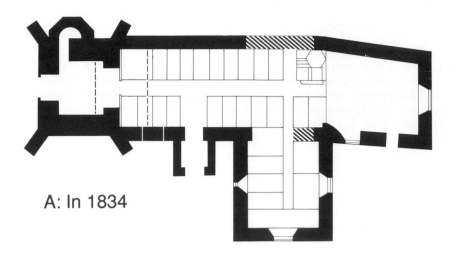

A: In 1834

B: As rebuilt, 1851-2

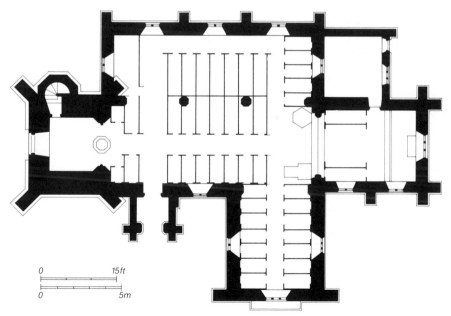

Fig. 13 Brampford Speke church, before and after 1851–2.
A: the old irregular building with three-decker pulpit, 'horsebox stalls' and gallery, in a
dilapidated state. B: as rebuilt, conserving the tower and medieval south aisle, but adding a
north aisle for a larger population, orderly pews, pulpit and reading desk. A non-Tractarian
church, no room was provided for ceremonial.

attend and were pronounced contumacious.[30] Thirteen votes in favour were enough for the chapter to report to the crown that it had elected the said Frederick Temple, but if you add the absent and the noes it was thirteen to ten, uncomfortably close. Of course Temple was not a dangerous sceptic, but a quintessential Victorian, rugged, tolerant and emotional; he resembled his predecessor only in his enormous energy.

The Victorian Achievement

The achievement of the Victorian age in churchmanship cannot be doubted. Indeed, it may almost be said to have created 'Anglicanism' as a definable and working mutation of Christianity in a pluralist society. There is a certain similarity in the age's approach to the Church as the clergy and the rest of the baptised and to the church as a building. In both cases it derived great inspiration from the past. Apostolic succession, Convocation, gothic architecture and ritualism make the point. But these things were not just archaic and archaeological. They spoke afresh to the age, and they were newer and more radical than they were often presented. The 'ideal' Church model of the bishop ruling his diocese and the parish priest ministering to his parish operated more completely in the nineteenth century than ever before, for it was the Victorians who abolished peculiars, limited pluralities, ended non-residence, raised the status of the parish clergy and began the rationalisation of incomes. It was they who accepted a degree of pluralism, in both doctrine and ritual, within the Church itself. It was they who made church buildings theatres of sacred music and liturgical drama, and because of this their own buildings, however lovingly gothic, showed significant differences from the middle ages they claimed to revere.[31]

It is more difficult—indeed impossible—to assess the precise part played by the South West in the process. Certainly the region was not backward or remote, nor had it any sense of waiting for a lead from London or elsewhere. When Anthony Trollope wrote the first Barchester novel, *The Warden* in 1855, he ranked Phillpotts with Blomfield and Wilberforce as a leading reformer; and if Cornwall was a low place of Anglican observance, this acted as a spur in ways we have seen. The *Exeter Diocesan Calendar* of 1870, the year after Phillpotts's death, listed the achievements of the episcopate. Apart from those already mentioned they included 129 new churches, and 27 rebuilt (*Figure 13*). The number restored could not be given because most of the diocese's ancient churches had received some degree of restoration. Phillpotts's prominence was not entirely enviable; his successors at Exeter and Truro provided, as we have seen, leadership of another sort.

A symbol of the new spirit of worship was provided by the cathedral organist,

Samuel Sebastian Wesley (Charles's grandson) who in 1842 left Exeter for a parish church (Leeds) where a surpliced choir of men and boys sang the services in a new building which acted as a model for many others.[32] Symbolic also of the fruitful combination of old and new was Sabine Baring-Gould, squire-parson of Lew Trenchard from 1881 to his death in 1924. Cosmopolitan, Tractarian and prolific, he had written 'Onward Christian Soldiers' during a Yorkshire curacy, and survived to the age of 90 to impress on Church and state that in the South West 'they were giants on the earth in those days'.

CHAPTER SIX

The Nineteenth Century: Nonconformity

Bruce Coleman

Revival ran along the hedge
And made my spirit whole
When steam was on the window panes
And glory in my soul.
                    (Betjeman, *Undenominational*)

The Nonconformist Revival

The period from the late eighteenth century to the mid-nineteenth century witnessed a major transformation of the English religious culture, one comparable to those experienced through less peaceful means in the sixteenth and seventeenth centuries. The South West of England was not exactly typical of the national experience in all aspects of this transformation—regional diversity was indeed a feature of the process—but it shared in it fully and underwent major changes in its religious character.

Nonconformity—to use the Victorian term for the (largely Protestant) denominations and congregations outside the established Church—was at the heart of this change. It grew in its numerical following: both absolutely and in relation to population, in its areas of strength, in the social groups to which it appealed and in its own range and diversity. After dissent (the older term for the phenomenon) had suffered what seems to have been a decline nationally in the mid-eighteenth century, it was expanding again by the end of the century and its growth accelerated in the first half of the nineteenth century. The explanations of this surge in religiosity outside the officially sanctioned channels are agreed by most historians to lie in the conjunction of various social and economic developments. These include the rapid growth of population (which doubled between 1801 and 1851), changes in its regional and local distribution, the great expansion of the commercial and industrial sectors of the economy which was accompanied frequently by a rapid growth of towns and cities, and also perhaps changes in the organisation of agriculture and fluctuations in its prosperity. The constitutional position of the Church of England meant that nonconformity inevitably had a political dimension, and the tensions of the troubled period of national politics from the 1780s to the 1840s fed into and interacted with the process of religious change.

In time the Church of England itself would start to respond to these developments, not least because its own privileged position had become threatened, but the earlier and more explosive response had come from nonconformity, which by 1851 accounted for slightly over half of the attendances at worship in England and Wales. Something of the rate of expansion of nonconformity over the preceding decades can be gauged from the returns of places of worship to the 1851 Census of Religious Worship. Of the recorded places of worship in England and Wales of all denominations, 48.8 per cent were identified as having been established during the previous fifty years, but that figure disguised a revealing discrepancy between the established Church and the voluntary denominations. Only 16.3 per cent of all Anglican places of worship had been founded 1801–51, but 71.3 per cent of the places belonging to other denominations. As *Table 6.1* shows, only just over a quarter of places of worship established before 1801 had been non-Anglican; the figure for all places recorded in 1851 had risen to nearly three-fifths:

Table 6.1: Census of Religious Worship, 1851

Ia: All Places of Worship recorded in 1851

	Church of England (%)	Other (%)
England & Wales	40.8	59.2
Devon	42.3	57.7
Cornwall	24.0	76.0

Ib: Places of Worship identified as established before 1801

	Church of England (%)	Other (%)
England & Wales	73.8	26.2
Devon	77.7	22.3
Cornwall	65.8	34.2

Ic: Places of Worship identified as established 1801-51

	Church of England (%)	Other (%)
England & Wales	13.6	86.4
Devon	8.6	91.4
Cornwall	7.7	92.3

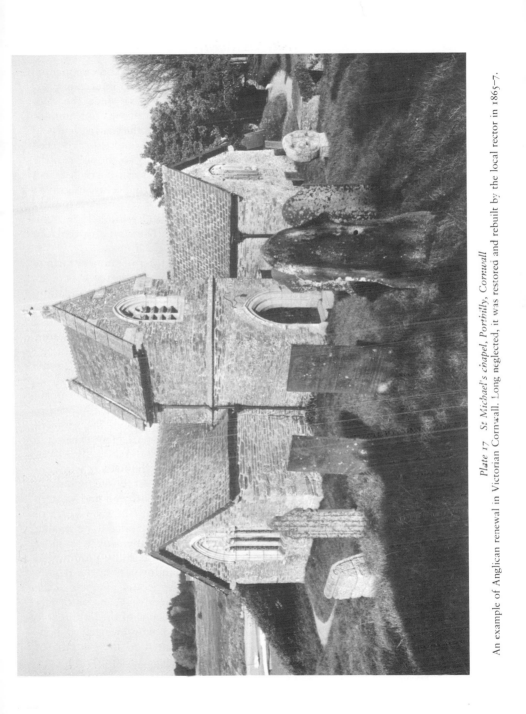

Plate 17 St Michael's chapel, Porthilly, Cornwall

An example of Anglican renewal in Victorian Cornwall. Long neglected, it was restored and rebuilt by the local rector in 1865–7.

The South West played a part in this change and experienced an exponential growth of nonconformity, though it was heavily concentrated in certain parts of the region. The region's population had been growing since the mid-eighteenth century, though more slowly than the nation's. It was not immune to the sharp changes in agricultural prosperity and to the fluctuating levels of government expenditure during and after the French wars, and it experienced contrasting industrial fortunes as mining expanded rapidly in the west of the region and as the old woollen textile industries in its eastern parts declined. One feature of this last change was that the region's industrial centre of gravity moved westwards, away from east Devon where dissent of seventeenth-century origins had once flourished on the strength of the local textile trades, and towards the mining areas of west Devon and Cornwall. The west now replaced the east as the most nonconformist part of the region.

In many parts of England and Wales the most rapid growth of nonconformity occurred where the Church of England was structurally weak—where its dioceses and parishes, still reflecting the medieval distribution of population, were over-large and where the pastoral clergy were now hard-pressed to cope with changing circumstances. Exeter was a large straggling diocese where episcopal supervision was handicapped by distance and poor communications. Much of the South West was uninviting territory to clergymen who wanted comfortable lives, and the general slackening of pastoral efficiency in the eighteenth century had left the more distant parts of the region suffering from the non-residence of incumbents, irregular performance of services and a generally low level of ecclesiastical provision. The diocese was ill-equipped to cope with the shift of industrial activity westwards and with the surge of evangelism associated with Methodism. Patterns of settlement (scattered hamlets and farmsteads rather than nucleated villages), the weakness of landlord influence and the paucity of significant towns with their concentrations of the professional classes, also limited the established Church's capacity to resist nonconformist expansion in much of Cornwall and western Devon. In eastern Devon, however, nearer to the cathedral city, the Church of England was better established and provided for. Parishes tended to be smaller and the problems of distance less acute, nucleated settlement was more common, the influence of the aristocracy and gentry was more pronounced and more effective (Lord Rolle, one of the largest landowners in the region, was particularly active against nonconformity) and the greater numbers of the professional classes in the country towns helped to give Anglican conformity a firmer social base. At the same time the continuing decline of the local textile industries limited the scope of both old dissent and new evangelical nonconformity for expansion. All these factors contributed to the patterns of nonconformist strength in the region by the mid-nineteenth century.

Methodism in the South West

The most spectacular growth of nonconformity in this period occurred through the Methodist denominations of eighteenth-century and subsequent origin. This was so both nationally and in the South West. In 1851 the largest nonconformist denomination in England and Wales would be the Wesleyan Methodist Original Connexion with about 1.5 million Sunday attendances at worship. Next came denominations of earlier origins—the Independents or Congregationalists (1.2 million) and the Baptists (nearly one million), then the Primitive Methodists with half a million, followed by a cluster of other Methodist denominations. Notable among these, in the region, were the Bible Christians, founded in Devon in 1815 by William O'Bryan, as an offshot of Wesleyan Methodism. Methodism in the aggregate of its variants accounted for over a quarter of the country's attendances at worship.

The Methodist phenomenon of the late eighteenth century owed little to the older dissenting denominations—the Independents, the Baptists, the Presbyterians, the Unitarians and the Quakers—which had ceased to grow and had even contracted in mid-century, often losing most of their rural congregations and falling back upon the towns. By the late eighteenth century old dissent had become heavily urban in character. Often, as in parts of the South West, its most marked retreat occurred in areas where the industries which had once sustained it were themselves in decline. Methodism originated rather within the Church of England, which many of its zealots continued to see as their natural home, and not for decades did it clearly separate itself as a distinct denomination or connexion. Its evangelical dynamic eventually made it too hot for the established Church to hold, though a strong Evangelical party remained within the Church of England. But soon Wesleyan Methodism itself was breeding and multiplying as further Methodist connexions established themselves, either as offshoots of Methodist endeavour or as formal secessions from the main body. By 1851 there would be seven forms of Methodism calling themselves Wesleyan, as well as two forms of Calvinistic Methodism. Some of these denominations were politically more radical than mainstream Wesleyanism, the leadership of which had shown itself to be intensely loyalist during periods of political tension; others were more radical only in terms of connexional government and practice, relations between ministers and laity often being at the heart of the disputes. Nearly all of the Methodist variants, however, were more self-consciously nonconformist than the Original Connexion.

There was some Methodism nearly everywhere in England and Wales by 1851, but its incidence was uneven. In some parts it had only a modest presence, in others it was strong enough to rival or even outdo the established Church

Plate 18   Roseworthy Wesleyan Methodist chapel, Gwinear, Cornwall
Humble, thatched and dating from 1825, Roseworthy chapel stands in the Wesleyan heartlands of west Cornwall.

in the extent of its popular following. It was a rather different pattern of strength from that of old dissent. Methodism had reached out into the rural areas, scattered industrial settlements and mining villages which the older denominations had hardly or never touched, and it was much less dependent than them on the boroughs and on urban society generally. In the South West these contrasts were readily apparent. In 1851 the strength of old dissent still lay in east Devon and particularly in the towns with a history of the textile industry. Of 98 nonconformist places of worship identified in 1851 as having been established in Devon by 1801, 72 were from the Independent, Baptist, Quaker and Unitarian denominations and only 18 were Methodist. In Devon Methodism had made a modest start: later and on a much smaller scale than in Cornwall. The comparable figures from the 1851 Census for Cornwall, where old dissent had never been strong, showed a very different picture: of 78 nonconformist places of worship identified as established by 1801, only 17 were of the old denominations but 56 were Methodist. By 1851 Devon would have 748 nonconformist places of worship (to 549 Anglican), of which 379, around half, were Methodist. Cornwall had 839 nonconformist places (to 265 Anglican), of which 737 were Methodist. Though the older dissent, particularly the Independents and Baptists, had resumed growth in the intervening half century, most of the recent nonconformist expansion—the larger part even in Devon and overwhelmingly so in Cornwall—had been in the Methodist connexions.

Some of the reasons for the remarkable success of Methodism in Cornwall have been mentioned. John Wesley had certainly found the county to be receptive territory and had visited it frequently. Was there anything special about Cornish culture and society which helped this Methodist impact? R.R.Currie has suggested that Cornwall was particularly responsive because it was one of the parts of the country 'where pre-christian religion survived at its strongest'.[1] It might be more accurate to say that in Cornwall, more than in most parts of England, a popular rather than an officially determined religious culture had always continued, so that the potential for something comparable to the Methodist upsurge had always existed and could realise itself once the legal and political pressures to Anglican conformity had weakened and once helpful economic conditions pertained. London, Canterbury and Exeter had never put their stamp effectively upon Cornwall. But the reasons for this failure and the reasons why it became even more manifest in this period were much more to do with those structural factors of distance, settlement, population and industrial change than with anything uniquely Cornish or Celtic. Methodism itself had an uneven impact even within Cornwall and it was most successful in those parts of west Cornwall where the growth of mining and of population was most rapid. The eastern districts of the county went more modestly Methodist and they were not very different from the rural parts of west Devon. The most significant frontier for religious practice in the South West ran not along the Tamar but down through mid-Devon.

The Character of Nonconformity

In both counties the rate of establishment of nonconformist places of worship had accelerated in the 1820s with the peak decade of growth being the 1830s. This surge coincided with the phase of constitutional and religious upheaval in national politics mentioned in the previous chapter. The upheaval began with the repeal of the Test and Corporation Acts (and of most dissenters' civil disabilities) in 1828 and Catholic Emancipation in 1829, and continued with the parliamentary Reform Act of 1832 and the Municipal Corporations Act of 1835, It produced major controversies and developments over Church reform, tithes, church rates and dissenters' marriages, and culminated with the threats to the political establishment offered by Chartism and the Anti-Corn Law League. What all this represented was the cracking of a Tory Anglican establishment (the Tory hegemony in national government ended in 1830–31) and a political sea-change which gave nonconformity an enhanced social and political consideration. Though not all nonconformity was self-consciously political in character—Wesleyan Methodism had been distinctly conservative in tone for most of its formative period—yet its great expansion has to be seen as a major shift within English society and one with political as well as cultural dimensions. The South West, though not one of the most prominent areas for the political assertiveness of nonconformity, was contributing its share to this change.

What was the social base of the region's expanding nonconformity? It is clear that nonconformity was almost entirely without the support the Church of England derived from the landowning classes and, only slightly less so, from the professional classes. Its support varied to some extent according to locality. In mining districts Methodism won a following among numbers of miners as well as from craftsmen and small employers. In the older towns, where the old dissenting denominations often flourished, its support came predominantly from tradesmen, craftsmen and merchants. In larger towns like Exeter and Plymouth it also reached into the wealthier elites. When it established itself in rural areas, as the Bible Christians did in much of west Devon and east Cornwall, it appealed not just to tradesmen and craftsmen but to farmers and even to labourers, a class which nonconformity hardly reached elsewhere. The leadership of nonconformity in particular continued to come from levels of society which, though distinct from the elites which dominated Anglicanism, were not without some status and means within their own localities. William O'Bryan, the prime mover of the Bible Christian movement, was a farmer with money of his own to spend on evangelism.

In all this the South West was probably not very different from other parts of the country. Yet one feature perhaps merits some emphasis. Except in the case of Plymouth, which receives attention later in this chapter and which certainly developed characteristics different from those of the rest of the region, the South West experienced little major urbanisation in the formative period of nonconformity. The religious changes in the region were largely characteristic of and characterised by small towns, rural parishes and scattered farmsteads and industrial settlements. To that extent the developments displayed a rather traditional character, not the sharp social and cultural discontinuities which characterised the rapid growth of cities and industrial towns elsewhere, and in certain respects a rather conservative character too. The relative weakness in the South West of the Primitive Methodists, the most radical of the Methodist connexions politically, was probably significant. New as much of the region's nonconformity was, its tone was not that of a wilful modernity.

Though Exeter, the cathedral city of the region, would be one of the declared models for Anthony Trollope's Barchester, by the 1850s the diocese of Exeter hardly displayed, if it had ever done so, the timeless and effortless Anglican dominance of Barsetshire. It would, however, be wrong to lurch to the opposite assumption and to see the South West as a kind of anti-Barsetshire simply overrun by nonconformity. At this point impressionistic analysis needs some quantitative assistance. Happily for this purpose the unique official Census of Religious Worship was held in 1851 at what was probably near the peak of nonconformist success in the region.

The South West in 1851

The national Census of Religious Worship was much the fullest and, for all its limitations, most reliable record of religious attendance made in the modern period. Attendances at each service at every identified place of worship were recorded (or were supposed to be) on the Census Sunday, 30 March 1851, with missing or defective returns being completed, so far as possible, at a later date. The original returns survive in the Public Record Office, but the present analysis utilises the summary tables published in a volume of the Census Report.[2] This material is presented most conveniently in terms of two indices: first, the index of attendance (IA)—the aggregate of all the attendances as a percentage of the population of the area in question;[3] secondly, the percentage share (PS) which a particular denomination or group of denominations had of the total attendances for all denominations. These calculations provide the content of *Tables 6.3* and *6.4* below. *Table 6.2*, also based on the Census material, shows the numbers of places of worship and of attendances for the various denominations in Devon and Cornwall respectively.

Table 6.2: Census of Religious Worship, 1851

	Devon (pop. 567098)		Cornwall (pop. 355558)	
	Places of Worship	Attend.	Places of Worship	Attend.
Church of England	549	227443	265	68122
Independents	142	43081	37	9965
Baptists (all)	112	29939	39	15361
Friends	8	315	12	608
Unitarians	12	2584	2	31
Moravians	1	420	—	—
Wesleyan Original Conn.	219	51240	412	99973
New Connexion	—	—	3	974
Primitive Methodists	—	—	38	8374
Bible Christians	146	20936	182	30038
Wesleyan Association	7	962	93	14513
Wesleyan Reformers	7	1669	6	833
Lady Huntingdon's Conn.	—	—	3	962
New Church	1	83	—	—
Brethren	36	4418	6	636
Isolated Congregations	43	13803	10	601
Roman Catholics	8	1813	7	946
Catholic & Apostolic Ch.	1	193	1	110
Latter Day Saints	3	438	—	—
Jews	2	202	2	51
Total	1297	399559	1104	241494

The South West's overall IA (i.e. for all faiths) was 69.5 (Cornwall 68.0, Devon 70.5), a figure which was significantly above the England and Wales average of 60.8 but not particularly high among southern counties with little major urbanisation. The religiosity of the two counties, at least as reflected in attendances at worship, was nothing remarkable, as some of the comparisons

Plate 19   Catholic and Baptist churches, South Street, Exeter

Respectively built in 1881–6 and rebuilt in 1823, they show nonconformity taking root under the very walls of the cathedral.

Table 6.3: Census of Religious Worship, 1851

	Index of Attendance (Aggregate)	Non-Anglican Denominations	
		Index of Attendance	Percentage Share
England & Wales	60.8	31.3	51.4
Registration Division V			
Wiltshire	85.7	41.0	47.8
Dorset	77.6	29.4	37.8
Devon	70.5	30.4	43.1
Cornwall	68.0	48.7	71.8
Somerset	70.3	27.0	38.4
Other Registration Counties			
Bedfordshire	104.6	63.6	61.4
Cambridgeshire	84.3	47.2	56.0
Durham	42.6	28.3	66.4
Yorkshire (West Riding)	52.9	34.8	65.8
North Wales	86.6	71.5	82.6
South Wales	83.4	67.7	81.2

Note: The registration counties in the second group are a selection from those where nonconformity was strongest. As such, they provide a standard against which Devon and Cornwall can be measured.

provided in *Table 6.3* show. Nor was the region's level of Church of England attendances, 32.0 against a national average of 29.5, though the first figure disguised a sharp contrast between Devon's 40.1 and Cornwall's 19.3. The IA for all non-Anglican denominations combined was 37.5, some way above the national figure of 31.3, but here the two counties again pulled apart, Devon's 30.4 falling far short of Cornwall's 48.7. The nonconformist PS (the percentage share of all attendances) was 53.9 against the national figure of 48.6, though Devon's 43.1 and Cornwall's 71.8 were again sharply contrasted. Cornwall's non-Anglican share of attendances was, indeed, the highest figure for any county except the two Welsh registration counties. Though the peninsula was thus rather more nonconformist than the average for England and Wales, Devon was hardly exceptional while Cornwall's condition was far enough from the norms of southern England to place it firmly in the 'Celtic fringe' of religious practice. It is thus hardly right to treat the South West as if it were a single, integrated region for religious purposes.

Table 6.2 fleshes out this picture with the numbers of places of worship and

Table 6.4: Census of Religious Worship, 1851

Registration District	Total IA	Anglican IA	Anglican PS	Non-Anglican IA	Non-Anglican PS	Old Dissent IA	Old Dissent PS	Methodism IA	Methodism PS	Roman Catholicism IA	Roman Catholicism PS
Devon											
Axminster	82.9	53.9	65.1	29.0	34.9	20.4	24.7	7.9	9.5	—	—
Honiton	76.8	50.4	65.6	26.4	34.4	17.9	23.3	8.2	10.7	—	—
St.Thomas	63.5	48.5	76.4	15.0	23.6	6.7	10.6	4.6	7.2	—	—
Exeter	84.5	54.7	64.7	29.8	35.3	12.8	15.2	10.0	11.8	0.8	0.9
Newton Abbot	75.9	45.5	60.0	30.4	40.0	16.4	21.6	10.0	13.2	0.7	1.0
Totnes	78.5	45.9	58.4	32.6	41.6	16.7	21.2	12.4	15.8	0.1	0.1
Kingsbridge	96.9	52.2	53.9	44.7	46.1	17.8	18.4	21.7	22.4	—	—
Plympton St Mary	50.1	32.2	64.4	17.9	35.6	3.7	7.3	12.4	24.9	—	—
Plymouth	55.1	24.5	44.5	30.6	55.5	9.6	17.4	7.5	13.7	—	—
East Stonehouse	54.5	21.7	29.8	32.8	60.2	10.1	18.5	14.4	26.5	8.3	15.3
Stoke Damerel	57.2	22.1	38.7	35.1	61.3	15.9	27.8	14.2	24.9	—	—
Tavistock	60.1	26.2	43.6	33.9	56.4	8.5	14.1	24.7	41.2	—	—
Okehampton	59.4	35.5	59.7	23.9	40.3	9.1	15.4	13.4	22.5	—	—
Crediton	64.9	42.6	65.6	22.3	34.4	12.5	19.2	6.4	9.8	—	—
Tiverton	69.0	39.3	57.0	29.7	43.0	19.0	27.5	10.1	14.6	0.2	0.3
South Molton	88.1	60.0	68.1	28.1	31.9	9.3	10.5	16.5	18.7	—	—
Barnstaple	71.5	39.6	55.4	31.9	44.6	16.9	23.6	12.2	17.0	—	—
Torrington	75.1	37.0	49.2	38.1	50.8	15.0	20.0	22.6	30.1	—	—
Bideford	81.0	35.0	43.2	46.0	56.8	13.6	16.8	32.1	39.6	—	—
Holsworthy	76.0	32.1	42.2	43.9	57.8	1.8	2.3	42.1	55.4	—	—
Cornwall											
Stratton	73.7	29.0	39.4	44.6	60.6	—	—	44.6	60.6	—	—
Camelford	76.7	19.7	25.7	57.0	74.3	—	—	57.0	74.3	—	—
Launceston	90.8	30.1	33.2	60.7	66.8	12.3	13.6	46.7	51.4	—	—
St Germans	72.7	37.6	51.8	35.1	48.2	10.4	14.4	24.6	33.9	—	—
Liskeard	58.9	18.4	31.2	40.5	68.8	3.9	6.6	35.7	60.6	0.4	0.7
Bodmin	74.2	24.7	33.2	49.5	66.8	—	—	48.8	65.8	0.5	0.7
St.Columb	77.8	22.1	28.4	55.7	71.6	4.1	5.2	50.6	65.0	1.0	1.3
St.Austell	72.2	10.9	15.2	61.3	84.8	6.7	9.3	53.0	73.5	—	—
Truro	84.0	22.3	26.5	61.7	73.5	5.0	5.9	56.7	67.4	—	—
Falmouth	68.4	20.7	30.2	47.7	69.8	10.7	15.6	34.9	51.0	0.8	1.1
Helston	46.5	15.0	32.2	31.5	67.8	1.7	3.7	29.8	64.1	—	—
Redruth	55.7	9.8	17.7	45.9	82.3	1.5	2.7	44.3	79.6	—	—
Penzance	63.8	17.6	27.7	46.2	72.3	3.0	4.8	42.3	66.3	0.7	1.1
Scilly Islands	106.6	53.8	50.5	52.8	49.5	—	—	52.8	49.5	—	—

of attendances for the separate denominations. In Devon the Church of England remained much the largest, returning over four times as many attendances as its nearest rival, the Wesleyan Original Connexion, with the Independents not far behind the latter. This bore some similarity to the overall national pattern. In Cornwall, however, the Wesleyans were comfortably the largest denomina-

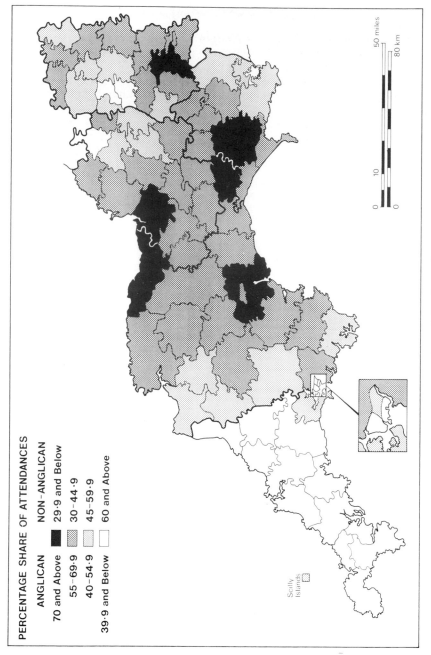

PERCENTAGE SHARE OF ATTENDANCES

ANGLICAN   NON-ANGLICAN

■ 70 and Above   29·9 and Below

55–69·9   30–44·9

45–54·9   40–54·9

39·9 and Below   60 and Above

Scilly
Islands

50 miles

80 km

10

0   0

Fig. 14 Percentage share of church attendances, 1851.

tion, while the Church of England's attendances were almost equalled by the total of those of other forms of Methodism, of which the Bible Christians were the most numerous. As for places of worship, the Church of England found itself outnumbered in both counties. Devon contained 549 Anglican places and 748 non-Anglican, Cornwall 265 and 839. In Devon the Church still possessed many more places of worship than any other single denomination, though the Wesleyans, the Bible Christians, the Independents and the Baptists all commanded sizeable numbers of chapels and meeting-places. In Cornwall the Wesleyans alone had over 400 places; the established Church came a clear second ahead of the Bible Christians and the Wesleyan Association, a Wesleyan offshoot which had some importance in the county. As *Table 6.1* shows,[4] most of the increase in non-Anglican places of worship had occurred since the century's start. Though Cornwall's take-off had been earlier and more dramatic than Devon's, both counties had experienced a surge in nonconformist foundations in the century's second quarter. For both 1831–41 had been the peak decade, Cornwall gaining at least 233 nonconformist places of worship and Devon at least 186. By that time the older dissenting denominations were contributing significantly to the number alongside the Methodist connexions. Even the Roman Catholics, a small denomination in this highly Protestant region, had founded over half their recorded places of worship between 1821 and 1851.

Table 6.2 confirms that, though both counties had complicated denominational patterns, the older, pre-Methodist denominations remained much better represented in Devon than in Cornwall. In fact the Baptists were to be found in all twenty of Devon's registration districts, the Independents in nineteen and even the Unitarians in nine. The equivalent figures for Cornwall's fourteen districts were ten, nine and two. The only old denomination stronger in Cornwall than in Devon was the tiny sect of the Friends (Quakers). Wesleyan Methodism had places in all twenty Devon districts and the Bible Christians in eighteen. Old dissent and the newer Methodism were roughly in balance, but in Cornwall the latter had overwhelmed the former numerically. The Wesleyans had places in all fourteen districts, as did the Bible Christians; the Wesleyan Association appeared in ten and the Primitive Methodists (apparently entirely absent from Devon) in six. Methodism had a certain luxuriance in Cornwall. Its success not only gave a special character to Cornish nonconformity; it also put it outside the frame of reference of the older denominations who still dominated nonconformity in much of Devon as in much of the rest of southern England, and who had seized the political leadership of national nonconformity by 1851. The only significant exception to the tendency for newer forms of nonconformity to be stronger in Cornwall than in Devon was provided by the recently-established sect of the (Plymouth)

Brethren. They were recorded in at least eleven districts in Devon but only three in Cornwall.

The Diversity of the Region

Was all this a matter of a simple contrast between Devon and Cornwall: the former a county with a 'normal' level of nonconformity, the latter exceptionally, indeed rampantly, Methodist? Though the aggregate figures for the counties might suggest this neat division, their breakdown into separate registration districts (see *Table 6.4*) indicates that the boundary between the counties was not a real frontier for religious purposes.[5] The district figures suggest that, in broad terms, there were three, not two, main zones of religious performance within the South West, a conclusion supported by the character of the Somerset and Dorset districts beyond Devon's eastern boundary (*Figures 14 and 15*, pp 142, 145). The most eastern zone included the western districts of Dorset and Somerset and the eastern half of Devon. The second covered west Devon and the eastern districts of Cornwall. The third consisted of central and west Cornwall. The first zone was characterised by the strong Anglicanism common across so much of southern England and by fairly modest levels of nonconformity which was here dominated by the older dissenting denominations; in the second both the Church of England and the older dissent were much weaker and the Methodist denominations were considerably stronger than in the first; and in the third, where old dissent had probably never appeared in force, the established Church was reduced to the bedrock of its support and the new nonconformity, above all Wesleyan Methodism, had established a dominant position. This analysis reduces the significance of the Tamar as a frontier. The registration districts either side of the Devon/Cornwall boundary were not very different from each other in religious (or indeed socio-economic) character. The boundaries between the main religious zones ran not between Devon and Cornwall but across the two counties very roughly north-to-south, the first dividing Devon and the second Cornwall.

This analysis of three main zones within the South West may, however, be somewhat too simple. Even within each one there were significant variations among the registration districts and this was particularly true within Devon, a large and heterogeneous county with major internal contrasts. The range spanned by the various indices of religious performance was greater within Devon than within any of Cornwall, Somerset, Dorset and Wiltshire. Within Devon the aggregate IA ranged from 50.1 to 96.9, the Anglican IA from 21.7 to 60.0, the nonconformist IA from 15.0 to 46.0 and the nonconformist PS from 23.6 to 60.2. This heterogeneity amounted to more than a simple east-west or north-south divide, rather a pattern of *pays* (in the sense used by Alan Everitt),[6]

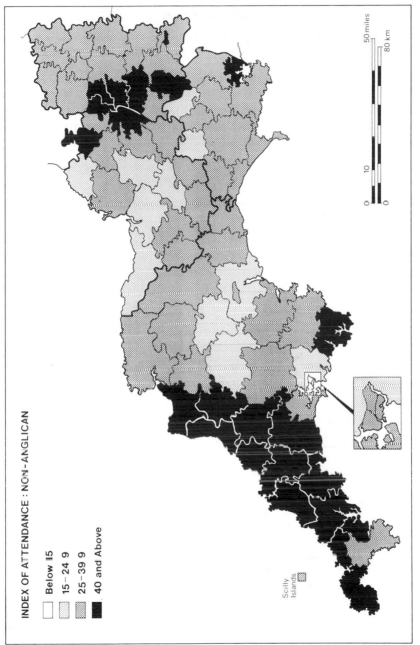

INDEX OF ATTENDANCE : NON-ANGLICAN

☐ Below 15

▨ 15 – 24 9

▨ 25 – 39 9

■ 40 and Above

Scilly
Islands ▨

0 ____ 10 ____ 50 miles

0 ____ 80 km

Fig. 15 Index of church attendances, non-Anglicans, 1851.

i.e. a complex of localities of distinctive socio-economic characteristics. Devon
fitted this conception even better than most other counties. Its large size, but
also the position of Dartmoor at its centre, the importance of its small towns
as local centres (it had long been much more a county of towns than Cornwall),
the influence which the once-powerful woollen industry had had on its eastern
half, linking it with political and religious developments further east, and the
influence of Exeter and Plymouth/Devonport, the two cities of the South West
(and very different cities too)—had all helped to give Devon an unusual degree
of local and sub-regional diversity.

Its patterns of religious attendance in 1851 showed this clearly. Alongside
local variations in aggregate attendances at worship and in levels of Anglican
worship, there was a marked unevenness in the incidence of nonconformity.
In east Devon, particularly the areas of the largely decayed woollen industry,
nonconformity had a minority status alongside the well-supported Church of
England and was probably weaker than it had been in the period covered by
Chapter 4, but it remained a significant force in the towns. The leading
denominations were the Unitarians and the Quakers. Though Methodism was
not completely absent here, it had not spread as successfully as further
westwards; it was still weaker than the older dissent and it was probably
competing more successfully outside the towns where the older denominations
were concentrated. The Bible Christians had made hardly any impact on this
territory. In parts of both north and south Devon, however, this pattern was
modified somewhat. Here, within rather lower levels of aggregate attendance,
the older denominations were significantly weaker and the new nonconformity,
though still predominantly Wesleyan in character, rather stronger. In several
of these registration districts the established Church no longer possessed a
majority of the places of worship, as it normally did in east Devon. In west
Devon and particularly in the north-western districts of Bideford, Torrington
and Holsworthy the picture was different again. Nonconformity now had a
clear majority of attendances, but these were overwhelmingly from the varieties
of Methodism—older dissent was only marginally represented here—and the
Bible Christians rivalled (in two districts even exceeded) the Wesleyans in
attendances. The places of worship of the new nonconformity, some of them
cottage meetings, were now spread through the rural parishes, not concentrated
in the towns as old dissent had usually been. Though Devon was unique among
English counties in having no Primitive Methodism recorded in 1851, its western
districts provided dramatic examples of the way the spread of the Methodist
denominations had transformed religion since the start of the century.

That point can be made even more strongly about Cornwall, where twelve
of the fourteen districts (St Germans in the east and the Scillies were the
exceptions) had majorities of non-Anglican attendances. Nowhere here was

nonconformity as weak as in some eastern parts of Devon. Yet, though Cornwall was the more homogeneous of the two counties, its religious practice was far from uniform. Aggregate attendances were higher in east and central Cornwall, as also were Anglican attendances. Nonconformity was strongest in the western parts of the county. Old dissent was generally weak and made no returns at all in four districts, but it had a significant presence in two of the easternmost districts, and in Falmouth. As we have seen, the phenomenon of Cornish nonconformity lay in Methodism, yet even in this respect the picture was uneven. In parts of east Cornwall the Bible Christians were the strongest nonconformist denomination, though they had a wider and more even spread across the whole county than in Devon. In the west, however, Wesleyanism was dominant over both its nonconformist rivals (including other forms of Methodism) and the established Church. Here lay most of the eight registration districts in which the Wesleyan Connexion was the largest denomination. The six districts in which Primitive Methodism showed were all in the western half of the county, where they seem to have drawn support from mining communities. The Wesleyan Association, a secession from the main body of Wesleyanism in 1836, was spread rather patchily but was strongest in some central and western districts. In west Cornwall particularly the issue of teetotalism had divided Wesleyanism and added to the tensions that produced secession.[7] Even within the Cornish context the western districts had something of a character of their own.

Exeter and Plymouth

Cornwall had no major urban centres, a fact of some influence on its religious experience. Devon included the region's only large towns: Exeter, the ancient county town and cathedral city, and Plymouth (with Devonport), the naval town which was divided into three districts for registration purposes (Plymouth, East Stonehouse and Stoke Damerel). They were sharply contrasting towns. Exeter, located in the Anglican east of the county and enough of an archetypal southern cathedral city to be among Trollope's models for Barchester, recorded high levels of attendance for a city of its size and had two-thirds of those attendances provided by the established Church. Its minority nonconformity was predominately of the older dissenting denominations, though the decline of the local textile trade had sapped some of their earlier vitality. Plymouth, a larger, newer and faster-growing city than Exeter, recorded some of the lowest levels of attendance in the region (all three registration districts had Anglican IAs between 20 and 25) and a clear nonconformist majority of attendances. Here nonconformity was an almost bewildering denominational mix of fourteen different non-Anglican faiths, the largest number anywhere in the region, though in line with the experience of many of the nation's larger cities. In Plymouth there was no one clearly dominant denomination.

Two of Plymouth's features deserve further comment. It had been one of several centres for the establishment and growth of the Brethren (sometimes known as the Plymouth Brethren), one of the period's newer sects.[8] Though the Plymouth registration district itself recorded no Brethren places of worship under that designation, it had a remarkable number of what the Census report termed 'Isolated Congregations', a category too small in most districts to be of much significance, but here credited with ten places of worship, an IA of 12.9 and a PS of 23.4, the highest such anywhere in the country. Part of the explanation seems to be that the Brethren in Plymouth (but not elsewhere) declined to return themselves as a distinct denomination. Secondly, the Stonehouse district returned much the largest number of Roman Catholic attendances (an obviously estimated 1000) anywhere in the region. This was in part a reflection of Irish immigration into the city. Otherwise there was very little Catholicism in the South West, which was in this respect (and others too) a notably Protestant region. The figure for Stonehouse, which presumably attracted Catholics from other parts of Plymouth too, shows how a greater and more rapid urbanisation within the region would have modified the South West's religious character by sucking in more Irish labour. As it was, fifteen Devon and nine Cornish districts recorded no Catholic attendances in 1851, while Plymouth was to become the seat of the new Roman Catholic diocese for the South West after the restoration of the Roman hierarchy in 1851.

Plymouth sat perhaps rather oddly in its regional context. Rawer, more dissident, more idiosyncratic and less godly than the county town, it was also more obviously a nineteenth-century type of city than Exeter. It was also less obviously of a piece with its rural hinterland. The author of the Census Report lamented the low levels of attendance and what he believed to be an advance of secularism in the nation's cities. Plymouth was the only major case in the South West where this worry might have been seen as justified—and, so far as it was, it represented a long-term threat to nonconformity as well as to the established Church.

1851: An Assessment

The South West in 1851 did, therefore, display significant nonconformist strength, though this strength was more apparent as one moved westwards within the region. Nonconformity had minority status in the almost Barsetshire-like east but was a majority force (at least amongst those religiously disposed at all) from west Devon onwards through Cornwall. By 1851 Cornwall was a much more nonconformist county than Devon, a reversal of the situation for most of the eighteenth century. The Tamar was not, however, a major boundary in this respect, for west Devon showed similar characteristics to contiguous districts in Cornwall. The main changes showed within counties rather than along their formal boundaries. Nonconformity itself was heterogeneous and this aspect showed in its geographical distribution. In the east of the region, particularly in the towns, the older dissenting denominations had survived most strongly. They were a marginal force further west in districts which seventeenth- and eighteenth-century dissent had never penetrated effectively and in Cornwall they verged on insignificance. Methodism in one or more of its variants had established a presence almost everywhere in the peninsula by 1851, though only in west Devon and Cornwall had it become a dominant force. In those parts, however, it had made its mark more firmly than almost anywhere else in England. Both in the vigour of Cornish Methodism (noted for turbulence and revivalism within its own connexion) and in the emergence of the Bible Christians, a denomination which remained largely concentrated in the South West, the region had shown its capacity for religious vitality and even creativity.

For all its experience of rapid religious change in the century's first half, the South West was not one of those parts of the country where the expansion of nonconformity had been associated primarily with large-scale industrialisation and urbanisation. Though the advance of some forms of Methodism had certainly been assisted by the expansion of mining, particularly in west Cornwall, that was hardly so true of those mainly rural areas in east Cornwall and west Devon where Methodism, including its Bible Christian form flourished. The decline of the residue of the Devon textile industry had, however, helped to confirm, even to increase, east Devon's dominant Anglicanism. The region had only two major towns and they were sharply contrasted. Exeter's majority Anglicanism was countered by Plymouth's nonconformist majority within what were the lowest levels of overall religious observance in the region.

Generalisations about 'the nonconformist South West' thus need to be shaped with some care. Devon and Cornwall did not form a homogeneous and integrated region, but rather one which displayed considerable internal diversity and contrast, particularly within Devon, the larger of the two counties. Within the region there existed uneven levels and diverse forms of nonconformity, some of them the product of recent expansion and some the residue of much earlier historical developments. Some forms of nonconformity were predominantly urban, others more characteristically rural, some associated with the recent expansion of mining but others without any obvious industrial connection. The statistics produced by the Census of Religious Worship do not always do much to explain what they reveal, but any estimate of the nature and significance of nonconformity within the South West and of the region's

Plate 20   Methodist church, Sidwell Street, Exeter
Resplendent with its octagonal dome and cupola, it was opened for Wesleyans in 1905 at the
acme of Methodist prosperity.

differentiation from other parts of England should be sensitive to the patterns of worship exposed in 1851.

The Late Nineteenth Century

The fortunes of the region's nonconformity become less easy to chart after 1851. There was no further official census of worship and when in the early 1880s a series of local censuses of attendance were conducted across the country under the aegis of newspapers of Liberal nonconformist persuasion, none seems to have been held in the South West, an omission which suggests that the peninsula remained somewhat isolated from the main currents of national nonconformity. Late Victorian developments in the region have to be followed through the records of the separate denominations. Their figures do not lend themselves to easy inter-denominational comparisons and they are often national figures not disaggregated for the various regions, counties and localities. No overall picture based on standardised data like that of 1851 is possible for a later date.

Perhaps this does not matter too much. The heroic age of nonconformist growth was probably over for the South West by the 1850s, as it was for many other parts of England. For many denominations further growth was a matter of consolidation, of infill and of marginal extension, of keeping up more-or-less with the continuing growth of population, rather than the explosive expansion which some regions, among them the South West, had experienced in the first half of the century. Some of that consolidation consisted of building chapels where only house-meetings had existed before and the South West shows much surviving evidence of this. Wesleyan Methodism in particular never grew so much or so fast again after its experience of schism and fall-back in the late 1840s. Some of the most rapid mid-Victorian growth nationally came from the Baptists, a faith only modestly represented in much of the peninsula.

There were other, more specifically local reasons why nonconformity had nearly reached its limit in the South West by the 1850s. The economy of the region was already slowing by mid-century and it suffered a series of blows thereafter to add to the earlier near-elimination of its textile trades. Mining hit a sudden slump around 1860, the herald of long-term decline, and another sharp contraction came in the 1890s; the region's agriculture suffered from the sharp depression in prices from the 1870s. During the century's second half the growth of the region's population was well below the national level and Cornwall was actually losing population during its last four decades. Though Devon never suffered so badly, its population was almost static in the 1880s and it was undergoing a significant internal redistribution as many of its rural districts lost population heavily while some of the towns, notably Plymouth and various seaside resorts, continued to grow steadily. Economic and demographic contraction was not the recipe for nonconformist expansion, and some of the areas where nonconformity had been best established in 1851 were those experiencing the harshest fortunes.

By this time the Church of England was also providing more formidable resistance and competition. The foundation of the see of Truro in 1876 was only part of a much more extensive mobilisation of Anglican resources and endeavour on a national scale. Even before 1851 Anglican church-building had started to make an impact in the South West and new provision had accelerated in the last decade before the Census. Though nonconformity often remained the most active provider of Sunday schooling, the established Church became dominant in many areas in the provision of day schools for the lower classes. The 1870 Education Act, which set up local School Boards to administer the elementary schools, ushered in a period of often intense conflict between Church and Chapel over the establishment and then the control of the Boards. Two of the period's more conspicuous social developments, suburbanisation and the growth of resort towns, offered opportunities to the Church to recruit among annuitants, the retired and the professional and business classes. Nonconformity was not absent from these new kinds of communities—there were chapels founded in all the successful resorts of the South West—but it was never going to dominate them as it had some of the mining and the more isolated agricultural districts.

Nonconformity was not, however, static. Many of the changes apparent in the South West were, though, more a matter now of reflecting national trends than of anything indigenous to the region. The Primitive Methodists, a denomination growing fast elsewhere in the century's third quarter, made their appearance in Devon. Later the Salvation Army, a new movement, made some impact on the region's larger towns. Roman Catholicism continued its modest growth in the region, though still largely as a result of Irish immigration. Catholic chapels were established in many more towns of the new Catholic diocese centred on Plymouth. Two denominations with special associations with the region, the Bible Christians and the Brethren, expanded outside the South West, though still on a modest scale and partly through the emigration of members out of the region. None of this, however, amounted to a great upheaval. Nonconformity, taken as a whole, was in a period of stabilisation and of consolidation in the South West, a prelude to what for many of the denominations would be a longer period of decline.

Some of the signs of decline were already appearing by the late Victorian years. A Wesleyan Methodist survey of national membership in 1886 noted already a marked decrease in Cornwall. The 662 Methodist chapels in Cornwall at the time of Methodist union in 1932 (there had been 737 chapels for all forms of Methodism in 1851) represented, however, a fairly gentle decline from the probable peak in the mid-Victorian years rather than any catastrophic collapse. The Bible Christian membership of 16,582 in Devon and Cornwall in 1900, well over half the total national membership, stood up reasonably well against the 51,000 attendances the denomination had recorded in the counties in 1851, membership and attendances being very different matters, but the comparison also underlines the lack of any explosive growth of the movement in its regional heartland between the two dates. The large towns had probably not changed dramatically either. In 1890 the religious accommodation of Plymouth divided one-third Anglican to two-thirds nonconformist, a division not far from that of attendances in 1851. The city was still worrying the religious with some of the lowest levels of religious observance in the region.

In the first half of the century the nonconformity of the South West had been incorporated only gradually and imperfectly into the national political scene, where dissent was coming to feel its strength. Its local enthusiasms had tended to be moralistic causes like anti-slavery and temperance rather than ones of radical political significance. In the region, however, as elsewhere, nonconformity and Liberalism eventually became almost synonymous. As so much of the region's nonconformity was rural rather than concentrated in the boroughs, its political influence, at least for parliamentary purposes, was muffled until the 1884 franchise act brought householder suffrage and a more intense party rivalry to the county divisions. The consequences were immediate: in the 1885 general election thirteen of the twenty parliamentary seats in the two counties, including all seven in Cornwall, were won by the Liberals, the exceptions being the five borough seats for Plymouth, Devonport and Exeter and two county divisions in east Devon. In 1906, that peak of Liberal success almost everywhere, the Liberals, emphasising the issues of free trade and education, won seventeen of the twenty seats, the Unionists holding only three seats in the more Anglican and Conservative territory of south and east Devon. Yet Liberal nonconformity in the South West showed itself to be remarkably susceptible to disruption and demoralisation by the issue of Irish Home Rule. In 1886, an election dominated by Gladstone's conversion to that cause, the Liberals, in sharp contrast to the result of the previous year, held only four of their seats. In the second general election of 1910, when Home Rule again reared its unwelcome head, the region swung back markedly against a Liberal government in alliance with the Irish Nationalists. The reasons for the anti-Irish mood of the South West, a phenomenon remarked upon much at the time, included the fears of its fishing interests that Home Rule would mean the closure of Irish waters to them and a strong, traditional anti-Catholic feeling which was more pronounced in Methodism than in some other forms of nonconformity.[9] In this respect the South West was again showing an instinctive

Protestantism, one reinforced not, as in some other regions, by reaction against major Irish immigration but rather by a fundamentalist evangelicalism with deep popular roots. But though the Irish issue disrupted political Liberalism in the South West, it probably did little to undermine nonconformity itself. The great gainer from Liberal divisions in the peninsula was not old Anglican Toryism but rather Liberal Unionism, the element which had broken away from the main Liberal party in 1886 and many of whose candidates continued to identify with nonconformist positions on most issues except Ireland. Most of the traditionally nonconformist constituencies in the region were contested from 1886 to the Great War not between Liberals and Conservatives but between Gladstonian (loyalist) Liberals and Liberal Unionists. Often non-conformist causes like temperance and education reform were prominent on both sides of these contests. The 1906 result showed the continuing political potential of Liberal nonconformity in the region. Here was a bedrock of nonconformity which would survive substantially the Liberal party's mis-fortunes after 1914. In the 1930s a study would find Cornwall to be still the most nonconformist county in England (excluding Wales) in terms of the provision of ministers. The county had one nonconformist minister to every 2,635 inhabitants. Devon now ranked tenth among the counties with 1:3,671, while the mean for England was around 4,500. Cornwall's nonconformity was still predominantly Methodist (and as such much more united than in 1851), while Devon remained much the better provided of the two counties for non-Methodist nonconformity.[10] A survivor from 1851 would have found much that was familiar about the picture. The two maps which support this chapter could, at a pinch, do double-duty to illustrate the distribution of nonconformity in the 1930s too.

All this suggests a long-term decline, perhaps an atrophy, of the region's nonconformity rather than any sudden collapse. Arguably the long, slow economic drift of the South West, which helped to prevent any further rapid growth of Protestant voluntarism after 1851, also slowed nonconformity's decline in the twentieth century. A more dramatic experience of economic development, particularly one involving rapid industrial expansion and large-scale urbanisation, might have undermined nonconformity more rapidly, as it did in some other parts of England. As it was, the slower pace of change across most of the South West and the traditionalism and conservatism that accom-panied it underpinned a nonconformist strength that was itself already traditional in much of the region, that tended to be theologically conservative, even fundamentalist, in its dominant evangelicalism, and which in its charac-teristic cultural attitudes was provincial rather than metropolitan and 'modern'. The South West would be one of the areas where nonconformity ebbed only slowly in the twentieth century from its earlier highwater-mark. It would continue to present a political and cultural barrier not only to Tory hegemony but also to the new Labour party, which made little impact outside the two cities of Plymouth and Exeter. Long after its peak, nonconformity would continue to colour the character and the culture of the South West.

Plate 21   Truro Cathedral
J.L. Pearson's great work, planned in 1880 and finished in 1910: the symbol of the Anglican
revival in Cornwall.

CHAPTER SEVEN

The Twentieth Century

The old order changeth, yielding place to new,
And God fulfils Himself in many ways
Lest one good custom should corrupt the world.
(Tennyson, *Morte d'Arthur*)

Part 1: Cornwall

Michael Winter

The Contrasting Religiosity of Cornwall

In matters of religion, as in many other things, Cornwall is a land of contrasts. Together, these contrasts add up to a county which stands apart from the rest of southern England in a number of respects. The strength of the nonconformist tradition, as the previous chapter has shown, is unparalleled elsewhere in the South. In 1901 Methodism, chiefly represented by the Wesleyan and Bible Christian denominations, still dominated the religious scene in Cornwall. On the Anglican side, the see of Truro was not established until 1877, and the diocese could not boast the continuity of history enjoyed by its neighbours such as Exeter or Bath and Wells. In terms of the allegiance of the Cornish, the Church of England in 1901 was a minority Church, but it was a growing minority and had a higher degree of optimism and confidence than for many years. During the twentieth century, Anglicanism has continued to grow and strengthen itself, while nonconformity on the other hand has experienced a loss of support. This dual process is a principal theme of the chapter-section which follows.

The diocese of Truro was founded at a time when the Anglo-Catholic movement in England was growing significantly, during the last decades of the nineteenth century. Perhaps for this reason, high churchmanship has been a prominent characteristic of Cornish Anglicanism since 1877, and this, of course, has served to underline the differences between the Methodist and Anglican traditions. It has to be said, however, that contrasts within the two main traditions are also important, with Wesleyan Methodism for example offering more sacramental worship than the Bible Christians. So too it should not be forgotten that strong pockets of Anglican evangelicalism have long existed within the diocese. Nor, indeed, has every bishop been firmly of the catholic position. The popular war-time bishop Joseph Hunkin (1935–50), was a notable liberal evangelical and the son of a Wesleyan local preacher of Truro.[1] Frederick Sumpter Guy Warman (1919–23) was another low-church bishop in the diocese. But, with those exceptions, most have been high-church and in Bishop Walter Howard Frere (1923–35) the diocese boasted not only one of the leading figures of twentieth-century Anglo-Catholicism but also the first monk to be appointed to an English bishopric since the Reformation.

The strength of Anglo-Catholicism in Truro diocese at the turn of the century has been gauged by Miles Brown. Deriving statistics from the *Church Guide for Tourists*, published by the English Church Union (an Anglo-Catholic group) in 1901, he estimated that 25 per cent of the churches in Cornwall were using vestments at this time, compared to just 14 per cent in Devon.[2] Anglo-Catholicism in the early days flourished in the towns and cities, but Cornwall was one of the few country areas where it found a ready home. It is no coincidence that in Compton Mackenzie's satirical trilogy *The Altar Steps*, the hero moves from his curacy in a London church to an incumbency in a Cornish village.

Some of the more notorious controversies surrounding ritualistic practices occurred in Cornwall.[3] In the second decade of the century national Protestant attention was brought to bear over the practices of Sandys Wason in Cury with Gunwalloe on the Lizard. These included veneration of the Virgin Mary, the use of incense and benediction. It was the persistent use of this last rite which led to formal deprivation of Wason's living by Bishop Winfrid Burrows in 1919. When Wason refused to vacate his vicarage, local opponents forcibly, and without warrant, evicted him! More controversy erupted a decade later, when in 1932 militants of the Protestant Truth Society wrecked—with crowbars and hammers—the ornate interior of the church at St Hilary. The incumbent, Bernard Walke, was a far more thoughtful and creative pastor than the somewhat eccentric Wason. His church plays for All Souls and Christmas were broadcast, and he founded a children's home in the parish. But the opposition, led by two of his own parishioners with considerable backing from militant Protestants from outside the county, broke the man who resigned the living in 1936. The trouble continued even after that with attempts to block the appointment of Walke's successor, a moderate catholic churchman, by the expedient of manipulating the membership of the electoral roll, so as to

Plate 22   St Hilary parish church, Cornwall
The interior as it was in the time of Bernard Walke (rector 1912–36), before its destruction by
Protestant zealots in 1932.

influence the election of a new church council. Sadly a number of Methodists allowed their names to be used in this way.

But over most of the diocese the more extreme forms of catholicism and Protestant reaction were foreign. For many priests describing themselves as 'prayer-book catholics' the core of their ministry centred on a renewed emphasis upon the sacraments, especially that of holy communion, a quiet dignity in worship with due attention to the details of liturgy, and deep pastoral concern. It was this quiet catholicism, more in the tradition of Puseyite Tractarianism than Romanising Anglo-papalism, which led Cornish Anglicanism out of its nadir of the nineteenth century.

Cornish Methodism in the twentieth century has not been immune to controversies, although they have been far less public and dramatic than those surrounding ceremonialism in the Church of England. A chief cause of internal disquiet in the early years of the century revolved around successive unity schemes, which by no means found ready acceptance in Cornwall. As Robert Currie has pointed out, opposition was on pragmatic grounds rather than doctrinal. Schemes of union in the 1920s foundered on the vexed question of what would happen to spare buildings in localities where circuits and chapels overlapped. At the unsuccessful vote for union in 1924, Cornwall provided

> the classic case of overlap and excess capacity in the south of England. Nine circuits in a triangle sixty square miles in area, from Camborne to Helston west to Penzance, rejected union, while several other circuits in the area strongly opposed it. The four opposing Wesleyan circuits consisted of forty-eight chapels. These had an average of 330 seats and sixty members, the ratio of seats to members being 5.6:1. The nine circuits probably had 23,000 empty seats between them.[4]

At first sight this might seem prime territory for ecumenism. In practice, however fears were very real due to the commitment of congregations to their own chapels, the uncertainty of what union would mean to the future of particular chapels, and the feeling that chapels would be closed and resources transferred to suburban and metropolitan Methodism where congregations were outgrowing their existing buildings. Some of these fears may have been well founded, although it is hard to identify cause and effect relationships in such matters. In 1932 the present-day Methodist Church was formed through the unification of the three remaining strands of Methodism—the Wesleyans, the Primitives and the United Methodists. At union there were 662 chapels in the county, but by the mid-1960s this had dropped to under 500 and by 1986 it was down to 365.

Church Allegiance

METHODISM IN DECLINE

Many commentators have asserted, probably correctly, that the conspicuous Anglo-Catholicism of the county arose in conscious reaction to the strength of Methodism. However, it has to be said that Methodism was in serious decline even before the hey-day of the Anglo-Catholics between the wars. Whereas Methodism (inclusive of all its constituent parts) in Great Britain as a whole continued to grow in the first three decades of the twentieth century—from 791,968 members in 1902 to 838,734 in 1932, after a peak of nearly 844,000 in 1929[5]—in Cornwall it declined. The Wesleyans recorded 17,072 Cornish members in 1901 and only 13,784 in 1921. The United Methodist Church, formed as a unification of the Bible Christians and two other national Methodist denominations in 1907, fared little better. *Table 7.1* traces the numerical fortunes of Methodism in the Cornwall District and the nearby Plymouth and Exeter District since union in 1932.[6] It shows that the decline has continued, although over the period as a whole Cornwall has fared somewhat better than its Devon neighbour and Britain in general. Between 1932 and 1986 Cornish Methodism suffered a 39 per cent decline in membership compared to 48 per cent in the Plymouth and Exeter District and 46 per cent nationally. The lower rate of decline is due to an increase in Cornish membership (one of only six English counties to do so) in the decade from 1951 to 1961. But in the fifteen years from 1971 to 1986 Cornwall lost nearly a third of its membership—a 31 per cent decline compared to 22 per cent in Devon and 25 per cent nationally.

Table 7.1: Methodist Membership: Cornwall, Plymouth and Exeter, Great Britain

	Cornwall	Plymouth and Exeter	Great Britain
1932	20,539	34,179	838,019
1951	16,990	29,833	744,815
1961	21,271	24,675	668,452
1971	18,333	22,606	601,068
1981	14,134	18,515	480,104
1986	12,594	17,683	450,406
1989	11,820	16,941	431,459

Source: Minutes and Yearbook of the Methodist Conference.

Plate 23 Ebenezer Bible Christian chapel, Blisland, Cornwall
A typical wayside chapel, opened in 1880, and here in picturesque decay in 1969.

The picture is particularly bleak when it is remembered that the population of the county began to grow rapidly at the same time. Having been more or less static, due to outward migration throughout the first fifty years of the century, a modest increase of 22,000 between 1961 and 1971 became an explosion in the 1970s and 1980s. Between 1961 and 1986 the county grew by a third from 340,000 to 450,000. Assuming about 20 per cent of the population to be under 16 years of age, and therefore unlikely to be in Church membership, this means that Methodist members comprised perhaps 8 per cent of the adult population in 1961 but just 3.5 per cent in 1986. We can estimate that the figures might be adjusted upwards to around 9, and 4 per cent if the Bude, Saltash and Callington circuits are taken into account. Nationally, where population growth was limited, the respective proportions are 1.5 per cent and 1 per cent.

Since 1969 the Methodist Church has also held records, on a 'community roll', of those who are not in membership but who are associated in some manner with the Church. The community roll typically contains double the number of people in full membership, so tripling the total Methodist population. The roll, some Methodists would argue, by taking children into account allows a truer reflection of the Church's importance in the community. Using the figures in this way nearly 8 per cent of the Cornish population can still be claimed for Methodism. While the community roll clearly includes those regular attenders, perhaps younger people, who have not yet been received into full membership, there are a number of very real problems with the community roll as an accurate measure of Church allegiance. The composition of the roll will vary from minister to minister, but may include Sunday School children, whose parents are practising Anglicans at a church with no Sunday School, or alternatively lapsed Methodist members who have not attended a place of worship for many years. Thus in terms of regular worship attendance, the figures are just a little higher than the membership figures but far short of the community roll.

What might be expected in an area historically rooted in Methodism is for many non-attenders to acknowledge their Methodist roots through some form of nominal allegiance to an 'established' church. This was undoubtedly the case in the past—in 1962, for example, 290 out of every 1,000 marriages with a religious ceremony in Cornwall were conducted in a Methodist church.[7] The next highest figure for an English county is less than 130 for the Isle of Wight. But a recent social survey, based on a sample of 100 rural parishioners in each of five English dioceses (Durham, Gloucester, Lincoln, Southwell and Truro), showed 'nominal' Anglican allegiance to be as high in Cornwall as elsewhere with only a few nominal Methodists.[8] Even in 1962 Truro was numbered amongst the top eight English dioceses for Anglican Easter communion attendance as a ratio of the population as a whole.[9] The evidence seems to indicate that in the immediate post-war period Methodism and Anglicanism shared in a generally high level of religious allegiance in the county compared to most parts of England. Since that time both denominations have declined in their ability to command the active allegiance of the people, but the decline in Methodism has been far starker than that of Anglicanism. Well researched explanations for the sharply changing fortunes of Methodism are hard to come by. However we do know that the population figures mask a continued exodus of Cornish workers from the county,[10] especially in the wake of the declining fortunes of the tin mining areas, traditional strongholds of Methodism. They have been replaced by in-migrants to Cornwall predominantly from the South East and Midlands,[11] not areas (excepting parts of London) where Methodism has historically been particularly strong. Ironically many of the newcomers come in search of local or 'roots' culture which they find in a revived (or created?) Celtic culture,[12] rather than in Methodism which is arguably a far more authentic expression of twentieth-century Cornish identity.

In accounting for the spectacular decline of Methodism it is also important to remember the strong strand of anti-clericalism in Cornish Methodism, both in its Bible Christian (inherently anti-clericalist) and Wesleyan forms. By anti-clericalism I do not mean militant opposition to the clerisy *per se,* but rather an inherent disrespect for ministerial authority and a reluctance to accept wholeheartedly a central role for the ministry in ecclesiological terms. This has had two rather contradictory impacts in recent decades. On the one hand rooted and institutionalised anti-clericalism has led to very traditional chapels resisting changes suggested by ministers anxious to attract younger people. On the other hand some Methodist lay folk, influenced by the charismatic movement, have resisted ministerial authority and left the Methodist Church to establish or join fringe Protestant/evangelical groups. Some are quite anarchic in character, but in others a strong authority structure emerges of a very different character to traditional Methodist ministry.[13] This mirrors the situation in the last century when Cornish Methodists were notorious for their reluctance to appoint ministers, so much so that there were up to three times as many members per minister in some Cornish circuits as the national average.[14] Anti-clericalism is also evidenced in opposition to ceremonialism—Cornish Wesleyans were far less enamoured with liturgy than Wesleyans elsewhere,[15] and Bible Christians were even more sceptical.

Turning now to the Church of England we immediately encounter far greater difficulty in measuring allegiance than for the Methodists. The Anglican Church has no form of membership equivalent to that to the Methodist Church, and arguably, there are at least five (overlapping) groups of people who can claim membership:

a. Those who declare themselves as members purely due to the rights of citizenship in a country with an established church. Thus membership of the Anglican Church in social surveys is consistently higher than the rate of infant baptism or any other measure of membership.
b. Those who are baptised.
c. Those who are confirmed.
d. Those whose names appear on the church electoral roll.
e. Those who attend services regularly.

None of these categories encapsulates, or is mutually exclusive of, all the others. While electoral roll members have to be baptised members of the Church of England (no longer communicant members as was the case in the past), or of a Church in communion with the Anglican Church, the roll may contain names of those who do not attend church regularly. Similarly not all regular attenders or communicants are on the church electoral roll. At different times and in different places electoral rolls have been criticised for being too all-embracing —containing large numbers of purely nominal members, or alternatively as being kept deliberately low to limit liability for financial payments to the diocese! Frequently Easter or Christmas attendances have been used to gauge levels of commitment to the Church, although these suffer from an added disadvantage that in some localities those of other denominations join Anglicans for these services. This is less likely for Easter Communion services than for Christmas services, and this measure has been presented in *Table 7.2.*

The figures in this table present an interesting contrast to the trends recorded for Methodist membership. Over the period as a whole the number of Anglican Easter communicants has increased, whereas Methodist membership declined sharply. This should not be seen as a direct comparison, as the emphasis placed upon communion has not been constant over the years. The figures may reflect the greater stress on liturgical and sacramental worship in the Anglican Church as the century has progressed, though it has to be said that even before the parish communion movement Easter was seen as an obligatory feast for

Table 7.2: Number of Easter Communicants in the Church of England

	Truro Diocese	Exeter Diocese	Provinces of Canterbury and York (to nearest '000)
1911	17,170	65,045	2,429,000*
1921	17,553	65,508	2,214,000
1931	21,087	70,304	2,288,000
1950	21,577	60,361	2,004,000
1960	30,253	77,919	2,347,000
1970	24,671	64,535	1,814,000
1982	28,200	58,600	1,674,000
1985	26,700	54,500	1,550,000

Notes: *The figure for 1911 is inflated due to the inclusion of the Welsh dioceses at this time prior to the implementation of disestablishment in Wales in 1920. The data is not strictly presented for census years due to unavailability in some instances.

Source: Church Statistics (Annual), Central Board of Finance of the Church of England.

communicants. If Truro held its own from 1931 to 1950, when its own population was static and the number of Easter communicants declined elsewhere, it was perhaps because of the readiness of a diocese steeped in the catholic tradition to implement weekly communions.[16] It also probably reflects the lasting influence of Bishop Frere. Since 1950 Truro has shared the general downward decline of other parts of the country, although once again it appeared to buck the general trend by registering an increase between 1970 and 1982. This must almost certainly have been a consequence of the massive population increase of the period, although Exeter diocese shared the inmigration but not the increasing number of Easter communicants.

Another measure of allegiance is the number of infant baptisms as shown in *Table 7.3*. Once again Truro, although sharing in the general decline of religious adherence, can be seen to have greater cause for encouragement than its neighbour Exeter. In 1960 the rate of Anglican infant baptisms was lower in Truro than nationally and considerably lower than in Exeter. Now the situation is reversed with Truro having a higher rate than either Exeter or England as a whole, although it must be difficult for the diocesan clergy to take comfort in the 'success' of a lower level of decline:[17]

Plate 24 Walter Howard Frere, bishop of Truro
Liturgist, historian and the first member of a religious order to hold a Church of England see
since the Reformation.

Plate 25 March of Christian Witness at Saltash, Cornwall, 1935

The evangelical Bishop Hunkin leads the personnel of Saltash church (who were 'higher'), with some mutual anxiety!

Table 7.3: Church of England Infant Baptisms: Rate per 1,000 Live Births

	Truro Diocese	Exeter Diocese	Provinces of Canterbury and York (to nearest '000)
1960	533	616	554
1970	489	498	466
1982	428	392	347
1985	390	366	356

Source: Church Statistics (Annual), Central Board of Finance of the Church of England.

Interestingly, on another key indicator, the annual number of confirmations, a dramatic rate of decline is almost identical to that experienced in Exeter and only a little less than the national figure. Confirmations have declined from 1,520 a year in 1961 to 588 in 1986. But the numbers on the electoral roll have shown only a slight decrease during the period, whereas nationally the electoral roll has fallen from nearly two and a half million to one and a half.

Together these statistics add up to a highly complex and mixed picture. More research is clearly needed on the changing nature of religiosity reflected in these sometimes contradictory figures. Research on religious views within the Cornish countryside shows a continuing high level of belief in a number of tenets of traditional Christian teaching, but these do not always result in religious commitment through activity and participation.[18] One commentator has recently identified this as a distinguishing feature of religion in late twentieth-century Britain, and coined the phrase 'believing without belonging' to describe the phenomenon.[19] For many sociological and cultural, not to mention doctrinal, reasons the Methodist Church is likely to suffer more than the Anglican Church under such a scenario and this certainly seems to have been the case in Cornwall in recent decades.

The Church of England: Diverse Responses to Change

If Methodism has been preoccupied with declining membership during recent years, Anglican concerns with change have been somewhat broader. Whereas in Methodism the decline in the number of ministers is more or less a direct consequence, and perceived as such, of the decline in membership, Anglicanism during these years has witnessed a radical redeployment of its clergy nationally from rural to urban benefices, largely irrespective of church attendance. This is, of course, a consequence of the historic parochial system, and its inherent bias in favour of rural areas. Although much has changed since the report produced by Leslie Paul in 1964 showed that half the benefices in the Church of England held only 10 per cent of the population, rural populations still have more priests pro rata than do urban areas.[20]

The Church of England during the last twenty years has been attempting to redress this imbalance in its deployment of manpower. Many of Paul's recommendations were embodied in the Pastoral Measure of 1968, which established a pastoral committee in every diocese with considerable powers for pastoral reorganisation if required. Whereas the Exeter committee was one of the first to use the new structure to establish a diocesan strategy (in 1974), Truro lagged behind and did not produce a report on pastoral needs until 1978. Moreover, under Bishop Graham Leonard, the diocese resisted the full implementation of the 1974 Sheffield Report which suggested ways in which reform might be achieved by proposing norms for numbers of parishioners in the charge of one clergyman. The Sheffield formula still retained a rural bias in provision, to reflect the larger geographical areas that clergy have to cover in the country (as well as the higher proportion of rural people attending a place of worship). In time it led to a speeding up of the process of joining parishes in a single benefice under one incumbent. There was more to these developments than a mere increase in the size of benefice in the charge of one priest. They also contained the possibility for a far more radical reorganisation of the parochial system. The Pastoral Measure 'provided for the alteration of ecclesiastical boundaries, for the preservation or disposal of redundant churches, and for the setting up of group and team ministries'.[21] Synodical government was introduced in 1970, which gave a new impetus to the possibilities for joint and united action by groups of parishes brought together in deanery synods. The same year also saw the authorisation of a non-stipendiary ministry.

Even more radical implications were contained in a report published in 1983, entitled 'A Strategy for the Church's Ministry'.[22] Its author Canon John Tiller has become one of the most persuasive advocates of a fundamental overhaul of the parochial system and an end to a locally based clergy. Tiller has focused

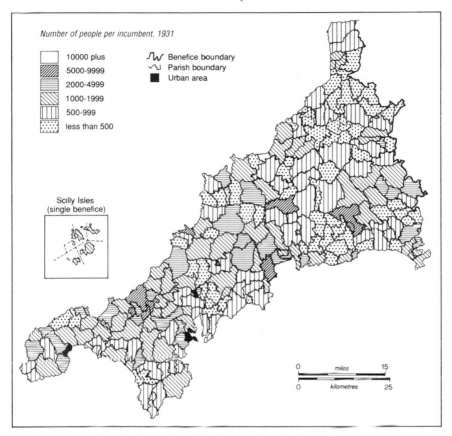

Fig. 16   Population of Anglican parishes in Cornwall, 1931.

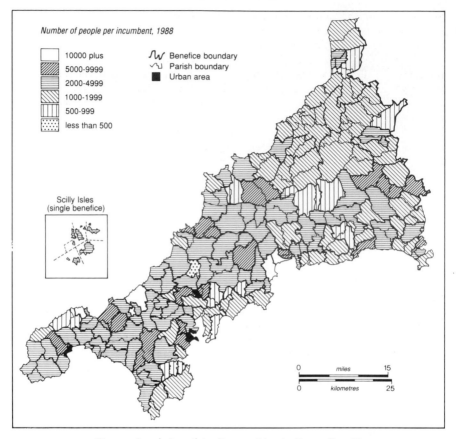

Fig. 17   Population of Anglican parishes in Cornwall, 1988.

his assault on the undue expectations placed upon the clergy in the parish ministry, especially the rural parish, which he sees as enervating to the development of the ministry of the body of the Church as a whole. He accuses the Church of nurturing a view dominated by clericalism.[23] There is strong resistance to Tiller's views from many parochial clergy and parishioners, but that such a senior churchman (he is chancellor of Hereford Cathedral) can make them so forcefully and attract such widespread interest suggests that the story of parochial reorganisation may not be over yet.

The two maps (*Figures 16* and *17*) show the numbers of people per incumbent in Cornwall in 1931 and 1988, revealing the dramatic changes that have taken place.[24] In 1931 52 per cent of the incumbencies within the diocese contained fewer than 1,000 souls and more than a quarter of the benefices had less than 500. Parochial organisation in 1931 was dominated by the single parish benefice, which comprised 88 per cent of the benefices. By 1988 the situation had been transformed with a threefold rise in the number of benefices of between 2,000 and 4,999 people. The number of incumbents declined from 222 to 146 and only two in 1988 held benefices with populations of less than 500. Only 49 per cent of the clergy now hold single-parish benefices and many of those have grown in size due to population growth or parish amalgamation.

The changes in parochial organisation and ministry add up to a more pluralistic and diverse Church organisation. Arguably even more radical changes have taken place in liturgy with the advent of the rites of the Alternative Service Book (ASB) alongside the time-honoured Book of Common Prayer. But it would be a mistake to assume that the ASB has replaced the Book of Common Prayer as the norm throughout the diocese, as demonstrated in *Table 7.4* which shows the mean number of different types of service per benefice in the Truro diocese for a four-week period from 16 October to 6 November 1988.[25] Although ASB holy communion is strongly developed, the Book of Common Prayer is still relatively widely used and for evensong remains the norm. Resistance to modern developments is strongest in the remoter countryside, where the use of Prayer-Book services is more common than in urban areas, and where lay ministry is also less developed.

Conclusion

This section has attempted to cover a great deal of material in a short space. In many ways it provides an agenda for further research, for as is often the case with very recent history, much of the available data is somewhat raw and has been subjected to very little sustained analysis. That is true for the data on Church attendance which has been well utilised by a number of scholars for the first half of the century, but there is an urgent need for much more

Table 7.4: Mean Number of Services per Benefice over Four Weeks in Truro Diocese, 1988

Holy Communion:
Book of Common Prayer	2.22
Alternative Service Book	7.22
Family	0.31
Other	0.20

Morning Services:
Book of Common Prayer	1.23
Alternative Service Book	0.15
Family	0.42
Other	0.05

Evensong:
Book of Common Prayer	3.12
Alternative Service Book	0.31
Family	0.00
Other	0.09

detailed work than has been possible here, especially on the whole of the post-war period and on denominations other than the Anglicans and Methodists. Modern Church records, such as the minutes of pastoral committees, are a largely untapped source of rich data on the thinking behind so much of the parochial reorganisation of recent years.[26] But probably the most neglected and challenging research possibility of all would be to conduct a detailed historical sociology of changing religiosity in post-war Cornwall or Devon. This paper provides some of the statistical bones of such a project and indicates some of the key themes that should be explored. I have already gathered much contemporary sociological material from clergy and people in Truro diocese in my work in 1988 and 1989 for the Archbishops' Commission on Rural Areas, but like all commissions its concerns are of the moment.[27] A full historical project requires a longer time horizon, and more time-consuming archival and oral history methodologies.

Part 2: Devon and General

Nicholas Orme

Changes and Problems

To a casual visitor, Devon today presents a picture of Christian England as it was in the days of Edward VII. Visually, the land appears to remain an occupied territory for Christ. Cathedrals, parish churches and chapels still dominate the high streets and the countryside. A few churches, chiefly in central Exeter and Plymouth, disappeared at the hands of Hitler's bombers.[1] Many more places of worship have been closed less violently in city centres as a result of population shifts, and in rural areas where congregations have united, making separate places of worship unnecessary. But the churches that most visitors notice—the Anglican churches—survive, projecting images of strength and glory with their battlemented medieval towers and soaring Victorian spires.

Churches and chapels are indeed a source of strength in the religious life of today. Buildings are solid reassuring symbols of Christianity, and many people find them easier to relate to than doctrine or even the liturgy. Each attracts a congregation, in which children and adults grow accustomed to the surroundings, usages and fellowship of the place. Churches acquire deep personal associations through one's baptism, confirmation or marriage, or through the burials of friends and relatives. They link us with the past, and challenge us to pass on something to the future. They advertise the Christian faith to the outside world, and may reveal the Lord to those who visit them in search of history or simply out of curiosity. They can be icons, too, for Christians who do not attend them or ever outwardly affirm their faith. Any attempt to declare a church redundant is sure to produce a protest. Unfortunately, buildings have other, less helpful characteristics. They are often too large for modern use, expensive to heat and maintain, yet difficult to adapt for changing needs. The Victorians in particular built on a grand scale, confident that congregations would grow as evangelism flourished and the population increased. In 1910 the Wesleyan Methodists estimated their resources in England as 8,606 churches, 520,000 members, and 2,500,000 seats—five for every church member. In Exeter diocese in the same year, the Church of England reckoned its seating as about 218,000—over three times the number of those who received communion on Easter Day, and more than enough to cope with all the other people who came to church that day, the busiest festival of the year. We should not think that seats were always filled.

Paradoxically, therefore, the existence of so many church buildings, inspiring strong and sometimes fierce loyalties, has also proved to be a problem for the Churches of the twentieth century, especially the Anglican and Free Churches. The energy and skill of Christians, lay and ordained, becomes absorbed in plant maintenance instead of in the task of congregation building by mission, evangelism and teaching. And to those on the fringe of Church life, buildings may obscure the other causes and activities for which the Churches stand; a contribution to a restoration appeal seems all that Christianity expects. Large numbers of buildings, too, disperse a Church's strength into numerous small groups, rather than bigger, more effective ones. There are said to be in Devon today at least a hundred more churches in use (of all denominations) for a population of one million, than there are in the diocese of London north of the Thames, with a population three times as large. But the disposal or adaptation of churches is not easy, either. Small Free Church premises may be closed if they have no architectural merit, but exacting legislation often means that Anglican churches have to be maintained as pieces of national heritage even if they are superfluous. One solution is to turn them into resource or counselling centres as is now done in central Exeter. Another is to maintain them with the Redundant Churches Fund of 1968, subsidised by the state, but this can cater for only a few special cases: Luffincott, Parracombe, Revelstoke, Torbryan and West Ogwell. In recent years, English Heritage, the Devon Historic Buildings Trust and other bodies have made generous grants to help keep churches open, but the main burden still falls heavily on congregations and local people in most cases.

The problems posed by church buildings arise in part from demographic changes, which have often transformed the communities for which the churches were built. The population of Devon as a whole has risen from 662,196 in 1901 to an estimated 1,010,000 in 1987, but the rise has not been uniform in all areas, and in some there has been a considerable fall. In Barnstaple, Exeter, Torquay and Plymouth depopulation has robbed the old central churches of their parishioners, and they can survive only by attracting an eclectic congregation from elsewhere. In smaller towns and in the suburbs, on the other hand, churches remain well supported and even need more space for their activities. Some would benefit from enlargement or the creation of daughter churches, but this involves problems of expense and planning regulations. Seaside areas also tend to retain larger numbers of church-goers, due to the high proportion of retired immigrants and the greater spirituality associated with retirement and old age. Rural Devon is another area that has suffered depopulation,

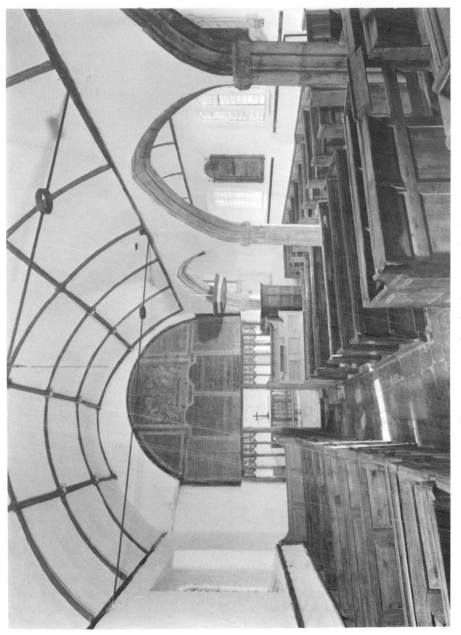

Plate 26   St Petrock's church, Parracombe, Devon

especially in the centre, but this is nowadays being reversed near towns through the spread of housing for commuters and retired people. Disparities have grown up between the size of the rural population and its share of Church resources—especially in the Church of England and the Free Churches. In 1960, when the urban and suburban population was some 85 per cent of the national total, the distribution of Anglican clergy was 42 per cent in the countryside, 27 per cent in the suburbs, and 28 per cent in the inner cities.[2] This reflected the ancient parochial system, inherited from the English rural past but increasingly out of date. During the twentieth century, first the Free Churches and then the Church of England have had to reduce the imbalance and increase the proportion of clergy in the towns and the suburbs.

Next to demographic changes there have been economic ones. These have had less effect, perhaps, on the Catholic Church and the Free Churches, which have always functioned on the basis of the voluntary contributions of their members. The Church of England, on the other hand, has undergone a major shift from its historic economy, based on endowments, to a more voluntary one. In 1901 it was still recognisably traditional, with a wide variety of clergy incomes. At the top stood the bishop with £4,200, then the cathedral dean with £2,000 and the canons with £1,000. Beneath them came the parish clergy with benefices ranging in value from Stoke Damerel with £929 to poor ones like Landcross with £54 and St Giles-in-the-Wood with £41, requiring supplementation from central funds:

Table 7.5: Net Values of Benefices, Exeter Diocese, 1901

£901–£1000	1	£401–£500	26
£801– £900	–	£301–£400	68
£701– £800	3	£291–£300	161
£601– £700	7	£101–£200	191
£501– £600	9	£100 or less	41

Source: Exeter Diocesan Calendar (1901), pp 74-111.

Also at the lower end were the 182 curates, poorly paid and without security of tenure. But during the twentieth century this has changed. Tithes, the great historic endowment, were phased out after 1936.[3] Many glebe lands have been sold. Inflation has eroded endowment income, and has had to be countered by greater voluntary giving. First in the poor parishes, then in the less poor, the authorities have had to augment the clergy's stipends to a reasonable level till, by the 1950s, virtually all the stipends were augmented and everyone received the same total. In 1957 the *Exeter Diocesan Directory* ceased to print the benefice values, and even the increments of the bishop and the dignitaries became very small. For the first time ever there were no really poor clergy, but neither were there any very rich ones since all the stipends—even the bishop's—fell well below those of comparable lay professions. This has had several consequences. Patronage of benefices, though it still exists, has lost its appeal, since it does not give the right to appoint to positions of wealth. Children of rich parents no longer enter the Church expecting to have an affluent way of life. The large old clergy houses, often built with the private wealth of their occupants and staffed with their servants, have ceased to be viable and many have been replaced with smaller dwellings. Most Anglican clergy in 1990 lived more modestly than their predecessors, and with a lower social status.

Intellectual and social changes have also acted on Devon, as elsewhere.[4] By 1900 not only were the ideas of Charles Darwin and Karl Marx tightening their holds, but there was a steady assimilation of the thought of the Enlightenment which made God an optional extra, not the basis of the understanding of life. The First World War was also influential, though in a more equivocal way. Some people experienced loss of faith due to the problem of evil which it presented, while the faith of others was strengthened; both world wars were followed by an increase of vocations to become clergy or ministers. Religion has also been weakened by the growth of the power of a secular state, notably in the sphere of education. Prior to 1944 there were about 9,000 Church of England schools in England as a whole, but the Education Act of that year left only about 2,000 with 'aided' status which allowed the Church to retain considerable influence. The rest became 'controlled' schools, where the Church's role was more formal and less effective.[5] In most English schools, except for Catholic and independent ones, religious instruction has declined to a very low level since 1944. Finally, church attendance has been undermined by the enhancement of private life and the weakening of the community, caused by greater prosperity, leisure and mobility. Churches no longer have their former monopoly as places of learning, culture and society for the population. They have to compete on Sundays with private leisure activities, and during the week—in their social, ethical and charitable work—with the immense number of voluntary organisations which have grown up in the twentieth century. As a result, most of the Churches (with the Catholics and the house churches as partial exceptions) have experienced a significant decline in the number of church attendances, requests for sacramental rites (baptisms, confirmations and marriages), and vocations to become full-time clergy or ministers.

Plate 27   Lord William Cecil, bishop of Exeter
Robed as a DD (a degree then automatically conferred on bishops), Lord William tries to
remember something he has forgotten.

The Church of England

Seven bishops have presided over the diocese of Exeter in the twentieth century: three scholars, three ex-parish priests, and one maverick nobleman.[6] At the beginning of the century, bishops were often still appointed (as Temple and Benson had been) from scholars and educationists with little or no experience of parish work, and the first two of the seven belonged to this group. Herbert Edward Ryle (1901–3) was an authority on the Old Testament, Hulsean professor of divinity at Cambridge and president of Queens' College—distinguished enough to be promoted to the see of Winchester after two years at Exeter. Archibald Robertson (1903–16) had been principal of King's College (London), vice-chancellor of London University, and a writer on St Paul and St Athanasius. Robertson was a dour hard-working administrator whose health broke down, forcing him to retire prematurely; this was followed by the oddest appointment of the century. Lord William Cecil (1916–36) was a son of the former prime minister, Lord Salisbury, whose brains he had not inherited (he only managed to get a 'third' in law at Oxford). Rector of the family church of Bishop's Hatfield (Herts.) for 28 years, the Cecils (allegedly tired of his incoherent sermons) are said to have lobbied for his removal to a cathedral canonry, but Asquith the prime minister, who was about to be toppled from power and wanted their goodwill, thought he would please them better with a bishopric! Accordingly, Lord William came to Exeter: a bearded eccentric figure who refused to live in the bishop's palace and rode into the city from the suburbs on a yellow bicycle. Vague, informal, the patron of tramps, he was also low-church, hostile to Anglo-Catholics, legalistic in a pernickety way and prone to maladroit interventions against his clergy. Yet somehow he won hearts, and died sufficiently beloved to be reproduced, beard and all, as St Peter on the top of the bishop's throne in the cathedral. Even today he still lives in the stories of his epic absentmindedness, like the telegram sent to his spouse ('Am in Ilfracombe. Why?') or the tender enquiry 'how is your dear wife' to the vicar of Pinhoe, a widower of long standing. Nor was that all, for he repeated the enquiry an hour later and received the tart reply, 'still dead, my lord'.[7]

In his odd way, Lord William marked a change towards bishops with more parochial experience. His successor, Charles Edward Curzon (1936–48) moved, after graduating, to a curacy, a string of parish benefices and the suffragan bishopric of Stepney (London), in what has come to be a common path to promotion in the late twentieth century. Eric Mercer (1973–85) and Hewlett Thompson (1985–) both accord with this pattern, the former having been a parish priest, diocesan missioner and bishop of Birkenhead in Chester diocese, and the latter incumbent of Wisbech and Folkestone and suffragan bishop of

Willesden. That leaves Robert Mortimer (1949–73), the longest serving bishop of the seven, who belonged to the academic group: Oxford double-first, lecturer on canon law and regius professor of moral and pastoral theology. As bishop, Mortimer was one of the Church's leading spokesmen on moral matters. Thoroughly at home in Parliament and the Church Assembly, he had a major influence on the Divorce Law Reform Act of 1969 and held generally progressive views on moral issues (as well as supporting Anglican-Methodist union). In Devon, on the other hand, he often appeared to be bored, though helpful to people in trouble (for nothing ever shocked him). Tall, distinguished, aloof, and one of the last to wear gaiters, he could deliver Olympian dismissals to bothersome lay readers ('bishop of Plymouth looks after that') or acolytes deputed to carry his bag ('in the boot'), and once astounded a village by leaving the parish buns and sandwiches to burst forth, wearing his episcopal garments, into the nearby public bar where he ordered large gins and tonics. Bishops are human like the rest of us, and the fact that Cecil and Mortimer have left behind such strong and affectionate memories is a reminder, perhaps, that a little eccentricity is no bad thing.

Ryle, Robertson and Cecil ruled a diocese which still possessed its ancient strength in terms of churches and clergy. In 1901 there were 588 parish churches and chapels, 127 other places of worship, and 666 full-time parish clergy, in a county of 662,196 people.[8] There was one parish clergyman to every 993 laity, and more than one per church—reflecting the fact that nearly every parish had its own rector or vicar while about 142 had one or more curates too. Lay support was less strong, with only 52,637 men and women receiving communion on Easter Day (7.9 per cent of the county population), but others would have gone to church that day (uncounted) without receiving communion, and Easter communicants in Devon increased in the early twentieth century (as they did in England generally), peaking at 74,746 in 1927. Thereafter, however, the diocese began to suffer from the economic and social changes already mentioned, as can be seen from *Table 7.6*. During the middle and second half of the century, the number of full-time parish clergy gradually fell by nearly half to 344. This partly reflected fewer vocations, and partly arose from the Church's economic inability to support so many clergy. The population, on the other hand, continued to rise, so that by 1990 each parish cleric had to serve, as it were, 2,935 people, and there were also fewer clergy than churches—whose numbers had stayed roughly constant. There were now only 64 curates, and most clergy had two or more churches to serve, either alone or in a team ministry. The number of Easter communicants fell likewise to 47,000 in 1990—less both absolutely and as a percentage of the whole population (5 per cent), though it was a little higher than the national percentage (about 3 per cent). Figures for baptisms, confirmations and

Plate 28   Robert Mortimer, bishop of Exeter
Almost prelatical in this portrait, Robert Exon was nevertheless divorce reformer, ecumenist
and reorganiser of the parish ministry.

Table 7.6: The Anglican Clergy in Devon, 1901–90

Year	Churches & Chapels(a)	Rectors & Vicars	Assistant Clergy	Laity per Clergyman	Ordinations, last 10 years(b)
1901	588	484	182	993	181
1911	594	488	146	1,055	138
1921	590	507	114	1,141	97
1931	622	476	90	1,293	77
1940	604	465	98	1,325	92
1951	605	415	74	1,628	63
1961	615	372	81	1,815	143
1971	605	337	100(c)	2,054	126
1981	600	306	55	2,654	90(d)
1990	630	256	88(e)	2,935	82(f)

Notes: (a) Rough figures, as the source is not consistent.
(b) Ordinations of deacons.
(c) Including some clergy later designated as team vicars.
(d) Including 25 non-stipendiary clergy.
(e) Including 24 parish deacons.
(f) Figures for 9 years only, including 22 non-stipendiaries.

Source: Exeter Diocesan Calendar (later *Directory*)

Table 7.7: The Anglican Laity in Devon, 1901–82

Year	Devon Population	Baptisms Infant	Other	Confirmations	Easter Communicants
1901	662,196	10,486	119	5,415	52,637
1911	669,703	10,520	306	7,214	65,045
1921	709,614	9,948	276	5,175	65,508
1931	732,869	7,599	275	3,646	70,304
1940	746,790	7,282	329	5,005	65,503
1950	796,621	8,219	296	3,926	60,361
1962	822,699	7,673	327	4,806	71,907
1973	848,404	6,024	245	2,446	55,090
1982	958,745	4,200	860	2,062	52,100

Source: The Official Year-Book of the Church of England

weddings have also declined from their heights in the earlier part of the century, so that the last four bishops have been leading a Church of fewer and fewer clergy and active lay people (*Table 7.7*).

The consequence was, eventually, that the diocese had to deploy its clergy among larger numbers of churches than before. For centuries the Church had permitted unions of two small parishes under one clergyman, but after the Second World War the authorities began to encourage bigger federations under two or more clergy working together. This arrangement has some similarities to the Anglo-Saxon pattern of minsters with large parishes, but in the modern case the individual small parishes remain with their own churchwardens and church councils, sharing clergy and ideally combining in joint activities. Nationally, a pioneer project of this kind was at South Ormsby in Lincolnshire, where in 1949 six rural churches (later twelve) were federated under a team of priests.[9] In Devon, the earliest scheme was set up by Bishop Mortimer in 1962 at Washfield near Tiverton, under the Rev. R.G. Herniman, later archdeacon of Barnstaple. Four parishes were grouped under a team rector and two assistant clergy, whose successors now serve twelve churches with the name of the Exe Valley team ministry.[10] In 1968 the national Church Assembly gave the diocesan authorities legal power to reorganise parish ministry in this way, and further unions were arranged in Devon by Bishops Mortimer and Mercer. Exeter indeed was one of the leading dioceses in making the change, so that by 1990 there were 30 federations of parishes designated as team ministries, the largest (South Molton) consisting of five clergy, twelve parishes and fifteen churches.[11] It was not at first a popular development, especially in the parishes which lost their resident clergy, nor has it always worked smoothly afterwards. True, it saves money, deploys the clergy more fairly and stimulates lay ministry, but it also produces problems. Most team clergy and their congregations are used to functioning individually, and learning to co-operate in a larger structure takes a long time.

It would be insufficient, however, to describe Anglican history in the twentieth century simply in terms of declining resources. Decline has been accompanied by, and has encouraged, positive developments. The most influential Anglican leader of the century was a west-countryman by birth, William Temple, born in the bishop's palace at Exeter in 1881 but subsequently active elsewhere as bishop of Manchester (1921-9), archbishop of York (1929-42) and finally of Canterbury (1942 till his death in 1944).[12] Temple envisaged at least three objectives for the Church of England in the twentieth century. The Church should govern itself (in 1901 its law-making was still largely in the hands of Parliament), there should be lay as well as clerical participation in its government, and there should be institutional unity with other Churches to give credibility to the Gospel as an agent of reconciliation.

Self-government of the Church by clergy and laity was the first to be achieved; it had indeed begun to develop in the late nineteenth century. A diocesan 'conference' including laymen was established in Exeter diocese by Bishop Frederick Temple in 1872, rural deanery conferences followed in the 1880s, and in 1897 lay parochial church councils were allowed on a voluntary basis. In 1904 the first national 'Representative Church Council' met, bringing together clergy and laity from all over England, so that a four-tier system of Church government came into existence, with lay involvement at all levels.[13] At first the system had no legal powers, but in 1919, partly due to William Temple's efforts, Parliament passed an Enabling Act, allowing the Church to make laws subject to some parliamentary supervision. The 'Representative Church Council' was renamed the Church Assembly for this purpose in 1920, and the other three tiers of government all became statutory, the chief subsequent change occurring in 1970 when the Church Assembly became the General Synod and the diocesan and deanery conferences were renamed synods too.[14] During the 1970s and 1980s the synods became important places for discussing moral, social and economic issues, though the local bodies have not always been in tune with the national one. The Exeter diocesan synod did not discuss the General Synod's report on 'The Church and the [Nuclear] Bomb' of 1982, and it voted 'no' to the ordination of women in 1973–4 and again in 1984–5. In contrast, another national project—the Church Urban Fund—has achieved strong support in Devon, despite the county's rural character.

Ecumenism, in the sense of goodwill and understanding between Anglicans and other Christians, has also made much progress. In 1888 a young ordination candidate, R.J.E. Boggis, asked the bishop of Exeter (E.H. Bickersteth) 'what should be my relations to nonconformist ministers?' The bishop returned no answer. By the 1930s Boggis was organising ecumenical services with the Free Churches in Torquay, and Lord William Cecil presided at one.[15] National discussions about Church union began between Anglicans and Methodists soon after 1946, and between Anglicans and Catholics in 1967. Under Michael Ramsey, archbishop of Canterbury 1961–74, ecumenical activity was considerable and hopes were high.[16] A South West Ecumenical Conference was held at Bristol in 1973, well supported throughout the region, at which Ramsey claimed justifiably that 'we have at last begun to lose our miserable denominational selfishness'. But formal arrangements to unite the Church of England with other denominations have made slow progress. The major enterprise, the scheme for Anglican-Methodist reunion, achieved a majority of support in the General Synod in 1972 but not the 75 per cent required, and the scheme foundered. No other plan of union has since been presented. Instead, ecumenism has made its advances locally and informally. Notable in Devon is the Estover Ecumenical Project in north-east Plymouth, in which Anglicans,

Baptists and Methodists have combined to build a church for common use, which is also shared by Catholics. At present this is the only such arrangement in Devon, compared with seventeen in Bristol, but recent changes in legislation have allowed a formal ecumenical sponsoring body to be formed in Devon early in 1991, and this will bring new opportunities for co-operation. Meanwhile, united worship often takes place in churches on special occasions like the week of prayer for Christian unity in January, and non-Anglicans are admitted to communion on an occasional or even regular basis. In this way goodwill continues to be fostered between the Churches of Devon, despite continuing formal separation.

Worship has been another area of change and development. At the beginning of the century change still meant Victorian change, as the Victorian innovations in worship (especially those of the Oxford Movement) continued to spread through Devon. In 1900 they were still often controversial. Bishops Ryle, Robertson and Cecil all tried to put a stop to 'ritualism', especially in Plymouth where it was strong, but they were not successful. Incense, confession and reservation of the sacrament became established in a minority of 'high' or Anglo-Catholic churches, and other Victorian practices grew very common indeed by the 1930s. Altars were decorated with a cross, candles and a coloured frontal. Clergymen ceased to stand on the north side of the altar during communion and moved to the west side, frequently wearing vestments matching the altar and changing with the seasons. Choirs were transferred from the west end of the church to the chancel, in the manner of a cathedral. Gradually, innovations which at first had been bitterly contested became almost universally accepted and taken for granted. The Oxford Movement triumphed in a decorative sense, but this did not always bring about the spiritual renewal which the movement's pioneers had intended.

That which appeals to one generation often fails to satisfy another. By the 1960s, the Victorian model of worship—dignifying and distancing the altar, clergy and choir—began to seem outdated in a more egalitarian and informal society. What has been called the 'Liturgical Movement' developed among Anglicans, Catholics and some Free Churchmen, though it was more of a school of thought than an organised group. The movement emphasised the eucharist as the normal Sunday service: a eucharist which was to come closer in form to the eucharist of the early Church, be more easily understood by the people, and incorporate them more in its words and actions. In 1965 the Church Assembly passed a measure allowing the introduction of new experimental services, which duly appeared in traditional Tudor language (1967) and modern English (1971). These services eventually became definitive in the Alternative Service Book (ASB) in 1980. Bible translations into modern English had already been published, notably the New English Bible in 1961–70. During the 1970s

Plate 29   The Church of the Ascension, Crownhill, Plymouth
Sunday in a new suburban church, built in 1956 with a free-standing altar. A layman helps to
give communion.

and 80s some Devon churches remained faithful to the traditional Prayer Book, but most changed to the ASB. In some places it was used in the existing setting, but in others the furnishings were altered as well. The altar was moved away from the east wall of the chancel so that the priest could face the congregation from behind it, or it was brought into the nave to be closer to the people. The church of the Ascension, Crownhill (Plymouth) was built in 1967 with an altar placed west of the east wall, while at Exeter Cathedral the main Sunday eucharist was moved to a central altar in the nave in 1982.[17] Some traditionalists have regretted these changes, especially the disuse of Cranmer's services, and a Prayer Book Society has been formed to defend them. This is ironic, given that Cranmer's objectives were so similar to those of the Liturgical Movement.

The liturgical reforms, in modifying the role of the priest and developing that of the congregation, reflected educational as well as social changes. Not only were the clergy becoming fewer, but their educational pre-eminence over the laity was also weakening. In 1901 80.8 per cent of the clergy in Devon were graduates, and the non-graduates were mostly curates or incumbents of poorer benefices. In 1950 the percentage was 56.9 per cent and in 1990 50.9 per cent, though it is now expected to rise through the growth of degree courses in theological colleges.[18] Lay education, on the other hand, expanded at university level during the period, especially after 1945. New universities were founded like Exeter (1955), and graduates came to dominate the legal professions, accountancy and the higher tiers of industry and local government. A non-graduate clergyman in 1990 might be faced by several graduates on his parochial church council. With fewer clergy and more highly trained laity, it became logical to widen the range of people able to become clergy or allowed to carry out clergy functions. The Free Churches have had a long tradition of lay ministry; the Church of England was slower to follow, but in 1866 lay readers were first introduced in the diocese of Gloucester, and in Devon Bishop Frederick Temple began to license lay 'assistants' (as they were originally called) in 1871.[19] Readers (men only) soon became common in the diocese and won acceptance, so successfully perhaps that nearly a century passed before the Church was moved to enlarge its ministry further. Here too the 1960s were important. First, there was the beginning of the ordination of men to the non-stipendiary ministry (NSM), in which they kept their jobs or professions while assisting as clergy in their spare time. This began in Southwark diocese and spread to Exeter in the late 1960s. Next, the ministry of women was developed. They were allowed to become lay readers in 1969 (the earliest two in Devon being appointed in the following year) and deacons in 1987, with the prospect of admission to the priesthood in the near future. Most recently, in the 1980s, the practice has grown for lay people to lead family services, take parts of communion services and administer communion—even though they are not lay readers.[20]

The role of women in the Church has particularly developed in the twentieth century. This is a complicated subject, and only the merest sketch is attempted here.[21] Traditionally, women were allowed little formal part in Church affairs, though they could be churchwardens (which was rare) and patrons of parish churches (which was limited to the propertied classes). In 1901 there were 39 parishes in Devon partly or wholly in the patronage of women, who thereby had the power of choosing the clergy and influencing parish life.[22] Normally, however, they made their contributions to the Church as clergy wives or in the home as informal teachers and counsellors. Once again it was the Victorians who started giving women more to do. Sisterhoods were established under Bishop Phillpotts; convents eventually followed. Deaconesses were introduced in 1887 to do pastoral work in Devon, but were always few and outnumbered by other women workers.[23] Societies and committees were founded for women at home, the Mothers' Union (1876) being the best known.[24] At first, the Church authorities envisaged women only in the spheres of social work and family life, not in running Church affairs. They were not allowed to be elected to the conferences and councils set up in the late nineteenth century,[25] but when Church government was reorganised in 1919–21 the prohibition was relaxed and they became eligible to serve on all Church bodies. Not that this was easy to achieve at the higher levels. Only one or two of the nine Exeter diocesan members of the Church Assembly were usually women, and up to 1942 they were the wives of the bishop and the dean! In the 1930s deaconesses were allowed to take mattins and evensong in churches, but this made little difference when there were so few of them. In 1950, for example, there were 9 active deaconesses to 177 male lay readers; in 1970, 5. Only in the 1970s and 1980s did women become more widely involved in leading worship, and even in 1990 they numbered only 29 lay readers out of 172 and 26 women deacons out of 429 parish and other clergy. The priesthood, and the higher dignities in the Church, remained to be conquered.

Other Churches and Denominations

The Anglican experience of the twentieth century has been shared in most respects by the Free Churches. Declining numbers of members and ministers have been accompanied by unions and closures of churches, the admission of women to the ministry, liturgical changes and schemes of denominational union. Indeed, in these developments the Free Churches have often been ahead of the Church of England. By 1900 Devon was well, in fact over, supplied with Free Church places of worship. From about 1830 the Baptists, Congregationalists and Methodists had pursued a policy of expansion in the villages around their older town churches. During the Victorian period the Plymouth Brethren also came into being and established themselves across the county. Smaller groups such as the Unitarians and Quakers did not witness such growth, but had their centres. There was a degree of regional distribution, in that the older denominations (Baptists and Congregationalists) tended to be stronger in the east of Devon, and the various Methodist groups in the west: the Bible Christians in the north-west, and the Primitive Methodists on the south coast.

Already by 1900 some Free-Churchmen were aware that there were too many competing ministries and places of worship, and by the 1920s falling numbers of members produced a further strong argument for denominational unity. First, in 1907, the Bible Christians, Methodist New Connexion and United Methodist Free Churches came together to form the United Methodist Church.[26] In Devon, the Bible Christians were the predominant group in this union, which was intended to form a united church of liberal Methodists complementing the more clerical, traditional Wesleyans. By 1932, however, differences between all Methodists had declined sufficiently for the three remaining groups—Primitive, United and Wesleyan—to enter into a further union, creating the modern Methodist Church. The hope was to forge a more effective instrument of evangelism, with a more economic use of chapels as part of the plan. In Devon, both the Methodist unions resulted in widespread reorganisation and closures of redundant buildings. Villages such as Bere Alston came into the century with chapels of all three main Methodist denominations, and as such provision could not be maintained, amalgamations and closures were inevitable. Finally, in 1972, the Congregational and English Presbyterian Churches united nationally to form the United Reformed Church (URC). In Devon, however, there was only one Presbyterian congregation, at Plymouth, and the union was not embraced by all the Congregationalists. Some of their churches in Devon joined the URC, but others insisted on retaining their congregational independence, associating themselves within a new Congregational Federation; yet others joined neither organisation, being technically 'unaffiliated'.

Unions of individual congregations have also taken place in Devon. About the turn of the century there were a few examples of 'union' churches, jointly built and supported by Baptists and Congregationalists, both of whom were congregationalist in Church government though they differed about Christian initiation. Such churches were more common in west Somerset, and later tended to become independent or revert to one denomination. The best example in Devon is Union Chapel at Feniton. The Estover project in Plymouth, where Anglicans, Baptists and Methodists share a joint church, has already been mentioned. In the years since the Second World War, Free Church congregations have also been amalgamated across denominational boundaries, mostly between the Methodists and the URC, but the United Church in Totnes was formed from Baptist and Congregational churches. The reasons for such amalgamations and the way in which they have been achieved have varied. Buildings requiring excessive expenditure have been one catalyst, as at Central Church, Torquay. Here two ageing Methodist chapels were sold and a new building erected on the site of the Belgrave URC chapel, providing a new home for three congregations joined into one. The same happened at Braunton, where Christ Church was built on the site of the URC chapel for a united Methodist and URC congregation. Sometimes a dwindling congregation has been glad to be welcomed into a nearby thriving church of another denomination. The URC community in Newton Abbot closed its great ornate building, and now worships at The Avenue Methodist Church. At Colyton, the Methodists closed their old chapel and purchased the Congregational one, inviting its few surviving members to stay. Unions have been projected at Ottery St Mary and Tiverton between the URC and Methodist churches which have not succeeded, but around Shebbear in north-west Devon, a group of Baptist and Methodist churches has been linked together with the closure of only one building. And despite the failure of the scheme for Anglican-Methodist union in 1972, some Free-Church congregations whose chapels have closed have joined the local Anglican church where this has been the nearest Christian fellowship: for example the Methodists at Christow.

Not all the Churches of the South West have experienced loss of support in the twentieth century. Anglicanism, as Michael Winter has shown, has strangthened itself in Cornwall, and Catholicism has done so there and in Devon as well. By 1901 the Catholic Church had established a secure but modest presence in the region, with a bishop and cathedral at Plymouth and a diocese covering the three counties of Cornwall, Devon and Dorset.[27] It boasted 111 priests, 52 places of worship, and by 1916 there were 53 schools teaching 4,645 children, with an estimated Catholic population of 19,895. The main strength was in Plymouth, with seven churches and religious houses, and there were single churches in Exeter, a few of the smaller towns (especially the seaside resorts), and one or two rural centres such as Chudleigh in Devon and Lanherne in Cornwall where Catholicism had survived for centuries under the protection of local aristocracy. There were also 5 religious houses of men and 11 of women in Devon and Cornwall, notably Syon Abbey at South Brent (Devon). The Bridgettine nuns of Syon originated near London in the fifteenth century, regrouped on the Continent after the Reformation and returned to England at the French Revolution. They are the only modern English monastic community with an unbroken history going back to pre-Reformation times.

During the twentieth century, Catholic organisation and support have

Plate 30   Buckfast Abbey, Devon
The undoing of the Reformation: Buckfast, a medieval Cistercian abbey, was rebuilt between
1883 and 1932 for a modern Benedictine community.

increased significantly. The 1930s was a particularly important decade in this respect, when 31 churches were built, enlarged or consecrated in Cornwall and Devon. The lay population has risen steadily throughout, and the number of clergy did so until the 1970s (in 1969 there were 229 priests attached to the diocese) but has declined again in recent years, reflecting the general fall in clergy vocations. By 1988 the three counties of the diocese contained 161 priests, 191 places of worship and 51 schools—the latter a similar total to that of 1916 but catering for three times as many children (13,718). The Catholic Church, unlike the Church of England, has benefitted from the 1944 Education Act, seizing the opportunities offered to develop education and being more resolute in financing it. The Catholic population of the diocese had more than tripled by 1988 to 71,228. The number of male religious houses in Cornwall and Devon had increased to 11 and those for women to 29, though the latter represented a decline from 35 in 1916. One Catholic house in Devon has achieved particular prominence during the twentieth century: Buckfast Abbey, belonging to the Benedictine order and consecrated in 1932 on the site of the medieval Cistercian abbey. Although Buckfast is only one of many Catholic communities, its classic monastic architecture in a major holiday area has enabled it to rival Exeter Cathedral as a place of resort for tourists. While satisfying the popular curiosity about monks, it must have done a good deal to teach and reassure non-Catholics about the Catholic Church.[28]

Another area of Christian growth, nationally and locally, has been that of house churches, community churches, or Restoration churches as they are also known.[29] They are the major new religious sector to have appeared in the second half of the twentieth century, though they frequently consist of members withdrawing from the older nineteenth-century denomination of the Plymouth Brethren, under the influence of the early twentieth-century movement of Pentecostalism. The South West of England played an important part in the origins of the house-church movement. In 1956 Sidney Purse, a former member of the Brethren, established an evangelical, charismatic church at South Chard (Somerset), which influenced the formation of similar churches in England during the 1960s and 1970s. In the 1960s, Arthur Wallis, also from the Brethren and eventually a national figure, helped found house churches in east Devon, including Cullompton, Hemyock, Ottery St Mary, Pinhoe and Talaton. Two early charismatic conferences were held at Okehampton in 1961 and Mamhead in 1962. During the 1970s and 1980s house churches developed at Barnstaple, Exeter, Exmouth, Plymouth, Tavistock, Torbay and other major centres in the county. As their name suggests, they began in private houses and still involve house meetings on weekdays, but on Sundays they often move to schools or halls to accommodate their growing numbers. House churches (not to be confused with house groups within the other Christian denominations) are congregational in organisation—self-governing and only informally linked to one another. They share their ministry among their members and try to recreate the apostolic Church of the New Testament. Services are free in form and include prophecy, interpretation and speaking in tongues. There is baptism of adults by total immersion, and a communion or 'breaking of bread'. Social work is done and money is raised for charity, for example by operating a Crisis Pregnancy Centre and a shop selling goods from the Third World. About 70 per cent of the membership is reckoned to have come from other Christian denominations, especially from the Brethren, and about 30 per cent from people not previously active in churches. Altogether, the commitment and activity of the house churches give them a high profile in relation to the size of their membership, which was probably about 3,000 people in Devon in 1990.

There are many other denominations in the South West with interesting histories and distinctive features, requiring a proper account in a larger book. The Jews returned to the region in the mid-eighteenth century. They may have been in Exeter by 1728 and were certainly in Plymouth by 1745, Falmouth by 1766 and Penzance by 1781, establishing cemeteries and places of worship. The Plymouth synagogue dates back to 1762, making it one of the oldest in Britain, and Exeter's was founded a year later. In 1847 the four communities numbered about 481 people, but since then Plymouth has declined to about 150 and Exeter to 80, while Falmouth and Penzance have disappeared.[30] Many of the Churches founded in England and America in the nineteenth century have also penetrated the region. Of the English ones the Plymouth Brethren (1830)—or Christian Brethren as they prefer to be called—are strong in Devon where they originated, with about 100 churches (usually called Gospel halls), but are weak in Cornwall. The Wesleyan Reform Union (1849), which separated from Wesleyan Methodism, has two churches at St Just-in-Penwith, and the Salvation Army (1865) works and worships in about 26 places all over the region. The American denominations include the Mormons (1830), Seventh Day Adventists (1844), Christadelphians (1848), Jehovah's Witnesses (1878) and Christian Scientists (1879). All these have places of worship in the three main conurbations—Exeter, Plymouth and Torbay—and most have spread to a few of the smaller towns. So have the Pentecostalists, who originated in the early twentieth century: the Elim Foursquare Gospel Alliance (founded in Ireland in 1915) and the Assemblies of God (formed in England in 1924). The Russian Orthodox Church holds services in English at a small Church in Exeter and at Combe Martin and Truro, while the Greek Orthodox Church organises worship in its own language for the Greek communities in Torquay and Plymouth. Finally, Exeter has an Islamic Centre for the Moslem students who attend the University and other local colleges.

Plate 31   All-age worship at St Matthias's, Torquay
The rector, Peter Larkin, deacon Priscilla Cooke and 'doves of peace', with a lively all-age
congregation in 1990.

Conclusion

The age-old forces with which this book has been concerned still operate in the South West of England. Unity remains a preoccupation. It is encouraged within each Church, and it is increasingly stressed at a local level in the Church of England through the grouping of parishes and the growth of more diocesan institutions. Moreover all the major denominations now have a sense of unity within a wider Church, and share activities and hopes to achieve it. Uniformity, on the other hand, tends to be weaker except in some of the smaller Churches, and a good deal of variety is tolerated in belief, worship and conduct. Most Church communities in Cornwall and Devon include a mixture of natives and immigrants with different experiences, needs and priorities. Party strife is relatively weak, and disputes are restrained even on contentious issues like abortion, sexuality and the ordination of women. Even vandalism, though it takes place, is far less common than indifference among non-church goers. Sectarian violence like the Protestant eviction of Sandys Wason from Cury vicarage in 1919 and the smashing of the images in St Hilary church in 1932 seems to belong to another age or another country—the last gunfire of a far-off Reformation.[31] Between the sixteenth and the early twentieth centuries, unity and variety found it hard to coexist. As the twentieth century draws to a close, we seem to have entered one of those periods when they live together in relative harmony.

Plate 32   Edward Henry Bickersteth, bishop of Exeter
A late Victorian bishop: evangelical and poetical, a gentler influence after the dynamism of
Phillpotts and Temple.

Lists of Bishops

The following lists are reprinted from *The Handbook of British Chronology* and *The Catholic Directory* (see below, pp 223, 228) by kind permission of The Royal Historical Society and Gabriel Communications Ltd., respectively. The sign x denotes an unknown point of time within two dates, while - indicates the whole period of time between them.

Bishops of Cornwall

Kenstec	occurs 823 x 870
? Asser	occurs 888 x 893, till 909
Conan	924 x 931, till 953 x 955
Daniel	955 x 956, till 959 x 963
Wulfsige Comoere	959 x 963, till 981 x 990
Ealdred	981 x 990, till 1002 x 1009
? Aethelsige	1002 x 1009, till 1011 x 1012
Buruhwold	1011 x 1012, till 1019 x 1027
Lyfyng	1027-1046
Leofric	1046-1050

Bishops of Crediton

Eadwulf	909-934
Aethelgar	934-952 x 953
Aelfwold I	953-972
Sideman	973-977
Aelfric	977 x 979, till 986 x 987
Aelfwold II	986 x 987, till unknown
Aelfwold III	unknown, till 1011 x 1015
Eadnoth	1011 x 1015, till 1019 x 1027
Lyfyng	1027-1046
Leofric	1046-1050

Bishops of Exeter

Leofric	1050-1072
Osbern FitzOsbern	1072-1103
William Warelwast	1107-1137
Robert Warelwast	1138-1155
Robert II	1155-1160
Bartholomew	1161-1184
John the Chanter	1186-1191
Henry Marshal	1194-1206
Simon of Apulia	1214-1223
William Briwere	1223-1244
Richard Blund	1245-1257
Walter Bronescombe	1258-1280
Peter Quinel	1280-1291
Thomas Bitton	1291-1307
Walter Stapledon	1308-1326
James Berkeley	1326-1327
John Grandisson	1327-1369
Thomas Brantingham	1370-1394
Edmund Stafford	1395-1419
John Catterick	1419
Edmund Lacy	1420-1455
George Nevill	1456-1465
John Booth	1465-1478
Peter Courtenay	1478-1487
Richard Fox	1487-1492
Oliver King	1492-1495
Richard Redman	1495-1501
John Arundel	1502-1504
Hugh Oldham	1504-1519
John Veysey	1519-1551
Miles Coverdale	1551-1553
John Veysey, restored	1553-1554
James Turberville	1555-1559
William Alley	1560-1570
William Bradbridge	1571-1578
John Woolton	1579-1594
Gervase Babington	1594-1597
William Cotton	1598-1621
Valentine Carey	1621-1626
Joseph Hall	1627-1641
Ralph Brownrigg	1642-1659
John Gauden	1660-1662
Seth Ward	1662-1667
Anthony Sparrow	1667-1676

Thomas Lamplugh	1676-1688
Jonathan Trelawney	1689-1707
Offspring Blackall	1708-1716
Lancelot Blackburn	1717-1724
Stephen Weston	1724-1742
Nicholas Claget	1742-1746
George Lavington	1747-1762
Frederick Keppel	1762-1777
John Ross	1778-1792
William Buller	1792-1796
Henry Reginald Courtenay	1797-1803
John Fisher	1803-1807
George Pelham	1807-1820
William Carey	1820-1830
Christopher Bethell	1830
Henry Phillpotts	1830-1869
Frederick Temple	1869-1885
Edward Henry Bickersteth	1885-1900
Herbert Edward Ryle	1900-1903
Archibald Robertson	1903-1916
Lord William Cecil	1916-1936
Charles Edward Curzon	1936-1948
Robert Cecil Mortimer	1949-1973
Eric Arthur John Mercer	1973-1985
Geoffrey Hewlett Thompson	1985-

Bishops of Truro

Edward White Benson	1877-1883
George Howard Wilkinson	1883-1891
John Gott	1891-1906
Charles William Stubbs	1906-1912
Winfrid Oldfield Burrows	1912-1919
Frederic Sumpter Guy Warman	1919-1923
Walter Howard Frere	1923-1935
Joseph Wellington Hunkin	1935-1950
Edmund Robert Morgan	1951-1959
John Maurice Key	1959-1973
Graham Douglas Leonard	1973-1981
Peter Mumford	1981-1989
Michael Thomas Ball	1990-

Catholic Bishops of Plymouth

George Errington	1851-1855
William Vaughan	1855-1902
Charles Graham (co-adjutor 1891)	1902-1911
John Keily	1911-1928
John P. Barrett	1929-1946
Francis Joseph Grimshaw	1947-1954
Cyril Edward Restieaux	1955-1986
Christopher Budd	1986-

References

1: From the Beginnings to 1050 (pp 1-22)

1. Aileen Fox, *Roman Exeter* (Manchester, 1952), p 92, plate X(a).
2. On this topic, see C. Thomas, *Christianity in Roman Britain to AD 500* (London, 1981).
3. P.T. Bidwell, *The Legionary Bath-House and Basilica and Forum at Exeter* (Exeter, 1979), pp 112-13; C.G. Henderson & P.T. Bidwell, 'The Saxon Minster at Exeter', *The Early Church in Western Britain and Ireland*, ed. Susan M. Pearce (Oxford, 1982), pp 145-75.
4. The inscriptions are listed by R.A.S. Macalister, *Corpus Inscriptionum Insularum Celticarum*, 2 vols (Dublin, 1945-9); his readings, however, need correcting in places. For discussion, see C.A. Ralegh Radford, *The Early Christian Inscriptions of Dummonia* (Redruth, 1973); and M. Todd, *The South West to AD1000* (London & New York, 1987), pp 249-52. To their evidence, we may now add that of Professor Charles Thomas's current excavations in Tintagel Churchyard (1990), which appear to reveal a group of graves of noblemen, probably Christian and dating from the fifth to the seventh centuries.
5. Gildas, *The Ruin of Britain*, ed. M. Winterbottom (Chichester, 1978), pp 29, 99 (chapter 28). For a different translation, see Lynette Olson, *Early Monasteries in Cornwall* (Woodbridge, 1989), p 8.
6. *La Vie de Saint Samson*, ed. R. Fawtier (Paris, 1912), pp 143-4, translated by T. Taylor, *The Life of St Samson of Dol* (London, 1925), p 49.
7. Fawtier (above, note 6), pp 93-172; trans. Taylor, pp 8-59.
8. For individual studies of the Cornish saints, see G.H. Doble, *The Saints of Cornwall*, 5 vols (Truro, 1960-70). There is also much relevant historical comment in O.J. Padel, *A Popular Dictionary of Cornish Place-Names* (Penzance, 1988).
9. On the Saxon Conquest, see H.P.R. Finberg, 'Sherborne, Glastonbury and the Expansion of Wessex', *Transactions of the Royal Historical Society*, 5th series, 3 (1953), pp 101-24, and Todd (above, note 4), pp 267-75.
10. For this and other charter evidence, see H.P.R. Finberg, *The Early Charters of Devon and Cornwall*, Leicester, University College, Dept. of English Local History, Occasional Papers, 2 (1953); P.H. Sawyer, *Anglo-Saxon Charters* (London, 1968); and *Anglo-Saxon Charters*, vol 3: *Sherborne*, ed. Mary Anne O'Donovan (Oxford, 1988).
11. Aldhelm, *Opera*, ed. R. Ehwald (Berlin, Monumenta Germaniae Historica, AA 15,

1919), p 524; *The Poetic Works,* trans. M. Lapidge & J.L. Rosier (Cambridge, 1985), pp 171-9, where Aldhelm's authorship is asserted.

12. *Councils and Ecclesiastical Documents relating to Great Britain and Ireland,* ed. A.W. Haddan & W. Stubbs, 3 vols (Oxford, 1869-78), iii, 268-73; Aldhelm, *The Prose Works,* trans. M. Lapidge & M. Herren (Ipswich & Cambridge, 1979), pp 155-60.

13. Finberg (above, note 10), no 78; Sawyer (above, note 10), no 450.

14. On Cornish monasteries and minsters, see Olson (above, note 5), *passim;* on Saxon ones in general, *Minsters and Parish Churches,* ed. J. Blair (Oxford, 1988); and on those in Devon, C.A. Ralegh Radford, 'The Pre-Conquest Church and the Old Minsters in Devon', *The Devon Historian,* 11 (1975), pp 2-11.

15. Olson (above note 5), pp 9-17.

16. The Life of St Boniface, trans. in C.H. Talbot, *The Anglo-Saxon Missionaries in Germany* (London, 1954), p 28; Finberg (above, note 10), no 2; Sawyer (above, note 10), no 255; *The Anglo-Saxon Chronicle,* trans. Dorothy Whitelock, D.C. Douglas & Susie Tucker (London, 1961), p 31 sub anno 757.

17. Blair (above, note 14), pp 1-3.

18. Finberg (above, note 10), no 78; Sawyer (above, note 10), no 450; *The Itinerary of John Leland,* ed. Lucy Toulmin Smith, 5 vols (London, 1907-10), i, 179; *Domesday Book: Cornwall,* ed. Caroline & F. Thorn (Chichester, 1979), section 4.

19. Henderson and Bidwell (above, note 3), pp 146-7; H.P.R. Finberg, *Tavistock Abbey,* 2nd ed. (Newton Abbot, 1969); J. Stephan, *A History of Buckfast Abbey from 1018 to 1968* (Bristol, 1970).

20. On what follows, see Thorn (above, note 18), *passim,* and *Domesday Book: Devon,* ed. Caroline & F. Thorn, 2 parts (Chichester 1985), *passim;* and on Hartland, G.H. Doble (above, note 8), v, 65-78, and P. Grosjean, 'Vie de S. Nectan', *Analecta Bollandiana,* 71 (1953), pp 359-414.

21. Finberg (above, note 10), nos 5-6, 55; Sawyer (above, note 10), nos 1452, 1691.

22. F. Barlow *et al., Leofric of Exeter* (Exeter, 1972), p 11; Thorn (above, note 18), section 4.

23. Thorn (above, note 20), *passim.*

24. Thorn (above, note 18), *passim.* On St Petroc's church, see also C. Henderson, *Essays in Cornish History* (Oxford, 1935), pp 120-4.

25. N. Orme, *Exeter Cathedral As It Was: 1050-1550* (Exeter, 1986), pp 83, 112 note 1.

26. Olson (above, note 5), p 61.

27. *The Crawford Collection of Early Charters and Documents,* ed. A.S. Napier & W.H. Stevenson (Oxford, 1895), pp 23-4.

28. Barlow (above, note 22), p 34 (cf. p 12).

29. *Councils and Synods I: A.D. 871-1204,* ed. Dorothy Whitelock, M. Brett, & C.N.L. Brooke, 2 vols (Oxford, 1981), i, 97-8, 295-6.

30. Orme (above, note 25), pp 1-2.

31. See below, note 44.

32. *The Cartulary of Launceston Priory,* ed. P.L. Hull, Devon & Cornwall Record Society, new series 30 (1987), pp xxi, xxiv-vii.

33. Susan M. Pearce, *The Kingdom of Dumnonia* (Padstow, 1978), pp 67-75; Todd (above, note 4), pp 241-3.
34. F.M. Stenton, *Anglo-Saxon England*, 2nd ed. (Oxford, 1947), p 150.
35. Pearce (above, note 33) pp 108-9; Todd (above, note 4), pp 294-300.
36. Whitelock *et al.* (above, note 29), i, 97-8.
37. Bridget Cherry & N. Pevsner, *Devon*, The Buildings of England, 2nd ed. (London, 1989), pp 38-9, 391, 414, 732.
38. Finberg (above, note 10), nos 60, 68, 70; Sawyer (above, note 10), nos 1003, 1037, 1236; Exeter, Devon Record Office, Exeter City Archives, Book 53A (Cartulary of St John's Hospital), fo 36.
39. Lynette Olson & O.J. Padel, 'A Tenth-Century List of Cornish Parochial Saints', *Cambridge Medieval Celtic Studies*, 12 (1986), pp 33-71.
40. Finberg (above, note 10), nos 29-30; Sawyer (above, note 10), no 498.
41. Haddan & Stubbs (above, note 12), iii, 215.
42. Whitelock *et al.* (above, note 29), i, 46.
43. Ibid., pp 97-8.
44. *English Historical Documents, c. 500-1042*, ed. Dorothy Whitelock, 2nd ed. (London, 1979), p 605; Whitelock *et al.*, (above, note 29), i, 57-60.
45. *The Exeter Book of Old English Poetry*, ed. R.W. Chambers *et al.*, (London, 1933), pp 53-4, fo 7a-b.
46. Finberg (above, note 10), nos 5-6, 55, 68; Sawyer (above, note 10), nos 1236, 1452, 1691.
47. Asser, *Life of King Alfred*, ed. W.H. Stevenson, 2nd ed. (Oxford, 1959), pp 20, 221-5; transl. S. Keynes & M. Lapidge (Harmondsworth, 1983), pp 75, 239.
48. Fawtier (above, note 6), pp 142-4; trans. Taylor, pp 47-50.
49. Aldhelm, *Opera* (above, note 11), pp 481-2; idem (above, note 12), pp 155-6.
50. Haddan & Stubbs (above, note 12), i, 674.
51. Olson (above, note 5), pp 51-4, 63-4.
52. On what follows, see Finberg (above, note 9), pp 101-24.
53. Ibid., p 119; Olson (above, note 5), pp 75-8.
54. Whitelock *et al.* (above, note 29), i, 54.
55. On what follows, see Barlow (above, note 22), *passim*.

2: From 1050 to 1307 *(pp 23-52)*

1. The enthronement is mentioned in King Edward's charter of 1050: Dorothy Whitelock, M. Brett and C.N.L. Brooke, eds., *Councils and Synods with Other Documents Relating to the English Church I: A.D.871-1204*, 2 vols (Oxford, 1981), I, 525-33, esp. p 530.The crucial part is translated in Audrey Erskine, *Exeter Cathedral* (Exeter, 1988), p 6. Florence of Worcester called Leofric *Brytonicus;* cf. F. Barlow *et al.*, *Leofric of Exeter* (Exeter, 1972), p 1.
2. C. Morris, *The Papal Monarchy: The Western Church from 1050 to 1250* (Oxford, 1989), pp 79-89.
3. Whitelock, *et al.* (above, note 1), i, 525.

4. Barlow (above, note 1), pp 2-11.
5. Erskine (above, note 1), pp 7-9.
6. Barlow (above, note 1), pp 10-11; the early history of the cathedral is also discussed in N. Orme, *Exeter Cathedral: As It Was, 1050-1550* (Exeter, 1986), pp 12-14.
7. Caroline and F. Thorn, *Devon*, 2 vols (Chichester, 1985, being vol 9, *Domesday Book*, ed. J. Morris), i, section 2. For their recovery by Leofric see Barlow (above, note 1), p 11, and distribution, C. Holdsworth, 'The Church at Domesday' in Holdsworth, ed., *Domesday Essays* (Exeter, 1986), p 52.
8. Orme (above, note 6), and Holdsworth (above, note 7), pp 56-60.
9. E. Miller and J. Hatcher, *Medieval England: Rural Society and Economic Change 1086-1348* (London, 1978), pp 27-63.
10. Morris (above, note 2), pp 28-33, 103-4, 371-6.
11. Erskine (above, note 1), pp 10-19, and Orme (above, note 6), p 14.
12. Erskine, pp 19-20. Exeter was the last English cathedral to acquire a dean. Cf. Orme (above, note 6), p 34.
13. The archdeaconries and deaneries with the number of parishes in each are listed by R.J.E. Boggis, *A History of the Diocese of Exeter* (Exeter, 1922), pp 158-59 based on the 1291 Taxation of Pope Nicholas IV; the Exeter section is edited by F.C. Hingeston-Randolph, *The Registers of Walter Bronescombe (A.D. 1257-1280), and Peter Quivil (A.D. 1280-1291), Bishops of Exeter, with some records of the episcopate of Bishop Thomas de Bytton (1292-1307); and also the Taxation of Pope Nicholas IV (A.D. 1291)* (London and Exeter 1889), pp 450-81.
14. See R.N. Hadcock, *Monastic Britain, South Sheet*, 2nd ed. (Ordnance Survey, 1954).
15. I am indebted to Nicholas Orme for the next three paragraphs. On them see N. Orme, 'The Medieval Parishes of Devon', *The Devon Historian*, 33 (1986), pp 3-9, and Orme (above, note 6), pp 16-17.
16. See p 42 below.
17. E.B. Fryde, D.E. Greenway, S. Porter and I. Roy, eds., *Handbook of British Chronology*, 3rd ed. (London, 1986), pp 246-7. For royal exploitation of vacancies, see Margaret Howell, *Regalian Right in Medieval England* (London, 1962), p 35 and note. Exeter produced c. £300 in a year for Henry compared with c. £1,000 for Canterbury or York, £840-880 for Lincoln and Ely, and c. £600 for Durham.
18. Cf. the biographical studies in the *Dictionary of National Biography*, G. Oliver, *Lives of the Bishops of Exeter, and a History of the Cathedral* (Exeter, 1861), Boggis (above, note 13), and Marion Gibbs and Jane Lang, *Bishops and Reform, 1215-1272* (London, 1934), pp 185-99.
19. W.H. Hale and H.T. Ellacombe, eds., *An Account of the Executors of Richard Bishop of London 1303, and of the Executors of Thomas Bishop of Exeter 1310*, Camden Society, new series, 10 (1874), p 43. The will is summarised by Boggis (above, note 13), pp 170-2. See the fuller discussion pp 49-50 above.
20. For a full list see D.M. Smith, *Guide to Bishop's Registers of England and Wales* (London, 1981), pp 76-88.
21. Boggis (above, note 13), pp 129, 143, 193-4. Grandisson's absences were on average less than three weeks a year.
22. D. Blake, 'Bishop William Warelwast', *Devonshire Association Transactions*, 104

(1972), pp 15-33: A. Morey, *Bartholomew of Exeter* (Cambridge, 1937), pp 44-78; Jane E. Sayers, *Papal Judges Delegate in the Province of Canterbury, 1198-1254* (Oxford, 1971), p 10, notes that Bartholomew was appointed 60-70 times, putting him on a par with Gilbert Foliot and Roger of Worcester, the busiest judges.

23. Whitelock, *et al.* (above note 1), pp 718-19; Boggis (above, note 13), p 130; F.M. Powicke and C.R. Cheney, *Councils and Synods II: 1205-1265*, 2 vols (Oxford, 1964), i, 48; ii, 816.

24. Powicke and Cheney (above, note 23), i, 227-37, especially, clauses 1, 37, 24; the text is incomplete, there is no definite ascription to Bishop Brewer, but a reference to Exeter in cap. 6 (p 230) is a very strong indication.

25. Ibid. ii, 982-1077: *Summula*, cl. 37 (p 1076); cf. Brewer, cl. 2 (i, 228).

26. Ibid. ii, 907 note 3.

27. Hingeston-Randolph (above, note 13), pp 335-60.

28. Leofric had in his missal a mass to be said for the king at the time of synod (F. Barlow, *The English Church 1000-1066* (London, 1963), p 138 note); for Warelwast, see Blake (above, note 22), p 28, and for Bronescombe, Powicke and Cheney (above, note 23), i, 227.

29. C.R. Cheney, *From Becket to Langton* (Manchester, 1956), p 167, about Bartholomew; Maurice Bell, ed., *Wulfric of Haselbury by John, Abbot of Ford* (Somerset Record Society, 47, 1933), p 29, which may refer to a visitation before the death of Wulfric, 1154, probably under Robert Warelwast (1138-1155); Hingeston-Randolph (above, note 13), pp 294-302, discussed by C. R. Cheney, *Episcopal Visitation of Monasteries in the Thirteenth Century* (Manchester, 1931), pp 6, 96, 124 (which also discusses Quinel). Cheney, p 14, mentions the Launceston decisions (which should, however, be dated 1306-7, *not* 1306-10, since Bitton died in 1307).

30. F.C. Hingeston-Randolph, *The Register of Walter Stapeldon, Bishop of Exeter (A.D. 1307-1326)* (London and Exeter, 1892), p 107 and refs there. For Colebrook and Colyton, see pp 109-10, 111.

31. Estimates of the number of parishes are approximate, because the main source, the Papal Taxation of 1291, unaccountably leaves some out. The figures of 413 for Devon and 170 for Cornwall are based on N. Orme's maps of medieval parishes in R. Kain & W. Ravenhill, ed., *An Historical Atlas of South-West England* (University of Exeter Press, forthcoming).

32. Information on monasteries, based upon D. Knowles and R.N. Hadcock. *Medieval Religious Houses: England and Wales*, 2nd ed. (London, 1971) unless otherwise noted, is summarised in *Table 2.1*. I have omitted hospitals from what follows.

33. The best short account of western monasticism is now C.H. Lawrence, *Medieval Monasticism*, 2nd ed. (London, 1989). Morris (above, note 2), pp 237-62, 452-62, deals clearly with the new orders and friars.

34. C.J. Holdsworth, 'Hartland', in A. Baudrillart *et al.*, *Dictionnaire d'Histoire et de Geographie ecclésiastique*, vol 23 (Paris, 1989), cols. 430-33.

35. Knowles and Hadcock (above, note 32) provide such figures as survive. I have suggested reasons why Cistercian houses which established daughter houses may have had as many as 60 monks, and two or three times as many lay brothers, in

'Baldwin of Forde, Cistercian and Archbishop of Canterbury', *Friends of Lambeth Palace Library, Annual Report* (1989), p 17.

36. A.G. Little and Ruth C. Easterling, *The Franciscans and Dominicans of Exeter* (Exeter, 1927), pp 22, 52.

37. For parishes, see above note 31, and for the visitation material, above note 30.

38. Lawrence (above, note 33), pp 69-74.

39. G. Oliver, *Monasticon Dioecesis Exoniensis* (Exeter, 1846), p 193, no. 2

40. The proportion is approximate; Amicia countess of Devon and lady of the Isle of Wight had an annual income of c £2,500, and at the dissolution Buckland had a net income of about £242 (S.F. Hockey, *Quarr Abbey and its Lands* (Leicester, 1970), p 104, and Knowles and Hadcock (above, note 32), p 112).

41. Cf. Knowles and Hadcock for these figures.

42. Vera C.M. London, ed., *The Cartulary of Canonsleigh Abbey* (Devon and Cornwall Record Soc., new series, 8 (1965), p xv (for the acreage in 1323); Oliver (above, note 39), pp 232-5, 237-8 (for the later estates).

43. See above, p 27 and below, note 44.

44. Boggis (above, note 13), p 160, and R.A.R. Hartridge *A History of Vicarages in the Later Middle Ages* (Cambridge, 1930), p 84, who points out that Quinel's standard was low.

45. Holdsworth, 'The Cistercians in Devon', in C. Harper-Bill, C.J. Holdsworth and Janet L. Nelson, ed., *Studies in Medieval History presented to R. Allen Brown* (Woodbridge, 1989), p 188.

46. Holdsworth (above, note 7), pp 54-5.

47. A.L. Rowse, *Tudor Cornwall, Portrait of a Society*, new ed. (London, 1969), pp 158-60: 'Cornwall enjoyed, if that is the word, a much higher proportion of its Church revenues being devoted to the upkeep of the monasteries, than Devon or most other counties'.

48. Morris (above, note 2), pp 250-7, and Lawrence (above, note, 33), pp 261-3.

49. Little and Easterling (above, note 36), pp 15-16.

50. Holdsworth (above, note 45), pp 182-5, for William fitz Baldwin and William Brewer; for Matilda Peverel, see Alison Binns, *Dedications of Monastic Houses in England and Wales* (Woodbridge, 1989), p 113, I.J. Sanders, *English Feudal Baronies* (Oxford, 1963), p 15, and D. Williams, 'The Peverils and Essebies 1066-1166: a Study in Early Feudal Relationships', in D. Williams, ed., *England in the Twelfth Century* (Woodbridge, 1990), pp 244-8.

51. Little and Easterling (above, note 36), p 21; Oliver (above, note 39), p 166, for Stapledon's appointment of Franciscan and Dominican confessors to the nuns of Polsloe in 1319.

52. H.P.R. Finberg, *Tavistock Abbey*, 2nd ed. (Newton Abbot, 1969), p 22; A. Saltman, *Theobald, Archbishop of Canterbury* (London, 1956), pp 325-6.

53. Little and Easterling (above, note 36), pp 40-6; Hingeston-Randolph (above, note 13), pp 84-91, 39, discussed by Holdsworth (above, note 45), pp 179, 185-6 (Buckland), and 188 (gift to Newenham).

54. Centro di Documentazione Istituto per le Scienze Religiose–Bologna, ed., *Conciliorum Oecumenicorum Decreta* (Basle etc., 1962), p 65, cap. iv.

55. Holdsworth (above, note 35), pp 13-31.
56. C. Henderson, *The Cornish Church Guide and Parochial History of Cornwall* (Truro, 1925), pp 30-1, 52, 77, 155; S.F. Hockey, *Beaulieu, King John's Abbey* (Old Woking, 1976), pp 46-9.
57. Nicholas Orme has kindly drafted this paragraph, based on M. Adler, 'The Medieval Jews of Exeter', *Devonshire Association Transactions*, 63 (1931), pp 221-40, unless otherwise noted.
58. Morey (above, note 22), p 164; A. Cartellieri & W. Stechele, ed., *Chronicon Universale Anonymi Laudunensis* (Leipzig & Paris, 1909), p 36.
59. J.M. Rigg, ed., *Select Pleas, Starrs, and Other Records from the Rolls of the Exchequer of the Jews (1220-1284)*, Selden Society, 15 (1902), p 61.
60. C. Roth, *A History of the Jews in England*, 3rd ed. (Oxford, 1964), p 77.
61. Devon Record Office, Exeter Mayor's Court Roll, 16/17 Edward I m 25d.
62. Roth (above, note 60), p 43 note.
63. Hale and Ellacombe (above, note 19), *passim;* for the funeral expenses, legacies, and final account see pp 22-4, 29-35, 45. For Bitton's building work and the burial places, see Erskine (above, note 1), pp 29-30, 73-4, and Orme (above, note 6), pp 17-18, 28.
64. Erskine (above note, 1), p 30, which does not refer to the will and residuary legacy. As Mrs Erskine has pointed out to me, there is a mystery, since the legacy does not show up on the fabric rolls; see her *The Accounts of the Fabric of Exeter Cathedral, 1279-1353*, 2 pts, Devon and Cornwall Record Society, new series, 24, 26 (1981-83).

3: The Later Middle Ages and the Reformation (pp 53-80)

1. *The Register of Walter de Stapeldon, Bishop of Exeter, 1307-1326*, ed. F.C. Hingeston-Randolph (London & Exeter, 1892), pp 446-56. On Stapeldon's career, see M. Buck, *Politics, Finance and the Church: Walter Stapeldon* (Cambridge, 1983).
2. On diocesan administration, see D. Cawthron, 'The Administration of the Diocese of Exeter in the Fourteenth Century', *Devonshire Association Transactions*, 87 (1955), pp 130-64.
3. For the list, see above, p 200. For their biographies, see the introductions to Hingeston-Randolph's editions of their registers, *The Dictionary of National Biography*, and (most up-to-date) A.B. Emden, *A Biographical Register of the University of Oxford to A.D.1500*, 3 vols (Oxford, 1957-9), and similarly of Cambridge (Cambridge, 1963).
4. On Lacy and Raphael, see N. Orme, 'Two Saint-Bishops of Exeter: James Berkeley and Edmund Lacy', *Analecta Bollandiana*, 104 (1986), pp 412-14; on music, idem, 'The Early Musicians of Exeter Cathedral', *Music and Letters*, 59 (1978), pp 395-410; and on education, idem, *Education in the West of England, 1066-1548* (Exeter, 1976). The Oxford colleges were Exeter, founded by Stapledon, and Corpus Christi, by Richard Fox (but later, when he was bishop of Winchester). School benefactions include Stapledon's to Exeter, Grandisson's to Ottery St Mary, Fox's to Grantham

and Taunton, Oldham's to Manchester, and Veysey's to Sutton Coldfield.

5. On chantries, see also N. Orme, 'The Dissolution of the Chantries in Devon, 1546-8', *Devonshire Association Transactions*, 111 (1979), pp 75-123.

6. *Reg. Stapeldon* (above, note 1), pp 339-41; *The Register of John de Grandisson, Bishop of Exeter, 1327-1369*, ed. F.C. Hingeston-Randolph, 3 vols (London & Exeter, 1894-9), ii, 731-4, 852-5.

7. On these foundations, see J. Whetter, *The History of Glasney College* (Padstow, 1988); Buck (above, note 1) and W.K. Stride, *Exeter College* (London, 1900); and J.N. Dalton, *The Collegiate Church of Ottery St Mary* (Cambridge, 1917).

8. N. Orme, 'The Church in Crediton from Saint Boniface to the Reformation', in *The Greatest Englishman*, ed. T.A. Reuter (Exeter, 1980), pp 103-4.

9. On this topic, see also R.W. Southern, *Western Society and the Church in the Middle Ages* (Harmondsworth, 1970), pp 300-4; Guillaume de Lorris & Jean de Meung, *Le Roman de la Rose*, lines 11,033-57 (trans. H.W. Robins (New York, 1962), p 226.

10. N. Orme, 'Mortality in Fourteenth-Century Exeter', *Medical History*, 32 (1988), p 201.

11. N. Orme, 'Warland Hospital Totnes, and the Trinitarian Friars in Devon', *Devon & Cornwall Notes & Queries*, 36 (1987), pp 44-6.

12. On parishes, see N. Orme, 'The Medieval Parishes of Devon', *The Devon Historian*, 33 (1986), pp 3-9.

13. W.H. Hale, *A Series of Precedents and Proceedings in Criminal Causes . . . Diocese of London* (London, 1847); B.L. Woodcock, *Medieval Ecclesiastical Courts in the Diocese of Canterbury* (London, 1952), *passim*. The main series of Exeter consistory court records begins in 1511, but the earliest cases are chiefly civil not criminal actions (Exeter, Devon Record Office, Chanter 775-8, 854).

14. On what follows, see B.L. Manning, *The People's Faith in the Time of Wyclif* (Cambridge, 1919), pp 126-36, and *Reg. Grandisson* (above, note 6), ii, 1201-4.

15. N. Pevsner, *The Buildings of England: Cornwall*, ed. Edith Ratcliffe (Harmondsworth, 1970), p 21.

16. Orme in Reuter (above, note 8), p 122.

17. *A Relation . . . of the Island of England*, ed. Charlotte A. Sneyd, Camden Soc., 37 (1847), p 23.

18. On indulgences, see N. Orme, 'Indulgences in the Diocese of Exeter', *Devonshire Association Transactions*, 120 (1988), pp 15-32.

19. Devon Record Office, Iddesleigh, PW 1.

20. *The Accounts of the Wardens of Morebath, Devon, 1520-1573*, ed. J.E. Binney (Exeter, 1904), *passim*.

21. For a list, see R.J. Whiting, The Reformation in the South West of England, Exeter University, PhD thesis, 1977, p 402. Most are kept in the Devon or Cornwall Record Offices.

22. See above, p 18, and N. Orme, 'The Kalendar Brethren of the City of Exeter', *Devonshire Association Transactions*, 109 (1977), pp 153-69.

23. Joanna Mattingly, 'The Medieval Parish Guilds of Cornwall', *Journal of the Royal Institution of Cornwall*, new series, 10 part 3 (1989), pp 290-329.

24. Exeter Cathedral Archives, D&C 2526.

25. For these and other references, see below, note 26.

26. For these figures, and lists of the chapels involved, see the indexes to the bishops' registers concerned, edited by F.C. Hingeston-Randolph, 7 vols (London & Exeter, 1886-1906), and *The Register of Edmund Lacy: Registrum Commune*, ed. G.R. Dunstan, 5 vols, Devon & Cornwall Record Society, new series, 1963-72.

27. *Reg. Lacy: Registrum Commune* (above, note 26), i, 9.

28. John Heywood, *The Four PP* (London, 1544) and other editions, lines 1-50.

29. C. Henderson, 'Ecclesiastical History of the 109 Western Parishes in Cornwall', *Journal of the Royal Institution of Cornwall*, new series, 2 part 4 (1956), pp 195-7; J. Leland, *Itinerary*, ed. Lucy Toulmin Smith, 5 vols (London, 1906-10), i, 208; London, Public Record Office, E 315/126 no 16.

30. *Churchwardens' Accounts of Ashburton, 1479-1580*, ed. Alison Hanham, Devon & Cornwall Record Soc., new series, 15 (1970), pp viii, xii-xv.

31. J.J. Wilkinson, 'Receipts and Expenses in the Building of Bodmin Church, A.D. 1469 to 1472', *The Camden Miscellany Vol VII*, Camden Soc., new series, 14 (1875), pp 1-41.

32. On the cathedral, its shrines, worship and lay congregations, see N. Orme, *Exeter Cathedral: As It Was, 1050-1550* (Exeter, 1986), especially chapters 3, 6-9.

33. Joyce Youings, *The Dissolution of the Monasteries* (London, 1971), pp 164-5.

34. On the early chapels in Exeter, see Frances Rose-Troup, *Lost Chapels of Exeter* (Exeter, 1923). There is as yet no full account of the chapels founded after 1300.

35. On what follows, see *Reg. Lacy: Registrum Commune* (above, note 6), i, 285-8; ii, 36-8, 41-2, 150-1, 174-5, 211-21, 309-10.

36. See above, note 13. Tithe disputes feature in the early Tudor consistory court records of Exeter diocese, from 1511 (Devon Record Office, Chanter 775-6, 854).

37. *Reg. Grandisson* (above, note 6), ii, 751-2, 1147-9, 1179-81.

38. Emden, *Oxford* (above, note 3), iii, 1772.

39. Devon Record Office, Chanter XIII (Reg. Oldham), fos 144^v-5, 179^v-180^v; Gladys E. Tapley-Soper, 'Thomas Benet, M.A., Reformation Martyr of Exeter', *Devonshire Association Transactions*, 63 (1921), p 375.

40. For a survey of the pre-Reformation situation in the South West, see R.J. Whiting, *The Blind Devotion of the People: Popular Religion and the English Reformation* (Cambridge, 1989), reviewed with some reservations by the present author in *Devon & Cornwall Notes & Queries*, 36 (1989), pp 220-3.

41. For a standard history of the Reformation, see A.G. Dickens, *The English Reformation*, 2nd ed. (London, 1989); on the dissolution of the monasteries, D. Knowles, *The Religious Orders in England*, vol 3 (Cambridge, 1959), and Youings (above, note 33), and on the South West in particular, Whiting (above, note 40).

42. W.H. Frere & W. McC. Kennedy, *Visitation Articles and Injunctions of the Period of the Reformation*, 3 vols (London, Alcuin Club, 14-16, 1910), ii, 37-8.

43. Ibid., pp 5, 126.

44. Ibid., p 9.

45. Orme (above, note 5), pp 75-123.

46. Frere & Kennedy (above, note 42), ii, 116, 177-8, 242-3.

47. Binney (above, note 20), p 185.
48. On the rising, see Frances Rose-Troup, *The Western Rebellion of 1549* (London, 1913); J. Cornwall, *Revolt of the Peasantry* (London, 1977), and Joyce Youings, 'The South-Western Rebellion of 1549', *Southern History*, 1 (1979), pp 99-122.
49. Rose-Troup, (above, note 48), p 220.
50. On the use of church buildings after the Reformation, see G.W.O. Addleshaw & F. Etchells, *The Architectural Setting of Anglican Worship* (London, 1948).
51. Praying privately (presumably audibly) during service was actually forbidden by Bishop Hooper of Gloucester and Worcester in 1551-2 (Frere & Kennedy (above, note 42), ii, 293).
52. On what follows, see N. Orme, *English Schools in the Middle Ages* (London, 1973), especially pp 285-7, and idem, *Education* (above, note 4), especially pp 1-34.
53. For the legislation, see J.R. Tanner, *Tudor Constitutional Documents* (Cambridge, 1922), pp 469-500, and for discussion, W.E. Tate, *The Parish Chest*, 3rd ed. (Cambridge, 1969).
54. Hanham (above, note 30), pp 185-6.
55. On Harding and Jewel, see A.B. Emden, *A Biographical Register of the University of Oxford, A.D. 1501-1540* (Oxford, 1974), pp 265-6, 317-18; on John Hooker, *The Dictionary of National Biography;* on Richard Hooker, C. Morris, *Political Thought in England from Tyndale to Hooker* (London, 1953); on Carew, F.E. Halliday, *Richard Carew of Anthony* (London, 1953); and on Roscarrock, his *Lives of the Saints: Cornwall and Devon*, ed. N. Orme, Devon and Cornwall Record Society, new series, 35 (1992).

4: *The Seventeenth and Eighteenth Centuries* *(pp 81-108)*

1. One product of this continuing European dimension was the influx of Huguenots, notably to Plymouth in the 1620s and after 1685 (R. Gwynn and Alison Grant, 'Huguenots of Devon', *Devonshire Association Transactions*, 117 (1985), pp 161-94).
2. Episcopal efforts are documented sympathetically in M.G. Smith, *Fighting Joshua: A Study of the Career of Sir Jonathan Trelawney, Bart* (Exeter, 1986); idem, 'Bishop Trelawney and the Office of Rural Dean', *Devonshire Association Transactions*, 111 (1979), pp 13-30; A. Warne, *Church and Society in Eighteenth-Century Devon* (Newton Abbot, 1969); R. Beddard, 'Eighteenth-Century Episcopal Standards', *Devon and Cornwall Notes and Queries*, 34 (1978-81), pp 45-51.
3. *Devon and Cornwall Notes and Queries*, 21 (1940-1), pp 226-7, 285-7; P. Jackson, 'Nonconformity and Society in Devon 1660-88', Exeter University, PhD thesis, 1986, p 132. Another example is Uffculme, a Salisbury peculiar on the Devon-Somerset border: see H. Miles Brown, 'The Diary of the Rev. Samuel Short', *Devon and Cornwall Notes and Queries*, 23 (1947-9), pp 221-40 and 251-3.
4. Muriel E. Curtis, *Some Disputes between the City and the Cathedral Authorities of Exeter* (Manchester, 1932); W.T. MacCaffrey, *Exeter, 1540-1640*, 2nd ed.

(London, 1975); A. Brockett, *Nonconformity in Exeter 1650-1875* (Manchester, 1962).

5. G. Oliver, *Collections Illustrating the Catholic Religion* (London, 1857); K.Beck, 'Recusancy and Nonconformity in Devon and Somerset, 1660-1714', Bristol University, MA thesis, 1961, pp 43-75; K. McGrath, *Catholicism in Devon and Cornwall in 1767* (London, 1960); Warne (above, note 2), p 88.

6. I.W. Gowers, 'Puritanism in the County of Devon between 1570 and 1641', Exeter University, MA thesis, 1970, p 88; Jackson (above, note 3), pp 53-62, 132.

7. G.F. Nuttall, 'The Baptist Western Association, 1653-8', *Journal of Ecclesiastical History*, 11 (1960), pp 213-18.

8. R.N. Worth, 'Puritanism in Devon and the Exeter Assembly', *Devonshire Association Transactions*, 9 (1877), pp 250-91; *The Exeter Assembly (1691-1717)*, ed. A Brockett, Devon and Cornwall Record Society, new series, 6 (1963). Devon and Some.set ministers also continued to hold joint meetings in Exeter and Taunton during the decades around 1700. In the 1650s Cornwall had attempted its own Presbyterian organisation: see 'Minutes of the Cornwall Classis 1653-8', ed. W.A. Shaw, Chetham Society, new series, 4 (1898), pp 175-88.

9. M. Watts, *The Dissenters: From the Reformation to the French Revolution* (Oxford, 1978), pp 270-6, 509; J. Murch, *A History of the Presbyterian and General Baptist Churches in the West of England* (London, 1835) (Devon occupies pp 298-532, Cornwall pp 533-46!); D. Jackman, *Baptists in the West Country* (Bridgwater, 1953); A. Brockett, 'An Index to the Papers on Nonconformist History Printed in the *Transactions*', *Devonshire Association Transactions*, 96 (1964), pp 186-9; *Nonconformist Congregations in Great Britain: A List of Histories and Other Materials in Dr Williams' Library* (London, 1973). For Somerset and Dorset, see R. Dunning, *Christianity in Somerset* (Taunton, 1975), pp 43-69; J.H. Bettey, *Dorset* (Newton Abbot, 1974), pp 101-6.

10. D. Defoe, *A Tour through the Whole Island of Great Britain* (1724-6), ed. P. Rogers (Harmondsworth, 1971), p 228.

11. H. Miles Brown, *The Church in Cornwall* (Truro, 1964), pp 56-91; R. Ball, *Congregationalism in Cornwall* (London, 1955); L.V. Hodgkin, *A Quaker Saint in Cornwall* (London, 1927); A.D. Selleck, 'Plymouth Friends', *Devonshire Association Transactions*, 98 (1966), pp 282-326, and 99 (1967), pp 213-62.

12. T. Shaw, *A History of Cornish Methodism* (Truro, 1967); H. Miles Brown, *Episcopal Visitation Figures and Methodism*, Cornish Methodist Historical Association Occasional Publications, 3 (1962); Warne (above, note 2), pp 107-26.

13. C.E. Welch, 'Dissenters' Meeting Houses in Plymouth to 1852', *Devonshire Association Transactions*, 94 (1962), pp 579-612 and idem, 'Andrew Kinsman's Churches at Plymouth', ibid., 97 (1965), pp 212-36.

14. *Transactions of the Congregational Historical Society*, 6 (1913-15), p 54; Gowers (above, note 6), pp 32-3; R.J.E. Boggis, *History of the Diocese of Exeter* (Exeter, 1922), p 442; Warne (above, note 2), pp 37-8.

15. *The Works of Joseph Hall*, new ed., 12 vols (Oxford, 1837-9), i, p xxxix.

16. For Anglican church layout, see H. Miles Brown, 'Communion Table Furnishings in Eighteenth-Century Cornwall', *Devon and Cornwall Notes and Queries*, 23

(1947-9), pp 112-15; S, Lambe, 'Some Notes on Eighteenth-Century Furnishings in Parish Churches of Devon', *Devonshire Association Transactions*, 89 (1957), pp 216-24; G.W.O. Addleshaw and F. Etchells, *The Architectural Setting of Anglican Worship* (London, 1948).

17. Jackson (above, note 3), pp 32, 80, 356-8. Cosmo III, Grand Duke of Tuscany, who was of course a Roman Catholic, found much that was familiar when he attended the cathedral's services in 1669: see R.P. Chope, *Early Tours in Devon and Cornwall*, new ed. (Newton Abbot, 1967), pp 105-9.

18. Boggis (above, note 14), pp 459, 468; Warne (above, note 2), pp 44-8.

19. J. Newte, *The Lawfulness and Use of Organs in the Christian Church* (London, 1696); *A Letter to a Friend in the Country* (London, 1698); H. Dodwell, *A Treatise concerning the Lawfulness of Instrumental Musick in Holy Offices* (London, 1700); *Devon and Cornwall Notes and Queries*, 18 (1934-5), pp 272, 321; Boggis (above, note 14), pp 435-6.

20. *Devon and Cornwall Notes and Queries*, 21 (1940-1), p 227; Gowers (above, note 6), pp 175 and 200; Warne (above, note 2), p 104.

21. Brockett (above, note 4), pp 74-95.

22. *John Wesley in Devon*, ed. M. Wickes (n.p., 1985), p 18.

23. G.C.B. Davies, *The Early Cornish Evangelicals, 1735-60* (London, 1951), pp 62 and following, especially pp 90-92, 101-2, 130.

24. Hall (above, note 15), i, pp xxxv-vi, xxxix; Gowers (above, note 6), pp 261-6. For the ejections, see A.G. Matthews, *Walker Revised* (Oxford, 1948) and *Calamy Revised* (Oxford, 1934) for royalist and nonconformist clergy respectively. John Walker, author of *An Attempt towards Recovering an Account of the Numbers and Suffering of the Clergy of the Church of England* (London, 1714), was an Exeter clergyman.

25. Brockett (above, note 8), pp 100-1. Ham's visitation sermon, which started the controversy, was published as *The Duties and Advantages of National Unity* (Exeter, 1713).

26. Brockett (above, note 8), p 131.

27. *Transactions of the Congregational Historical Society*, 20 (1965-70), pp 141-3.

28. Quoted in Jackson (above, note 3), p 140. On the general theme, see J. Barry, 'The Parish in Civic Life: Bristol and its Churches, 1640-1750' in *Parish, Church and People*, ed. S. Wright (London, 1988), pp 152-78.

29. Gould is cited by R.L. Taverner in *Devonshire Association Transactions*, 100 (1968), p 81. See also Jackson (above, note 3), especially pp 294-5. The years after 1701 saw a bitter Devon debate about the nature of 'schism' and who was responsible for it, involving such figures as George Trosse, Robert Burscough, Joshua Bowchier and Humphrey Smith. *The Life of the Reverend Mr George Trosse* (Exeter, 1714), not only offers an inside view of Presbyterian developments since the Civil War but is also an eloquent plea for Presbyterians to be seen (and to see themselves) as 'non-schismatic', natural members of a Protestant national church.

30. *Devonshire Association Transactions*, 28 (1896), p 129 (the memoirs are reproduced on pp 129-73 and ibid., 29 (1897), pp 79-94); J. Pearce (ed.), *The Wesleys in Cornwall* (London, 1974), pp 35, 54, 76-8, 80, 85-6.

31. Defoe (above, note 10), p 209.
32. Ibid, p 246.
33. J. Triffitt, 'Politics and the Urban Community: Parliamentary Boroughs in the South West of England, 1710-30', Oxford University, DPhil thesis, 1985, pp 91-130, shows this convincingly for Dartmouth, Plymouth, Tavistock, Tiverton and Totnes, as well as Bridgwater and Taunton.
34. Quoted in W.P. Authers, *The Tiverton Congregational Church, 1660-1960* (Tiverton, 1960), p 23.
35. Rosemary O'Day, *The English Clergy: The Emergence and Consolidation of a Profession, 1558-1642* (Leicester, 1979); *The Axminster Ecclesiastica*, ed. K.W.H. Howard (Sheffield, 1976).
36. See A. Gordon, *Freedom after Ejection* (Manchester, 1917), pp 17-20, 30-3; *Transactions of the Congregational Historical Society*, 17 (1952-5), pp 92-3; Brockett (above, note 8) and, for academies, Beck (above, note 5), pp 192-7 and *Transactions of the Congregational Historical Society*, 4 (1909-10), pp 236-41; 5 (1911-12), pp 70-2, 155; 6 (1913-15), p 143; and 7 (1916-18), pp 98-101, 389-91.
37. Boggis (above, note 14), pp 459-73; Warne (above, note 2), pp 41-3.
38. *Devon and Cornwall Notes and Queries*, 21 (1940-1), pp 362-3; Gowers (above, note 6), pp 124-66; W.H. Wilkins, 'Vicars of Stockland', *Devonshire Association Transactions*, 71 (1939), pp 267-78; J. Triffitt, 'Believing and Belonging: Church Behaviour in Plymouth and Dartmouth 1710-30' in Wright (above, note 28), pp 179-202. For Plymouth's civic church and its choice in 1680, see also *Devon and Cornwall Notes and Queries*, 22 (1942-6), pp 109-12, 143, and *Plymouth Memoirs: A Manuscript by Dr James Yonge*, ed. J.J. Beckerlegge (Plymouth, 1951), pp 37-8, 61-8.
39. Davies (above, note 23), p 57.
40. Ibid, pp 57, 138, 178, 201.
41. H. Finberg, 'A Chapter in Religious History' in W.G. Hoskins and Finberg, *Devonshire Studies* (London, 1952), pp 366-95, at p 375; Shaw (above, note 12), p 78.
42. *Devonshire Association Transactions*, 28 (1896), pp 151-2.
43. Davies (above, note 23), p 121.
44. In 1708 the Exeter Assembly were faced with the case of South Molton where a temporary preacher, Mr Rutter, was favoured as the new minister by half the congregation but opposed by others ('they cannot profit by him . . . he is not popular, nor lively . . . he doth not rouse them'). This threatened to split the congregation; eventually another candidate was chosen: see Brockett (above, note 8), pp 69-73.
45. T. Shaw, *The Bible Christians* (London, 1965); idem (above, note 12); J.K. Hopkins, *A Woman to Deliver Her Own People* (Austin, Texas, 1982).
46. *Devon and Cornwall Notes and Queries*, 23 (1947-9), pp 212-15, 248-51.
47. Ibid., 16 (1930-1), pp 225-9 at p 226.
48. See for example the disputes and financial arrangements recorded in Short's diary (above, note 3), pp 236-7, 251-3.
49. For a dissenting example, see the Poole church book for 1777 in *Transactions of*

the Congregational Historical Society, 15 (1945-8), p 93. For Anglican seating see
Addleshaw and Etchells (above, note 16); surviving seating plans are listed in M.G.
Dickinson, 'Church Pews in the Diocese of Exeter;, *Devon and Cornwall Notes
and Queries*, 35 (1982-5), pp 331-4, and 36 (1986-9), p 132. For examples of disputes
see ibid, 17 (1932-3), pp 272-4; 33 (1974-7), pp 118-20; and *Devonshire Association
Transactions*, 19 (1887), pp 538-46; 34 (1902), pp 333-5; and 92 (1960), pp 293-301.
The classic use of church seating as a basis for describing the social structure of a
community is Richard Gough's analysis of a Shropshire parish in 1700: *The History
of Myddle*, ed. D. Hey (Harmondsworth, 1981).

50. Warne (above, note 2), p 76, notes prosecutions for non-attendance, the last being
in 1807. Jackson (above, note 3) lists the licences taken out in Devon 1689-99 (pp
353-5). Beck (above, note 5) counts 383 Devon licences before 1736 (p 168), far less
than Somerset's 1211, due to the greater prevalence of itinerant ministry by
Presbyterian and Congregational ministers in the latter county, leading to the
registration of many private houses.

51. Warne (above, note 2), pp 93-104; A. Brockett, 'Nonconformity in Devon in the
Eighteenth Century', *Devonshire Association Transactions*, 90 (1958), pp 31-54; 'A
View of English Nonconformity in 1773', *Transactions of the Congregational
History Society*, 5 (1911-12), pp 210 (Cornwall), 212-14 (Devon), and 379-80
(national totals with comparisons with 1715). Finberg (above, note 41), pp 383-93,
offers Tavistock as a case-study in decline, although his figures for baptisms in
parish church and chapel suggest that the dissenting proportion remained just under
20 per cent until the 1780s.

52. Shaw (above, note 12), p 21.

53. Ibid., Shaw (above, note 45); J.H.B. Andrews, 'The Rise of the Bible Christians
and the State of the Church in North Devon in the Early Nineteenth Century',
Devonshire Association Transactions, 96 (1964), pp 147-85.

54. Brockett (above, note 8), pp 74-5; Triffitt (above, note 38), pp 181-5; Watts (above,
note 9), pp 494, 500, 502. Jackson (above, note 3), pp 309-46, surveys the social
structure of late seventeenth-century nonconformity.

55. Such theories are usefully summarised in A.D. Gilbert, *Religion and Society in
Industrial England* (London, 1976).

56. Beck (above, note 5), pp 211-16; J. Bossy, *The English Catholic Community*
(London, 1975); R. Venn, *The Social Development of English Quakerism. 1655-1755*
(Cambridge, Massachusetts, 1969).

5: The Nineteenth Century: The Church of England   (pp109-28)

1. G.F.A. Best, 'The Constitutional Revolution, 1828-32', *Theology*, 62 (1959), pp
226-34.

2. Hesketh Pearson, *The Smith of Smiths* (London, 1934), p 267.

3. *The Diocese of Exeter in 1821: Bishop Carey's Replies to Queries before Visitation*,
ed. M. Cook, 2 vols, Devon & Cornwall Record Society, new series, 3-4, 1958-60,
i, p vii; ii, p vii.

4. B.I. Coleman, 'Southern England in the Census of Religious Worship, 1851', *Southern History,* 5 (1983), pp 154-88.
5. F.W.F. Smith (earl of Birkenhead), *Halifax* (London, 1965), p 19.
6. J. Keble, 'Preface to the Assize Sermon on National Apostasy, Oxford, 1833', *Sermons Academical and Occasional,* 2nd ed. (Oxford, 1848), p 127.
7. R.D. Middleton, *Magdalen Studies* (London, 1936), pp 3-28.
8. *Exeter Diocesan Calendar for 1869* (Exeter, 1868).
9. G.C.B. Davies, *Henry Phillpotts* (London, 1954), p 390.
10. See further, J.A. Thurmer, 'Henry of Exeter and the Later Tractarians', *Southern History,* 5 (1983), pp 210-20.
11. On Gorham, see *The Dictionary of National Biography,* and N. Orme, 'The History of Brampford Speke', *Devonshire Association Transactions,* 121 (1989), pp 67-76.
12. Though he did not live in Devon after his youth, Samuel Taylor Coleridge the poet (1772-1834) ought at least to be mentioned in this chapter. He was brought up at Ottery St Mary, and was a powerful influence on literature, society and religion. J.S. Mill regarded Coleridge as one of 'the two great seminal minds' of nineteenth-century England (the other was Bentham). Bentham asked of anything, 'Is it true?' Coleridge asked, 'What is the meaning of it?' See B. Willey, *Nineteenth-Century Studies* (London, 1949), pp 1-50.
13. E.F. Moore, *The Case of the Rev. G.C. Gorham against the Bishop of Exeter* (London, 1852), p 471.
14. *The Remains of the Rev. R H. Froude,* ed. J.H. Newman & J. Keble, 2 parts (London & Derby, 1838-9), part ii, vol i, p 274.
15. O. Chadwick, *The Mind of the Oxford Movement* (London, 1960), p 44.
16. W.N Yates, '"Bells and Smells"· London, Brighton and South Coast Religion Reconsidered', *Southern History,* 5 (1983), pp 122-53.
17. O. Chadwick, *The Victorian Church,* 2 vols (London, 1966-70), i, 218ff.
18. A manuscript account of the controversy was written by Dr T. Shapter for the Rev W.H.B. Proby in 1881 and is preserved in Exeter Cathedral Library.
19. R.J.E. Boggis, *History of St John's Torquay* (Torquay, 1930), pp 71-6.
20. P.F. Anson, *The Call of the Cloister,* 2nd ed. (London, 1964), pp 259-79.
21. Ibid., pp 404-5.
22. Ibid., pp 457-62.
23. Davies (above, note 9), p 317.
24. *The Law Reports: High Court of Admiralty and Ecclesiastical Courts,* 4 vols (London, 1867-75), iv, 297-379; *The Law Reports: Privy Council Appeals,* 6 vols (London, 1865-75), vi, 435-67.
25. Yates (above, note 16), pp 138-9.
26. P. Hinchcliff, *John William Colenso* (London, 1964).
27. *The Statutes of the Realm,* 11 vols (London, 1810-27), iii, 462-4 (25 Henry VIII cap. 20, 1534).
28. Chadwick (above, note 17), i, 237-50.
29. R. Barnes, *Report on the Case of the Deanery of Exeter* (Exeter, 1840), and R.C. Mortimer, 'The Exeter Case', *Devonshire Association Transactions,* 94 (1962), pp 26-41.

30. Chadwick (above, note 17), ii, 86-90.
31. See G.W.O. Addleshaw & F. Etchells, *The Architectural Setting of Anglican Worship* (London, 1948), chapter 7: an epoch-making work, if somewhat over-reacting against the Victorians.
32. Ibid., pp 209-19.

6: *The Nineteenth Century: Nonconformity   (pp 129-56)*

1. R.R. Currie, *Methodism Divided,* (London, 1968), pp 21- 2.
2. The original returns are held in the Public Record Office, London, as Home Office 129. Those for Devon have been published in an edited transcript by M.J.L. Wickes as *Devon in the Religious Census of 1851* (Appledore, 1990). The Census Report and the supporting statistical tables are in *Parliamentary Papers, 1852-53,* LXXXIX (1890), Census, 1851: Religious Worship (England and Wales).
3. The IA represents attendances, not the proportion of the population that accounted for those attendances. As many people attended more than one service that day, the total of attendances was certainly significantly higher than the number of people involved.
4. Based on Census, 1851: Summary Table D, pp ccxi-ccxli. The category of 'places of worship' was not confined to discrete buildings; it also included meetings in farmhouses, cottages and other private buildings, and these were of some importance for certain nonconformist denominations, particularly those strong in rural areas like the Bible Christians.
5. *Table 6.4* disaggregates the figures for non-Anglican denominations into those for old dissent (the denominations of pre-Methodist origins); the sum total of Methodism in all its variants; and Roman Catholicism.
6. A. Everitt, 'Country, County and Town: Patterns of Regional Evolution in England', *Transactions of the Royal Historical Society,* 5th series, 29 (1979), pp 79-108.
7. The best short account of the splits in Methodism is Currie (above, note 1), especially chapter 2.
8. The most useful modern account is P.L. Embley's chapter, 'The Early Development of the Plymouth Brethren', in *Patterns of Sectarianism,* ed. B.R. Wilson (London, 1967), pp 213-43.
9. For the region's parliamentary politics, see H. Pelling, *Social Geography of British Elections* (London, 1967), pp 158-174.
10. F. Tillyard, 'The Distribution of the Free Churches in England', *Sociological Review,* 27 part 1 (1935), pp 1-18.

7: *The Twentieth Century*

PART 1: CORNWALL   (PP 157-74)

* I gratefully acknowledge the financial support of the Leverhulme Trust which funded the research on which this paper is based. I am also indebted to my colleagues

on the Rural Church Project—Douglas Davies, Caroline Pack, Susanne Seymour, Christopher Short, and Charles Watkins—for many stimulating discussions on matters ecclesiastical during the past two years.

1. A. Dunstan and J.S. Peart-Binns, *Cornish Bishop* (London, 1977).
2. H.Miles Brown, *The Catholic Revival in Cornish Anglicanism,* privately published, quoted in W.S.F. Pickering, *Anglo-Catholicism: A Study in Religious Ambiguity* (London, 1989), p 102.
3. This paragraph draws heavily on the account of events in H.Miles Brown, *A Century for Cornwall: The Diocese of Truro 1877–1977* (Truro, 1977).
4. R.R. Currie, *Methodism Divided: A Study in the Sociology of Ecumenicalism* (London, 1968), p 199.
5. Figures taken from R.R. Currie, A. Gilbert and L. Horsley, *Churches and Church-goers: Patterns of Church Growth in the British Isles since 1700* (Oxford, 1977).
6. It should be noted that the Holsworthy Circuit of the Plymouth and Exeter District contains a few strong chapels located in north Cornwall, a stronghold of the Bible Christians. And several chapels in the Bude, Callington, Saltash and Torpoint circuits are located in Devon. Indeed the Callington and Saltash circuits although in the Plymouth and Exeter district are predominantly Cornish. Ian Haile has calculated the true membership in Cornwall for 1989 at 13,508. But with those exceptions, the Cornwall District figures represent a reasonably accurate reflection of Methodism in the county as a whole. This allows a reasonable comparison with data on Anglicanism in the Truro diocese which is contiguous with the county of Cornwall with the inclusion of two small Devon parishes: St Giles-on-the-Heath and Virginstow. Originally there were three other Devon parishes—Werrington, North Petherwin and Broadwoodwidger—in the Truro diocese. One—Broadwoodwidger—reverted to Exeter in 1922, and the other two became Cornish parishes as a result of civil boundary changes in 1966.
7. J.D. Gay, *The Geography of Religion in England* (London, 1971).
8. D. Davies, C. Pack, S. Seymour, C. Short, C. Watkins, and M. Winter, *The Views of Rural Parishioners,* Report to Archbishops' Commission on Rural Areas (Cirencester, 1990).
9. Gay (above, note 7).
10. R. Perry, 'Counterurbanisation in Cornwall', *South West Papers in Geography,* 8 (1983).
11. K. Dean, B. Brown, and R. Perry, 'Counterurbanisation and the Characteristics of Persons Migrating to West Cornwall', *Geoforum,* 15 (1984), pp 177-90.
12. R. Perry, 'Some Economic and Social Impacts of Recent Working-Age In-Migrants on West Cornwall', *Cornish Studies,* 2 (1986), pp 47-60.
13. Schismatic groups of a charismatic and/or fundamentalist nature seem often to have found fertile ground in the west country. The Bible Christian Church itself is one example. So too the Irishman, J.N. Darby, found fertile territory in Plymouth to launch the Brethren in 1831. More recently, in the 1960s a 'mini-revival' in Cornwall was associated with Bryn Jones, who subsequently, in Bradford, became one of the leaders of the house-church or Restorationist movement, arguably Britain's newest

denomination: A. Walker, *Restoring the Kingdom: The Radical Christianity of the House Church Movement* (London, 1985). Other independent evangelical groups have arisen in the 1970s and 1980s and the Assemblies of God have also experienced recent growth. These trends are not peculiar to Cornwall, but according to Ian Haile, currently chairman of the Cornwall Methodist District, such fringe movements seem to take a particularly 'independent' guise in Cornish religiosity (personal communication). Ian Haile is preparing a fascinating MA dissertation on these groups in Cornwall which promises to make a major contribution to our understanding of the issue.

14. D. Luker, 'Revivalism in Theory and Practice: the case of Cornish Methodism', *Journal of Ecclesiastical History*, 37 (1986), pp 603-19.

15. T. Shaw, *A History of Cornish Methodism* (Truro, 1967), p 132. The Reverend Thomas Shaw has modified his opinion subsequently, pointing out that although the morning service form was not extensively used, sacramental liturgy was (personal communication). However, this was only for the relatively infrequent communion services.

16. It is sometimes forgotten today how recently regular holy communion became the norm for weekly worship among Anglican congregations. It was not until the 1930s that such a pattern of worship was widely canvassed outside Anglo-Catholic circles. Crucial to this was the publication of a set of essays: A. G. Hebert, *The Parish Communion* (London, 1937).

17. Cornish Methodist infant baptism rates for 1961 and 1971 were respectively 220 and 186.

18. Davies *et al.*, (above, note 8).

19. G. Davie, 'Believing without Belonging', paper presented to the CISR, Helsinki (1989).

20. L. Paul, *The Deployment and Payment of the Clergy* (London, 1964).

21. A Russell, *The Country Parish* (London, 1986), p 240.

22. J. Tiller, *A Strategy for the Church's Ministry* (London, 1983).

23. J. Tiller and M. Burchall, *The Gospel Community* (London, 1986).

24. The maps and the data in this section are taken from D. Davies, C. Pack, S. Seymour, C. Short, C. Watkins, and M. Winter, *A Study of the Deployment and Work of the Rural Clergy in Five English Dioceses*, volume 1: Report to Archbishops' Commission on Rural Areas (Cirencester, 1990). I am particularly grateful to my colleague, Susanne Seymour, who painstakingly assembled the information necessary to compile the maps.

25. D. Davies, C. Pack, S. Seymour, C. Short, C. Watkins, and M. Winter, *A Study of the Deployment and Work of the Rural Clergy in Five English Dioceses*, volume 3: Report to Archbishops' Commission on Rural Areas (Cirencester, 1990). The data is based on the response to a postal questionnaire sent to all incumbents in the diocese: 92 out of 140 responses were made, a 66 per cent response rate.

26. Davies *et al.*, (above, notes 8, 24, 25).

PART 2: DEVON (PP 175-97)

1. Twenty-seven churches were destroyed or seriously damaged. For a list, see *Exeter Diocesan Directory* (Exeter, 1945), pp 10-11, and J.M. Slader, *The Churches of Devon* (Newton Abbot, 1968), pp 127-8.

2. For these and later Anglican statistics, see L. Paul, The *Deployment and Payment of the Clergy* (London, 1964), and *The Ordained Ministry: Numbers, Cost and Deployment* (London, General Synod Report No. 858, 1988).

3. Anthony Russell, *The Country Parish* (London, 1986), pp 232-3.

4. The best survey of English religion in the twentieth century is A. Hastings, *A History of English Christianity, 1920-1985* (London, 1986); for cultural change, see especially chapters 8-12.

5. Ibid., pp 417-22.

6. There are *Times* obituaries of H.E. Ryle (21 August 1925, p 12), A. Robertson (31 January 1931, p 14), Lord W. Cecil (24 June 1936, p 18), C.E. Curzon (24 August 1954, p 9) and R. C. Mortimer (13 September 1976, p 16). Ryle, Robertson and Mortimer appear in the 20th-century supplements to *The Dictionary of National Biography,* and there are studies of Ryle and Mortimer by M.H. Fitzgerald, *A Memoir of Herbert Edward Ryle* (London, 1928) and B.G. Skinner, *Robert Exon* (Bognor Regis, 1979).

7. I am indebted for these stories to the late Canon Frank Rice.

8. *Exeter Diocesan Calendar* (Exeter, 1900).

9. A.C. Smith, *The South Ormsby Experiment* (London, 1960).

10. *Exeter Diocesan Directory* (Exeter, 1963), confirmed by private information from the Ven. R.G. Herniman.

11. Teams have a leader, the team rector. There is also one 'group', Crediton and Sandford, where the clergy are equals.

12. For Temple's life, see F.A. Iremonger, *William Temple, Archbishop of Canterbury* (London, 1948), especially chapters 14 and 24.

13. O. Chadwick, *The Victorian Church,* 2 vols (London, 1966-70), ii, 201, 364-5; R.F.E. Boggis, *A History of the Diocese of Exeter* (Exeter, 1922), p 534; Hastings (above, note 4), pp 62-4. Rural deanery conferences were proposed at the diocesan conference in 1881, and appeared gradually in the following years (*Exeter Diocesan Calendar* (Exeter, 1882), p 178; (1883), p 180). Boggis founded a church council at St Mary Magdalene (Barnstaple) in 1907, but notes that this was unusual (R.J.E. Boggis, *I Remember* (Exeter, 1947), p 104).

14. Hastings (above, note 4), pp 546, 606-11.

15. Boggis, *I Remember* (above, note 13), pp 57, 121. However, Bickersteth, though doubtful about Church union, was kindly disposed to Free Church ministers and once entertained 200 of them at his palace (Boggis, *History* (above, note 13), p 541).

16. For Ramsey's life, see O. Chadwick, *Michael Ramsey: A Life* (Oxford, 1990).

17. On Crown Hill, see Bridget Cherry and N. Pevsner, *Devon* (Harmondsworth, 1989), p 640, and Slader (above, note 1), pp 126-7. At Exeter Cathedral, the moving of the main eucharist from the choir to the central altar in the nave was due to the growth of the congregation, but the solution and effect have been in line with

liturgical changes elsewhere. I am grateful to Canon J.A. Thurmer for this information.

18. Figures are taken from *Exeter Diocesan Calendar* and *Directory*, omitting retired clergy in 1950 and 1990. Analysis of the 1990 volume suggests that more non-graduate clergy were ordained than graduates in the 1960s. There has also been a recent increase in the ordination of candidates with other professional qualifications.

19. *Exeter Diocesan Calendar* (Exeter, 1871).

20. The involvement of the laity in all aspects of Church life, including leading worship, was stressed by the bishop of Exeter, Hewlett Thompson, at the quadrennial diocesan clergy conference at Paignton in November 1987.

21. For further information, see B. Heeney, *The Women's Movement in the Church of England, 1850-1930* (Oxford, 1988).

23. Ibid., p 136.

24. *The Oxford Dictionary of the Christian Church*, ed. F.L. Cross and E.A. Livingstone, 2nd ed. (Oxford, 1974), p 943.

25. Chadwick (above, note 13), ii, 201.

26. On Methodism in the twentieth century, see R. Davies, A.R. George and G. Rupp, *A History of the Methodist Church in Great Britain*, 4 vols (London, 1965-88), vol 3 (1983).

27. These and the following statistics are taken from *The Catholic Directory* (London, 1838, in progress).

28. On the history of Buckfast Abbey, see J. Stephan, *A History of Buckfast Abbey from 1018 to 1968* (Bristol, 1970).

29. On the house church movement, see A. Walker, *Restoring the Kingdom*, 2nd ed. (London, 1988), especially pp 34-5, 44-5.

30. The fullest account of the subject is now B. Susser, *The Jewish Communities of South-West England: Their rise and decline, 1100 to the present*, (Exeter, 1991). See also C. Roth, *The Rise of Provincial Jewry* (London, 1950), pp 59-63, 91-3, 110-11, and *The Jewish Yearbook*, ed. S.W. Massil (London, 1990), pp 123, 135.

31. H. Miles Brown, *A Century for Cornwall* (Truro, 1976), pp 80, 99.

Further Reading

The books in each section are divided into two categories: local, relating to the South West alone, and general, relating to Church history as a whole.

Basic Handbooks

These are useful for more than one period, and are not listed under the individual chapters.

LOCAL

R.J.E. Boggis, *A History of the Diocese of Exeter* (to 1900) (Exeter, 1922).
G. Oliver, *Monasticon Dioecesis Exoniensis* (Exeter & London, 1846). The best work on medieval religious houses in Cornwall and Devon.
G. Oliver, *Lives of the Bishops of Exeter and a History of the Cathedral* (Exeter, 1861). Superseded, but still useful.
F.C. Hingeston-Randolph (ed.), *The Registers of Walter Bronescombe,* etc., 9 vols (London & Exeter, 1886-1909). Indexes and transcripts of the medieval bishops' registers to 1455, completed by G.R. Dunstan (ed.), *The Register of Edmund Lacy,* 5 vols (Exeter, Devon & Cornwall Record Society, 1961-72).
C. Henderson, *Cornish Church Guide and Parochial History of Cornwall* (Truro, 1925).
H. Miles Brown, *The Church in Cornwall* (London, 1964).
H. Peskett, *Guide to the Parish and Non-Parochial Registers of Devon and Cornwall, 1538-1839* (Exeter, Devon and Cornwall Record Society, extra series, 2, 1979). A useful gazetteer.
R.F.S. Thorne, *Methodism in the South-West: A Historical Bibliography* (Topsham, 1983).
A. Erskine, V. Hope and J. Lloyd, *Exeter Cathedral,* 2nd ed. (Exeter, 1988).
N. Pevsner and E. Ratcliffe, *Cornwall* (The Buildings of England), 2nd ed. (Harmondsworth, 1970).
B. Cherry & N. Pevsner, *Devon* (The Buildings of England), 2nd ed. (Harmondsworth, 1989).
R. Kain & W. Ravenhill (ed.), *An Historical Atlas of South-West England* (Exeter, University of Exeter, forthcoming).

GENERAL

E.B. Fryde, D.E. Greenway, S. Porter & I. Roy (ed.), *Handbook of British Chronology,*

3rd ed. (London, 1986). The best lists of kings, bishops, officers of state and parliaments.

L. Stephen & S. Lee (ed.), *Dictionary of National Biography*, 63 vols (London, 1885-1900), plus supplements.

The Oxford English Dictionary, 2nd ed., 20 vols (Oxford, 1989). Invaluable for explaining terminology with dated historical references.

F.L. Cross & E.A. Livingstone (ed.), *The Oxford Dictionary of the Christian Church*, 2nd ed. (Oxford, 1974).

C.G. Herbermann & others, *The Catholic Encyclopaedia*, 15 vols (New York, 1907-14).

The New Catholic Encyclopaedia, 15 vols (New York, 1967).

D. Knowles & R.N. Hadcock, *Medieval Religious Houses, England and Wales,* 2nd ed. (London, 1971). The standard list of religious houses, now in need of some correction.

CHURCH HISTORIES

O. Chadwick, H. Chadwick, R.W. Southern, G.R. Cragg, A.R. Vidler, & S. Neill, *The Pelican History of the Church*, 6 vols (Harmondsworth, 1960-70).

D. Edwards, *Christian England*, 3 vols (London, 1982-4).

J.R.H. Moorman, *A History of the Church in England*, 2nd ed. (London, 1967).

D. Mathew, *Catholicism in England, 1535-1935* (London, 1936).

E.I. Watkin, *Roman Catholicism in England from the Reformation to 1950* (London, 1957).

A.C. Underwood, *A History of the English Baptists* (London, 1947).

R.T. Jones, *Congregationalism in England, 1662-1962* (London, 1962).

R. Davies, A.R. George & G. Rupp, *A History of the Methodist Church in Great Britain*, 4 vols (London, 1965-88).

B. Susser, *The Jews of South-West England* (Exeter, 1991).

1: *From the Beginnings to 1050*

LOCAL

A. Fox, *South-West England*, 2nd ed. (Newton Abbot, 1973).

S.M. Pearce, *The Kingdom of Dumnonia* (Padstow, 1978).

M. Todd, *The South-West to AD 1000* (London & New York, 1987).

G.H. Doble, *The Saints of Cornwall*, 5 vols (Truro, 1960-70).

L. Olson, *Early Monasteries in Cornwall,* Studies in Celtic History, 11 (Woodbridge, 1989).

H.P.R. Finberg, *The Early Charters of Devon and Cornwall* (Leicester, University College, Dept. of English Local History, Occasional Papers, 2, 1953).

M.A. O'Donovan (ed.), *Anglo Saxon Charters,* vol 3: *Sherborne* (Oxford, 1988).

C.A. Ralegh Radford, 'The Pre-Conquest Church and the Old Minsters in Devon', *The Devon Historian,* 11 (1975), pp 2-11.

O.J. Padel, *A Popular Dictionary of Cornish Place-Names* (Penzance, 1988).

A. Preston-Jones & P. Rose, 'Medieval Cornwall', *Cornish Archaeology*, 25 (1986), pp 135-85, with good bibliography.

GENERAL

C. Thomas, *Christianity in Roman Britain to AD 500* (London, 1981).
R.A.S. Macalister, *Corpus Inscriptionum Insularum Celticarum*, 2 vols (Dublin, 1945-9).
S.M. Pearce (ed.), *The Early Church in Western Britain and Ireland* (Oxford, British Archaeological Reports, British Series 102, 1982).
F.M. Stenton, *Anglo-Saxon England*, 2nd ed. (Oxford, 1947).
M. Deanesly, *The Pre-Conquest Church in England* (Cambridge, 1961).
J. Godfrey, *The Church in Anglo-Saxon England* (Cambridge, 1962).
D. Knowles, *The Monastic Order in England, 940-1216*, 2nd ed. (Cambridge, 1963).
F. Barlow, *The English Church 1000-1066*, 2nd ed. (London, 1979).
J. Blair (ed.), *Minsters and Parish Churches: the local Church in transition, 950-1200* (Oxford, 1988).

2: *From 1050 to 1307*

LOCAL

M. Adler, 'The Jews of Medieval Exeter', *Devonshire Association Transactions*, 63 (1931), pp 221-40.
D. Blake, 'Bishop William Warelwast', *Devonshire Association Transactions*, 104 (1972), pp 15-33.
L.E. Elliott-Binns, *Medieval Cornwall* (London, 1955).
H.P.R. Finberg, *Tavistock Abbey. A Study in the Social and Economic History of Devon*, 2nd ed. (Newton Abbot, 1969).
C. J. Holdsworth, 'The Cistercians in Devon', in *Studies in Medieval History presented to R. Allen Brown*, ed. C. Harper-Bill, C.J. Holdsworth and J.L. Nelson (Woodbridge, 1989), pp 179-91.
A.G. Little and R.C. Easterling, *The Franciscans and Dominicans of Exeter* (Exeter, 1927).
A. Morey, *Bartholomew of Exeter, Bishop and Canonist: a study in the twelfth century* (Cambridge, 1937).
D. Seymour, *Torre Abbey* (Exeter, 1977).

GENERAL

F. Barlow, *The English Church 1066-1154* (London, 1979).
K. Edwards, *The English Secular Cathedrals in the Middle Ages*, 2nd ed. (Manchester, 1949).
D. Knowles, *The Monastic Order in England*, 2nd ed. (Cambridge, 1963).
D. Knowles, *The Religious Orders in England*, vol 1 (Cambridge, 1948).
D. Matthew, *The Norman Monasteries and Their English Possessions* (Oxford, 1962).
J.R.H. Moorman, *Church Life in England in the Thirteenth Century* (Cambridge, 1955).

D.M. Robinson, *The Geography of the Augustinian Settlement in Medieval England and Wales* (British Archaeological Reports, British Series, 8, 2 parts, 1980).

S. Wood, *English Monasteries and their Patrons in the Thirteenth Century* (Oxford, 1955).

3: The Later Middle Ages and the Reformation

LOCAL

H.P.R. Finberg, *Tavistock Abbey*, 2nd ed. (Newton Abbot, 1969).

M. Buck, *Politics, Finance and the Church: Walter Stapeldon* (Cambridge, 1983). Bishop of Exeter, 1308-26.

N. Orme, *Education in the West of England, 1066-1548* (Exeter, 1976).

N. Orme, *Exeter Cathedral: As It Was. 1050-1550* (Exeter, 1986).

N. Orme, articles on parish churches, chantries, guilds and indulgences, listed in the notes to Chapter 3.

R.J. Whiting, *The Blind Devotion of the People: Popular Religion and the English Reformation* (Cambridge, 1986). On Devon and Cornwall.

Frances Rose-Troup, *The Western Rebellion of 1549* (London, 1915).

A.L. Rowse, *Tudor Cornwall* (London, 1941).

GENERAL

J.C. Dickinson, *An Ecclesiastical History of England: The Later Middle Ages* (London, 1979).

W.A. Pantin, *The English Church in the Fourteenth Century* (Cambridge, 1955).

B.L. Manning, *The People's Faith in the Time of Wyclif* (Cambridge, 1919).

D. Knowles, *The Religious Orders in England*, 3 vols (Cambridge, 1948-59).

Joyce Youings, *The Dissolution of the Monasteries* (London, 1971).

A.G. Dickens, *The English Reformation*, 2nd ed. (London, 1989).

J. Scarisbrick, *The Reformation and the English People* (Oxford, 1984).

C. Haigh (ed.), *The English Reformation Revised* (Cambridge, 1987).

W.E. Tate, *The Parish Chest*, 3rd ed. (Cambridge, 1969).

4: The Seventeenth and Eighteenth Centuries

LOCAL

A. Brockett, *Nonconformity in Exeter, 1650-1875* (Manchester, 1962).

A. Brockett, (ed.), *The Exeter Assembly 1691-1717*, Devon and Cornwall Record Society, new series, 6 (1963).

P. Jackson, 'Nonconformity and Society in Devon, 1660-1688', Exeter University, PhD thesis, 1986.

J. Murch, *A History of Presbyterian and General Baptist Churches in the West of England* (London, 1835).

A. Warne, *Church and Society in Eighteenth-Century Devon* (Newton Abbot, 1969).

GENERAL

J. Bossy, *The English Catholic Community* (London, 1975).

P. Collinson, *The Religion of Protestants: The Church in English Society, 1559-1625* (Oxford, 1982).

J.F.C. Harrison, *The Second Coming* (London, 1979).

A. Lloyd, *Quaker Social History, 1669-1738* (London, 1950).

G.F. Nuttall and O.Chadwick (ed.), *From Uniformity to Unity, 1662-1962* (London, 1962).

N. Sykes, *Church and State in England in the Eighteenth Century* (London, 1934).

M.R. Watts, *The Dissenters: From the Reformation to the French Revolution* (Oxford, 1978).

S. Wright (ed.), *Parish, Church and People: local studies in lay religion, 1350-1750* (London, 1988).

5: The Nineteenth Century: The Church of England

LOCAL

A.C. Benson, *The Life of Edward White Benson*, 2 vols (London, 1900).

P. Brendon, *Hurrell Froude and the Oxford Movement* (London, 1974).

M. Cook (ed.), *The Diocese of Exeter in 1821: Bishop Carey's Replies to Queries before Visitation*, 2 vols, Devon & Cornwall Record Society, new series, 3-4, 1958-60.

G.C.B. Davies, *Henry Phillpotts* (London, 1954).

J.C.S. Nias, *Gorham and the Bishop of Exeter* (London, 1951).

E.G. Sandford (ed.), *Memoirs of Archbishop Temple*, 2 vols (London, 1906).

B.G. Skinner, *Henry Francis Lyte* (Exeter, 1974).

GENERAL

S.C. Carpenter, *Church and People, 1782-1889* (London, 1933).

O. Chadwick, *The Victorian Church*, 2 vols (London, 1966-70).

O. Chadwick, *The Mind of the Oxford Movement* (London, 1960).

R.W. Church, *The Oxford Movement* (London, 1891).

R.P. Flindall, *The Church of England, 1815-1948: A Documentary History* (London, 1972).

D. Newsome, *The Parting of Friends* (London, 1966).

B. Willey, *More Nineteenth-Century Studies* (London, 1956).

6: *The Nineteenth Century: Nonconformity*

LOCAL

T. Shaw, *A History of Cornish Methodism* (Truro, 1967).
T. Shaw, *The Bible Christians, 1815-1907* (London, 1965).
J.C.C. Probert, 'The Sociology of Cornish Methodism: The Formative Years', *Cornish Methodist Historical Association, Occasional Publications*, 8 (1964).
M.J.L. Wickes (ed.), *Devon in the Religious Census of 1851* (Appledore, 1990).
B.I. Coleman, 'Southern England in the Census of Religious Worship, 1851', *Southern History*, 5 (1983), pp 154-88.
B.I. Coleman, 'Religious Worship in Devon in 1851', *The Devon Historian*, 18 (1979), pp 3-7.
B.I. Coleman, 'Exeter in the Census of Religious Worship, 1851', *The Devon Historian*, 23 (1981), pp 2-6.
P.L. Embley, 'The Early Development of the Plymouth Brethren', in B.R. Wilson (ed.), *Patterns of Sectarianism* (London, 1967), pp 213-43.

GENERAL

A.D. Gilbert, *Religion and Society in Industrial England: Church, Chapel and Social Change, 1740-1914* (London, 1976).
O. Chadwick, *The Victorian Church*, 2 vols (London, 1966-70).
I. Sellers, *Nineteenth-Century Nonconformity* (London, 1977).
R. Currie, *Methodism Divided* (London, 1968).
J.D. Gay, *The Geography of Religion in England* (London, 1971).
B.I. Coleman, *The Church of England in the Mid-Nineteenth Century: A Social Geography* (London, 1980).

7: *The Twentieth Century*

LOCAL

The Exeter Diocesan Calendar (later *Directory*) (Exeter, 1861, in progress).
The Truro Diocesan Year Book (Truro, 1926, in progress).
The Catholic Directory (London, 1838, in progress).
R.J.E. Boggis, *I Remember* (Exeter, 1946). A Devon autobiography.
B.G. Skinner, *Robert Exon* (Bognor Regis, 1979). A biography of R.C. Mortimer, bishop of Exeter 1949-73.
H. Miles Brown, *A Century for Cornwall: The Diocese of Truro 1877-1977* (Truro, 1976).
S. Foot (ed.), *Methodist Celebration: A Cornish Contribution* (Redruth, 1988).
B. Walke, *Twenty Years at St Hilary* (London, 1935). A Cornish autobiography.
C.S. Phillips, *Walter Howard Frere: A Memoir* (London, 1947). Bishop of Truro 1923-35.
A. Dunstan & J.S. Peart-Binns, *Cornish Bishop* (London, 1977). A life of John Hunkin, bishop of Truro 1935-50.

B. Deacon, A. George & R. Perry, *Cornwall at the Crossroads: Living Communities or Leisure Zones* (Redruth, 1988).

GENERAL

A. Hastings, *A History of English Christianity, 1920-85* (London, 1986).

D. Davies, C. Pack, S. Seymour, C. Short, C. Watkins & M. Winter, *The Rural Church*, 4 vols (Cirencester, Centre for Rural Studies, Occasional Papers, 11-14, 1990).

The Official Year-Book of the Church of England (London, 1883, in progress).

R. Lloyd, *The Church of England, 1900-1965* (London, 1966).

P.A. Welsby, *A History of the Church of England, 1945-1980* (Oxford, 1984).

A. Russell, *The Clerical Profession,* 2nd ed. (London, 1984).

A. Russell, *The Country Parish* (London, 1986).

D.W. Bebbington, *Evangelicalism in Modern Britain: a history from the 1730s to the 1980s* (London, 1989).

W.S.F. Pickering, *Anglo-Catholicism: A Study in Religious Ambiguity* (London, 1989).

F. Penhale, *Catholics in Crisis* (London, 1986).

F.R. Coad, *A History of the Brethren Movement* (Exeter, 1968).

A. Walker, *Restoring the Kingdom,* 2nd ed. (London, 1988). On the house-church movement and the Pentecostalists.

Plate 33   Molland parish church, Devon
Molland, like Parracombe, shows what churches were like before the Victorians, with box
pews, tympanum, and commandment tables.

Index